Francis Bacon

Also by Gilles Deleuze

Anti-Oedipus: Capitalism and Schizophrenia
(with Félix Guattari)

A Thousand Plateaus: Capitalism and Schizophrenia
(with Félix Guattari)

Kant's Critical Philosophy

Foucault

Cinema 1: The Movement-Image

Cinema 2: The Time-Image

Kafka: Toward a Minor Literature
(with Félix Guattari)

The Fold: Leibniz and the Baroque

Essays Critical and Clinical

Proust and Signs: The Complete Text

Francis Bacon

The Logic of Sensation

Gilles Deleuze

Translated and with an
Introduction by Daniel W. Smith
Afterword by Tom Conley

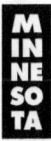

University of Minnesota Press
Minneapolis

Published by the University of Minnesota Press
111 Third Avenue South, Suite 290
Minneapolis, MN 55401-2520
http://www.upress.umn.edu

Library of Congress Cataloging-in-Publication Data

Deleuze, Gilles.
   [Francis Bacon. English]
   Francis Bacon : the logic of sensation / Gilles Deleuze ; translated
and with an introduction by Daniel W. Smith ; afterword by Tom Conley.
    p.   cm.
   Includes bibliographical references and index.
   ISBN 0-8166-4341-5 (HC/j : alk. paper)
   1. Bacon, Francis, 1909–1992—Criticism and interpretation.   2. Figurative
expressionism—England.   I. Bacon, Francis. II. Title.
ND497.B16 D413 2004
759.2'915—dc21   2003013280

12 11 10 09 08 07 06 05 04 03   10 9 8 7 6 5 4 3 2 1

Contents

Deleuze on Bacon: Three Conceptual Trajectories in *The Logic of Sensation*

Daniel W. Smith

Francis Bacon: The Logic of Sensation is a remarkable text in which Gilles Deleuze (1925–1995), one of the most original French philosophers of the twentieth century, confronts the work of Francis Bacon (1909–1992), one of the most original painters of that century.[1] The book originally appeared in 1981, when Bacon and Deleuze were both at the height of their powers. Although already well known at the time, Bacon was hardly a canonical painter and was even suspect in certain circles for his figural leanings. When Deleuze's book appeared, it received a number of favorable reviews but then was largely passed over in silence.[2] Today, *The Logic of Sensation* has come to be recognized as one of Deleuze's most significant texts in aesthetics. It was the first book Deleuze published after his decade-long collaboration with Félix Guattari on the two volumes of *Capitalism and Schizophrenia* (1972, 1980).[3] In the following years, Deleuze would publish a number of works on the arts, including the two-volume *Cinema* (1983, 1985), *The Fold: Leibniz and the Baroque* (1988), and the writings on literature collected in *Essays Critical and Clinical* (1993).[4] *The Logic of Sensation* can thus be read not only as a philosophical study of Bacon's paintings but also as a crucial text within Deleuze's broader philosophy of art.[5]

The original French version of *Francis Bacon: The Logic of Sensation* was published in Paris by Éditions de la Différence as a two-volume set. The first volume contained Deleuze's essay; the second volume consisted entirely of full-page reproductions of Bacon's paintings, allowing readers to view and study the reproductions directly alongside Deleuze's text. Regrettably, it has not been possible to include reproductions in the present edition. Images of Bacon's paintings, however, are widely available both on-line and in catalogs, and it goes without saying that Deleuze's book is best read with such images on hand. The paintings cited by Deleuze are designated by a number in brackets, which refers to the chronological list of Bacon's paintings at the end of the volume.

Deleuze has frequently insisted that he writes on the arts not as a critic but as a philosopher, and that his works on the various arts must therefore be read, as he himself says, as works of "philosophy, nothing but philosophy, in the traditional sense of the word."[6] In *What Is Philosophy?* (1991), Deleuze and Guattari define philosophy as an activity that consists in the creation or invention of concepts. "One can very easily think without concepts," Deleuze writes, "but as soon as there is a concept, there is truly philosophy."[7] Yet art itself is an equally creative enterprise of thought, but one whose object is to create sensible aggregates rather than concepts. Great artists are also great thinkers, but they think in terms of percepts and affects rather than concepts: painters think in terms of lines and colors, just as musicians think in sounds, filmmakers think in images, writers think in words, and so on. None of these activities has any priority over the others. Creating a concept is neither more difficult nor more abstract than creating new visual, sonorous, or verbal combinations in art; conversely, it is no easier to read an image, painting, or novel than it is to comprehend a concept. Philosophy, for Deleuze, can never be undertaken independently of art (or science); it always enters into relations of mutual resonance and exchange with these other domains, though for reasons that are always internal to philosophy itself.

As a philosopher, then, Deleuze's aim in his analyses of the arts is to create the concepts that correspond to these sensible aggregates. In *The Logic of Sensation*, Deleuze creates a series of philosophical concepts, each of which not only relates to a particular aspect of Bacon's paintings but also finds a place in "a general logic of sensation." The text is organized in quasi-musical fashion, divided into seventeen sequences that each develops concepts as if they were melodic lines, which in turn enter into increasingly complex contrapuntal relations and together form a kind of conceptual composition that parallels

Bacon's sensible compositions. In a similar manner, Deleuze's two-volume *Cinema* can be read as "a book of logic, a logic of the cinema" that sets out "to isolate certain cinematographic concepts," concepts which are specific to the cinema but which can only be formed philosophically.[8] Strictly speaking, there is no "philosophy of art" in Deleuze: "art" is itself a concept, but a purely nominal one, since there necessarily exist diverse problems whose solutions are found in heterogeneous arts. Hermann Broch wrote that "the sole *raison d'être* of the novel is to discover what only the novel can discover,"[9] and each of the arts, and each work of art, can be said to confront its own particular problems, using its own particular material and techniques. The cinema, for instance, produces images that move, and that move in time, and it is these two aspects of film that Deleuze sets out to analyze in *The Movement-Image* and *The Time-Image*: "What exactly does the cinema show us about space and time that the other arts don't show?"[10] Similarly, *Francis Bacon: The Logic of Sensation*, as its title indicates, is not only a study of Bacon's paintings but also an inquiry into a more general logic of sensation.

Readers who approach this book expecting a work of art criticism will thus be disappointed. There is little discussion of the socio-cultural milieu in which Bacon lived and worked; nor of his artistic influences or contemporaries, such as Lucian Freud or Frank Auerbach; nor of his personal life (his homosexuality, his lovers and friends, his drinking and gambling, his nights at the Colony Room Club), which played such an evident role in Bacon's work and in his choice of subjects. Even the secondary sources are sparse. Apart from two short texts by the French writers Michel Leiris and Marc Le Bot, the only secondary book Deleuze refers to is John Russell's 1971 now-classic study, *Francis Bacon*.[11] The links Deleuze establishes with Bacon's work are as often as not with writers (Conrad, Proust, Beckett, Kafka, Burroughs, Artaud) and musicians (Messaien, Schumann, Berg) that figure prominently in Deleuze's other writings, but whom Bacon may or may not have been influenced by or even read. In this sense, *The Logic of Sensation* is a highly personal book, though it is hardly written in a personal style.

Deleuze wrote his study of Bacon at the suggestion of Harry Jancovici, the editor of the series in which the book first appeared, which was titled La vue le texte. The aim of the series was to explore the resonances between the visual arts and domains such as philosophy and literature, and it would come to include texts by the philosopher Jean-François Lyotard and the writer Michel Butor.[12] Deleuze never explains why he chose to write on Bacon in particular. Bacon, however, had a strong presence in Paris during the 1970s and 1980s. He maintained a studio near the Place des Voges and was close friends with Leiris, whose portrait Bacon painted several times and who in turn wrote several important texts on Bacon.[13] It was the Grand Palais exhibition of 1971 in Paris that had cemented Bacon's international reputation, and the exhibition at the Galerie Claude Bernard in 1977 further solidified his position in the late 1970s.[14] Deleuze undoubtedly encountered Bacon's work at some point at an exhibition in Paris—in a later interview, Deleuze says that he frequently went to art exhibitions and films on weekends, on the lookout for precisely this kind of "encounter."[15] The book itself attests to the profound resonances Deleuze found between his own work and Bacon's paintings.

The relationship between the two men, however, was not personal. Deleuze and Bacon met only once, sometime after the book was published. Deleuze had sent the original manuscript to Bacon, who was intrigued by the book and delighted with the attention. The two arranged to spend an evening together, and Deleuze arrived with what Bacon described as a little "court" of admirers. Michael Peppiatt, in his biography *Francis Bacon: Anatomy of an Enigma*, reports that "although there was a perceptible sympathy and admiration between the two men, no friendship evolved."[16] Deleuze later recollected some of his impressions in an interview: "One senses in him a power and violence, but also a very great charm. After he is seated for an hour or so, he contorts himself in every direction, as if he were himself a Bacon painting.... When I met Bacon, he said that he dreamed of painting a wave, but dared not believe in the success of such a venture. It is a lesson of the painter, a great painter who comes to say to himself, 'It would be nice if I could trap a little wave . . .' It's very Proustian; or Cézannian: 'Ah! If only I could manage to paint a little apple!'"[17] According to Peppiatt, the two would never meet again.

Deleuze said that he wrote this book primarily with two things in front of him: reproductions of Bacon's paintings and the texts of David Sylvester's interviews with Bacon, which had been published in 1975 under the title *The Brutality of Fact*.[18] This approach reflects the tension between percept and concept: how does one talk in one medium (concepts) about the practices of another (percepts)? The dictum that one should heed what artists do, not what they say, is no less true for Bacon than for other artists. "I have often tried to talk about painting," he cautioned, "but writing or talking about it is only an approximation, as painting is its own language and is not translatable into words."[19] Nonetheless, Bacon's interviews contain penetrating discussions of the practice of painting, and have been favorably compared with Delacroix's journals and da Vinci's notebooks. Deleuze himself insists that we do not listen closely enough to what painters have to say. "The texts of a painter act in a completely different manner than the paintings," he notes. "In general, when artists speak of what they are doing, they have an extraordinary modesty, a severity toward themselves, and a great force. *They are the first to suggest the nature of the concepts and affects that are disengaged in their work*."[20] Deleuze thus uses the interviews not as definitive statements on Bacon's part but rather as the starting point for his own conceptual inventions. Deleuze once wrote: "We dream sometimes of a history of philosophy that would list only the new concepts created by a great philosopher—his most essential and creative contribution."[21] *The Logic of Sensation* is perhaps best approached in the same manner: as a book of philosophical concepts. The concepts Deleuze develops are sometimes drawn from everyday language, sometimes from specific scientific and art historical traditions, sometimes from Bacon's interviews, sometimes from Deleuze's own philosophical vocabulary. But the concepts themselves enter into multiple resonances and interactions, such that it is possible to trace numerous trajectories through the "rhizome" of the book: the brevity of the text belies its complexity. The remarks that follow attempt to isolate three such conceptual trajectories, which respectively concern Deleuze's formal analyses of Bacon's paintings, the general "logic of sensation" that underlies the book, and the techniques through which painters can be said to participate in such a logic of sensation (the "coloring sensation").

The first trajectory concerns the concepts Deleuze uses in his formal analyses of Bacon's work, which, he says, move "from the simplest to the most complex" aspects of Bacon's paintings. The question Deleuze poses to an artwork is not "What does it mean?" but rather "How does it function?" Deleuze thus treats Bacon's work as a *multiplicity* (although he does not use this term in the book) and attempts to isolate and identify the components of that multiplicity. Deleuze frequently returns to the three simplest aspects of Bacon's paintings—the Figure, the surrounding fields of color, and the contour that separates the two—which taken together form a "highly precise system" that serves to *isolate* the Figure in Bacon's paintings (chapter 1). But a first level of complexity immediately intervenes: the fields of color tend to curl around the contour and envelop the Figure, but at the same time the Figure itself tends to strain toward the fields, passing through washbasins, umbrellas, and mirrors, subjected to the forces that contort it, that *deform* or *contract* it in a kind of "derisory athleticism," revealing the intensive "body without organs" beneath the extensive organic body (chapter 3). In some cases, the Figure is dissipated entirely, leaving behind nothing but a sand dune or a jet of water—a pure Force that replaces the Figure (chapter 5). A second level of complexity appears in the works in which Bacon paints *coupled* Figures that nonetheless resonate together in a single "matter of fact" (chapter 9). A third level of complexity emerges in the triptychs, where this "matter of fact" includes not only the distances that separate the distinct panels but also the forced movement or *rhythms* that constitute the true Figure of the triptychs: the steady or "attendant" rhythm; an active, rising, or diastolic rhythm; and a passive, descending, or systolic rhythm (chapter 10). Deleuze not only identifies these three fundamental rhythms found in Bacon's triptychs, he also shows that even the simple paintings already function like triptychs, with their complex movements and combinatorial variability. A final level of complexity arises with regard to Bacon's handling of *color* (chapter 16), and his construction of a properly "haptic" space, since it is primarily through the use of color (relations of tonality) that he brings about all these effects in his works (isolation, deformation, coupling, rhythm...). Deleuze's book is marked throughout by extraordinarily specific and detailed analyses of individual paintings.

The fundamental concept in all these analyses, however, is that of the *Figure*. Modern art and modern philosophy can be said to have converged on a similar problem: both renounced the domain of representation and instead took the *conditions* of representation as their object. Deleuze suggests that twentieth-century art remained far ahead of philosophy in this regard, and that philosophers still have much to learn from painters. But he also suggests that there are two general routes through which modern painting escaped the clichés of representation and attempted to attain a "sensation" directly: either by moving toward *abstraction,* or by moving toward what Lyotard has termed the *figural.* An abstract art like that of Mondrian or Kandinsky, though it rejected classical figuration, in effect reduced sensation to a purely *optical* code that addressed itself primarily to the eye; by contrast, an abstract expressionism, like that of Pollock, went beyond representation, not by painting abstract forms, but by dissolving all forms in a fluid and chaotic texture of *manual* lines and colors (chapter 14). Bacon in effect followed a "middle path" between these two extremes, the path of the Figure, which finds its precursor in Cézanne. Whereas "figuration" refers to a form that is related to an object it is supposed to represent, the "Figure" is the form that is connected to a sensation, and that conveys the violence of this sensation directly to the nervous system. In Bacon's paintings, it is the human body that plays this role of the Figure: it functions as the material support or framework that sustains a precise sensation. This is Bacon's solution to the problem he shares with Cézanne: How to extract the Figure from its figurative, narrative, and illustrational links? How to "paint the sensation" or "record the fact"?

This brings us to the second trajectory, which concerns the nature of the "logic of sensation" that constitutes the object of Deleuze's analyses in this book. The notion of "sensation" one finds in Deleuze is taken initially from the phenomenological tradition. Erwin Straus, in his classic book *The Primary World of the Senses* (1935), had established a fundamental distinction between perception and sensation.[22] Perception, he argued, is a secondary rational organization of a primary, nonrational dimension of sensation (or "sense experience," *le sentir*). Earlier in the century, Marius von Senden had recorded the experiences of congenitally blind people who were given sight after the operation to remove cataracts was developed. Initially such patients were afflicted by a painful chaos of forms and colors, a gaudy confusion of visual *sensations* within which they could distinguish neither shapes nor space. They would acquire a *perception* of the world only after an often-painful process of learning and apprenticeship, during which they developed the schemata and "Gestalten" capable of providing this prereflective sense experience with the coordinates familiar to ordinary perception.[23] Studies of infants have revealed in them a similar sensory world populated by pure intensities (of sound, light, hunger, etc.) in which the baby cannot yet distinguish between itself and its world.[24] "In sensory experience," writes Straus, "there unfolds both the becoming of the subject and the happenings of the world. I become only insofar as something happened, and something happens (for me) only insofar as I become. . . . In sensing, both self and world unfold simultaneously for the sensing subject."[25]

This prerational world of sensation is not *prior* to the world of perception or representation, but strictly speaking is *coextensive* with it. It is precisely this world, the world of "lived experience," that phenomenologists have attempted to describe. Straus, for instance, drew a distinction between what he called geography and landscape. The geographical world, the world recorded on maps, is perceptual and conceptual; it is an abstract system of coordinates with an unspecified perspective. A landscape, by contrast, is sensory; it is a perspectival world, enclosed by a horizon that moves as our body moves. In a landscape, we do not so much move *in* space as space moves *with* us. Similarly, Maurice Merleau-Ponty, following Kurt Goldstein, distinguished between "touching" and "pointing": a patient who is able to scratch his nose at the point where a mosquito is biting him is unable, a moment later, to point to his nose with his finger. The former takes place within the "intentional" system of bodily space (sensation), whereas the latter requires an abstract coordination of points in external space (perception); in certain pathological cases the transition from the first to the second is blocked.[26] It is often difficult to separate sensation from perception, landscape from geography, since conceptual perception is such an integral part of our everyday experience of the world. For all his indebtedness to thinkers such as Straus, Merleau-Ponty, and Henri Maldiney, however, Deleuze is not a phenomenologist. Phenomenology is insufficient because it merely invokes the "lived body." But the lived body, says Deleuze, is still a "paltry thing in comparison with a more profound and almost unlivable Power," which is precisely the power of *rhythm* in its confrontation with chaos.[27] Sensation is itself constituted by the "vital power" of rhythm, and it is in rhythm that Deleuze locates the "logic of sensation" indicated in his subtitle, a logic that is neither cerebral nor rational. This linkage between sensation and rhythm can perhaps best be illustrated by means of a somewhat lengthy detour through Deleuze's reading of Kant's theory of perception, which forms a kind of complementary text to *The Logic of Sensation.*[28]

In the *Critique of Pure Reason*, Kant argues that perception requires a *synthesis* of what appears in space and time. In the first version of the transcendental deduction, Kant identifies three operations that make up a synthesis: apprehension, reproduction, and recognition. Since everything is a multiplicity and has a multiplicity of parts, perception begins when I synthesize these parts successively in an act of *apprehension*. I must also *reproduce* or "contract" the preceding parts when the following ones occur if a synthesis is to take place.

These two aspects of spatiotemporal synthesis—the apprehension and reproduction of parts—are activities of the productive imagination and no longer sensibility.[29] But a third moment is required for a perceptual synthesis to be complete: this sensible complex of space and time must now be related to the form of an object *(recognition)*. To be sure, one can imagine numerous sensations in which the diversity of space and time is *not* related to the object-form, such as hallucinations. It is rather *perception* as such that is constituted in such a manner that a sensible diversity is related to the form of an object. In other words, it is not so much that I perceive objects; it is rather my perception that presupposes the object-form as one of its conditions. Kant invented a famous formula for this object-form: the object $= x$. The object $= x$ is a pure form of perception, just as space-time is the pure form of sensation. The object $= x$ will receive a concrete determination (e.g., as a lion-object) only when it is related to the synthesized parts of a spatiotemporal diversity (a long mane, a loud roar, a heavy step...), such that I can say, "So it's a lion!" But the multiplicity of sensations that appear to us in the manifold of experience would never be referred to an object if we did not have at our disposal the empty form of the object $= x$, since there is nothing within sense experience itself that accounts for the operation by which I go beyond sensible diversity toward something I call an object. Where does this form come from? The object in general, Kant tells us, is the correlate of the "I think" or the unity of consciousness; it is the expression of the *cogito*, its formal objectivation. "Therefore the real (synthetic) formula of the *cogito* is: I think myself, and in thinking myself, I think the object in general to which I relate a represented diversity."[30] The predicates that are attributed to the object $= x$ are what Kant calls the *categories* or the pure a priori concepts of the understanding; and the subsumption of a sensible diversity under a concept is what Kant calls an act of *judgment*.[31]

The *Critique of Pure Reason* thus presents us with an analysis of the edifice of perception: the apprehension of successive parts, the reproduction of preceding parts, recognition by means of the form of the object in general. Kant's analysis in effect moves from the form of space and time (the pure form of sensation) to a determined spatiotemporal form (apprehension and reproduction as syntheses of the imagination) to the form of the object $= x$ (the pure form of perception). The philosophical adventure Deleuze explores in *The Logic of Sensation* begins at this point. The post-Kantians such as Hegel took as their starting point Kant's theory of the "transcendental *unity* of apperception." But Deleuze moves in the opposite direction, breaking with the form of recognition that grounds that unity. There are neither categories nor mediation in Deleuze, and one of his most insistent themes is "to have done with judgment" (Artaud). Deleuze effectively pushes to its limit a trajectory inaugurated in the *Critique of Judgment*, in which Kant explored the role of the imagination freed from the legislation of the understanding. Four elements of his analyses are particularly relevant to the themes of *The Logic of Sensation*.

1. *Aesthetic comprehension.* The first is the theme of "aesthetic comprehension" (measure). In the *Critique of Pure Reason*, Kant tells us that the act of synthesis begins with the apprehension of successive parts. In the *Critique of Judgment*, however, he in effect starts over and asks a question that went unformulated in the first critique: what counts as a part? To determine what constitutes a part, the imagination must have at its disposal a constant, or at least common, unit of measure. To be sure, the understanding could intervene and provide a mathematical evaluation of magnitudes in the fixed form of a *concept* of number (this object is "ten meters high" or "four inches wide"). But the imagination does not have recourse to concepts, and in the nature of objects there is no such constant measure. The imagination can thus begin to carry out its syntheses only by choosing a *sensible* or qualitative unit of measure. Kant notes, almost in passing, that such a unit of measure is found primarily in the *human body*: "A tree judged by the height of man gives, at all events, a standard for a mountain."[32] In other words, I can use the height of a human being as the unit of measure to apprehend the parts of a tree ("this tree is as tall as ten men . . ."); in turn, I can then use the height of the tree to measure the mountain behind it ("that mountain is as

high as twenty trees…"). Even at the level of simple perception, apprehension already implies something like a "lived evaluation" or "aesthetic comprehension" of a unit of measure, and, as Derrida notes, "this primary (subjective, sensory, immediate, living) measure proceeds from the body."[33] This is the moment of phenomenology in Kant: aesthetic comprehension presupposes the situatedness of our bodies in the world, our "being-in-the-world." In the *Phenomenology of Perception* (1962), Merleau-Ponty analyzed in detail the manner in which our body provides us with such a "corporeal or postural schema" on the world.[34]

2. *Rhythm.* This leads to a second theme, that of *rhythm*. What Kant is saying in the *Critique of Judgment* (§26) is that even the most elementary act of the synthesis of perception presupposes a logical act (though Kant here gives the term logic a new meaning). Beneath the successive apprehension of arts, there is a kind of logical synthesis that requires a purely aesthetic comprehension of the unit of measure. "All estimation of the magnitude of objects of nature is in the last resort aesthetic (i.e., subjectively and not objectively determined)."[35] Because the measure is subjectively determined, it is subject to constant evaluation and reevaluation, and is therefore in *constant variation.* The unit of measure varies in each case depending on the thing to be perceived, just as the thing to be perceived depends on the chosen unit. I may evaluate a tree in relation to the human body, but at night I may evaluate the rising moon in terms of a coin held at close range. From the viewpoint of aesthetic comprehension, I am continually in the process of changing my unit of measure according to my perceptions. Following Maldiney, Deleuze describes this aesthetic comprehension of units of measure as the grasping of a *rhythm* (though Kant himself does not use this term), which takes place *without a concept.*[36] Aesthetic comprehension is the grasping of a rhythm with regard to both the thing to be measured and the unit of measure. Beneath both the measure and the units, there is rhythm. In this sense, concepts are *metrical:* they give one the beat, but beneath the concept there is the rhythm. "Rhythms are always heterogeneous, we plunge into them in a sort of exploration," an experi-

mentation; even if you have a concept, "you do not yet have the rhythmicity of the things which are subordinated to it. A concept, at best, will give you the beat or the tempo."[37] Beneath concepts, one always finds rhythmic blocks or complexes of space-time, spatiotemporal rhythms, ways of being in space and in time. The *foundation* of perceptual synthesis is aesthetic comprehension, but the *ground* on which this foundation rests is the evaluation of rhythm.

3. *Chaos.* But once we have reached this point, we cannot stop. In the *Critique of Judgment*, Kant finally becomes aware of an impending catastrophe, as if the ground (rhythm) upon which the foundation of the synthesis rests were starting to tremble. Kant presents a disconcerting scenario: I look at something, but my imagination wavers, I become dizzy, vertiginous. First catastrophe: I seek an appropriate unit of measure, but I cannot find one; or I choose one, but it is destroyed. I choose another, but it too proves to be inadequate, as if what I am seeing is incommensurable with any unit of measure. Second catastrophe: In my panic, I can perhaps see parts, completely heterogeneous parts, but when I come to the next one, my dizzy spell only becomes worse; I forget the preceding part; I am pushed into going ever further, losing more and more. Third catastrophe: What is striking my senses is unrecognizable; it is something that goes beyond any possibility of aesthetic comprehension. My entire structure of perception, in other words, is in the process of exploding: I can no longer *apprehend* the successive parts, I cannot *reproduce* the preceding parts as the following ones arrive, and finally I can no longer *recognize* what the thing is. I can no longer qualify the object in general. Why does this happen? Because my aesthetic comprehension, that is, the evaluation of a rhythm that would serve as a foundation of measure, has become compromised, threatened. This is what Kant calls the experience of the *sublime*. The sublime takes place when the edifice of synthesis collapses: I no longer apprehend parts, I no longer reproduce parts, I no longer recognize anything. Instead of rhythm, I find myself drowned in a *chaos*.

What Kant discovers in the *Critique of Judgment* is that the synthesis of the imagination (apprehension, reproduction, recognition), which constitutes the edifice of knowledge, rests on a basis of a different nature—namely, an aesthetic comprehension of both the thing to be measured and the unit of measure. Aesthetic comprehension is not part of the synthesis, it is the foundation on which the synthesis rests, its soil. But at the same time that Kant discovers this foundation, he also discovers the extraordinary variability of its ground (rhythm) and its fundamental fragility (chaos). Between the synthesis and its foundation, there is the constant risk that something will emerge from beneath the ground and break the synthesis. Why this fundamental fragility? According to Kant, it is because there are infinite phenomena in space and time (such as the immense ocean or the starry heavens) that risk overturning the aesthetic comprehension of the unit of measure. The imagination finds itself overturned, blocked before its own limit; it discovers its own impotence, it starts to stutter. We here reach the point that Deleuze calls the "bend" in sufficient reason: it is at one and the same time that we discover both the ground of the synthesis (rhythm) and its ungrounded nature (chaos). Fortunately, we are not caught up in the sublime all the time, which would be a terrible experience; normally we manage to hold on to our perception, and to relate spatiotemporal diversities to the object-form. The sublime, however, entails a suppression of perception, an experience of the formless or the deformed. Yet chaos itself can also be a germ of order or rhythm, and it is this rhythm-chaos couple that lies at the heart of *The Logic of Sensation*.

When Deleuze was asked if the aim of *The Logic of Sensation* was to make readers see Bacon's paintings better, he conceded that it would necessarily have that effect if it succeeded. "But," he continued, "I believe that it has a higher aspiration, of which everyone dreams: to approach something that would be the common ground [fond] of words, lines, and colors, and even sounds. To write on painting, to write on music always implies this aspiration."[38] This "common ground" is, precisely, rhythm: "Rhythm appears as music when it invests the auditory level, and as painting when it invests the visual level. This is a 'logic of the senses,' as Cézanne said, which is neither rational nor cerebral. What is ultimate is thus the relation between sensation and rhythm, which places in each sensation the levels and domains through which it passes."[39] In painting, it was Cézanne and Klee who best exemplified this complex relation between chaos and rhythm. Cézanne said that the painter must look beyond a landscape to its chaos: he spoke of the need to always paint at close range, to no longer see the wheat field, to be too close to it, to lose oneself in the landscape, without landmarks, to the point where one no longer sees forms or even matters, but only forces, densities, intensities. This is what Cézanne called the world before humanity, "dawn of ourselves," "iridescent chaos," "virginity of the world"—a complete collapse of visual coordinates in a universal variation or interaction. Afterward, in the act of painting, the earth can emerge, with its "stubborn geometry," its "geological foundations" as "the measure of the world"—but with the perpetual risk that the earth in turn may once again disappear in a second catastrophe, in order for colors to arise, for the earth to rise to the sun.[40] Similarly, Paul Klee, in a famous text in *Modern Art*, wrote of how rhythm emerges from chaos, and how the "grey point" jumps over itself and organizes a rhythm, "the grey point having the double function of being both chaos and at the same time a rhythm insofar as it dynamically jumps over itself."[41] Translated into Kantian terms, both Cézanne and Klee mark the movement by which one goes from the synthesis of perception (apprehension, reproduction, recognition) to aesthetic comprehension (rhythm) to the catastrophe (chaos), and back again: the painter passes through a catastrophe (the diagram) and in the process produces a form of a completely different nature (the Figure).

4. *Force.* But there is a final moment to this Kantian trajectory. Kant himself presents us with a kind of consolation: at the very moment the imagination discovers its impotence, it makes us discover within ourselves a higher faculty that is stronger than the imagination: the faculty of *Ideas*, which is like a faculty of the infinite, of the supersensible. What is this faculty of Ideas? Kant famously identified two types of the sublime: the mathematical sublime and the dynamical sublime. For Deleuze, the latter is more profound than

the former because the dynamical sublime finds its figure in the "unformed" or the "deformed" (the undoing of the object-form). The forces of Nature are unleashed: a flood, a fire, an avalanche, a hurricane at sea. What do I experience? The fact that I am nothing! It is all too much for me, too strong, too overwhelming, and I experience a kind of terror. As a mere human, I am nothing compared to the might of Nature: my intensive power is reduced to zero faced with the unformed or deformed power of Nature. But at the same time, what is thereby awakened in me is a new power, a spiritual power, a faculty of Ideas that Kant identifies as the faculty of Reason, and by which humanity is revealed to be superior to Nature, pointing beyond Nature toward our *spiritual* destiny as moral beings (the noumenal as transcendent).[42]

But this is where Deleuze breaks with Kant and inverts the critical philosophy. For Deleuze, the faculty of Ideas is no longer identified with Reason; rather, Deleuze posits Ideas within sensibility itself and defines them not by their transcendence to Nature but rather in terms of their immanence to experience itself (the noumenal as immanent). Ideas remain suprasensible, but they now reveal the *forces* or intensities that lie behind sensations, and which draw us into nonhuman or inhuman *becomings*. In Deleuze, in other words, the power of Nature in the unformed or the deformed appears in the form of the *nonorganic life of things:* "The non-organic life of things, a frightful life, which is oblivious to the wisdom and limits of the organism.... It is the vital as potent pre-organic germinality, common to the animate and the inanimate, to a matter which raises itself to the point of life, and to a life which spreads itself through all matter."[43] Bacon's primary subject matter is the "body without organs" that lies beneath the organism, the body insofar as it is deformed by a plurality of invisible forces: the violent force of a hiccup, a scream, the need to vomit or defecate, of copulation, the flattening force of sleep. In Cézanne, similarly, mountains are made to exist uniquely through the geological forces of folding they harness, landscapes through their thermal and magnetic forces, apples through their forces of germination. Van Gogh even harnessed as yet unknown forces, such as the extraordinary force of a sunflower. Klee's famous formula echoes through Deleuze's writings like a kind of leitmotif: *not to render the visible, but to render visible*. Sensations are given, but it is force that constitutes the condition of sensation. The artistic question then becomes: How to render sensible forces that are not themselves sensible? How to render the nonvisible visible in painting, or the nonsonorous sonorous in music?

This leads us, finally, to the third line of concepts in Deleuze's book, which concerns the way in which painters, and Bacon in particular, produce this "logic of sensation." The aim of the book, Deleuze tells us, is not only to build a "general" logic of sensation, but to show how, in Bacon's work, its summit is found in the sensation of *color*. In arriving at this conclusion, Deleuze once again takes us through a kind of deduction of concepts. The first is the concept of the *cliché*. Clichés, Deleuze writes elsewhere, are anonymous and floating images "which circulate in the external world, but which also penetrate each of us and constitute our internal world, so that everyone possesses only psychic clichés by which we think and feel, are thought and felt, being ourselves one cliché among others in the world that surrounds us."[44] If Deleuze's philosophy is a *genetic* philosophy, the cliché is precisely what *prevents* the genesis of an image, just as opinion and convention prevent the genesis of thought. In this sense, one of the fundamental questions of Deleuze's philosophy is, What are the conditions for the production of the *new* (an image, a thought...)? Hence the essential role of the catastrophe: the condition for the genesis of the image (or the sensation) is at one and the same time the condition for the destruction of the cliché.

How then does the painter pass through the catastrophe and destroy the cliché? This is the role of what Deleuze calls the *diagram* or *graph* (chapter 12), a term he derives from the semiotic theory of C. S. Peirce. Peirce had noted the important and often overlooked role that diagrams play in mathematical thought. Although mathematics is usually presented as a purely deductive or axiomatic science, theorematic reasoning often involves the construction of diagrams and a kind of "ideal experimentation" with schemata consisting of points, lines, surfaces, and relations: "points are made and stretched ... pins are stuck in maps ... pages are covered in scribbles."[45] Mathematics, Peirce insisted, is as experimental as physics or chemistry, except that its experiments necessarily take on an ideal or "diagrammatic" form. In his semiological theory, Peirce had classified the diagram as a special case of the icon, "an icon of intelligible relations."[46] Although Deleuze admits his indebtedness to Peirce, he rejects the iconic status that Peirce assigned to the diagram, since it tends to conceive the diagram simply as a "copy" or graphic representation of intelligible relations or coordinates.[47] Deleuze, rather, prefers to assign to the diagram a much more strongly creative or genetic role: "the diagrammatic or abstract machine does not function to represent, even something real, but rather constructs a real that is yet to come, a new type of reality."[48] As Deleuze explains in chapter 13, the diagram acts as an analogical *modulator*, a conjunction of matter and function.

Painters, Deleuze argues, have their own type of diagrammatism. What he terms a painterly diagram (an operative set of nonrepresentational and nonsignifying lines and colors) is the means by which painters, in their own way, pass through the experience of catastrophe. The painter's diagram undoes the optical organization of the synthesis of perception (clichés), but also functions as the "genetic" element of the pictorial order to come. Every painter, Deleuze suggests, will pass through this process in a different manner. "The diagram is indeed a chaos, a catastrophe," he writes, "but it is also a germ of order or rhythm."[49] Using Wittgensteinian language, Deleuze says that the diagram constitutes a "possibility of fact," out of which the Fact itself will emerge. Plateau 11 of *A Thousand Plateaus* analyzes, in a more general manner, this complex emergence, out of chaos, of the elements of rhythm, with its territories and milieus.[50] The struggle against chaos in art, philosophy, and science is also one of the central themes of *What Is Philosophy?*, notably in its final chapter, "From Chaos to the Brain."[51]

If the summit of Bacon's own logic of sensation is found in the "coloring sensation," it is because it is primarily (though not exclusively) through the use of *color* that Bacon effects his diagrammatic procedures. In this regard, Deleuze identifies two fundamental uses of color in the history of painting. The first, more traditionally, emphasizes relations of *value* between colors, that is, the contrast of shadow and light (chiaroscuro). It has as its correlate the construction of what Deleuze calls a *tactile-optical* space, that is, the representational space that was inaugurated by Greek art and refined in the Renaissance. Figuration is itself a consequence of this tactile-optical space. In such a space, bodies are not merely perceived optically but take on a sculptural or tactile quality (depth, contour, relief, etc.), producing the illusion of a three-dimensional space behind the frame. In chapter 14, Deleuze shows how, in the history of art, this tactile-optical world would subsequently be broken and develop in two different directions: toward the exposition of a purely *optical* space, in which space is freed from its references to even a subordinate tactility (Byzantine art); and toward the imposition of a violent *manual* space, in which the hand begins to express itself in an independent way, producing a line that delineates nothing, and which the eye can barely follow (Gothic art). Deleuze's analyses of these developments draw heavily on the German art historical tradition of Aloïs Riegl, Heinrich Wölfflin, and Wilhelm Worringer, though without the last's appeal to a "will to art" *(Kunstwollen)*.[52] These developments, in turn, would be recapitulated in their own way in modern art: abstraction would develop a purely optical code (Mondrian), whereas expressionism would move toward the extraction of a purely manual line (Pollock).

In chapter 15, however, Deleuze will define Bacon's novelty in a twofold manner that breaks with these earlier conceptions of color and space. On the one hand, in his use of color, Bacon follows Cézanne and Van Gogh in replacing relations of value with relations of *tonality*, that is, with pure relations between the colors of the spectrum. Following Gilbert Simondon, Deleuze calls this a technique of *modulation* that relies on the relations between colors or the juxtaposition of tints. "The formula of the colorists is: if you push color to its pure internal relations (hot-cold, expansion-contraction), then you have everything." For the colorist, everything in painting—form and ground, light and shadow, bright and dark—is derived from pure relations of color. In this regard, Deleuze sees Bacon as one of the great colorists in the history of painting. Chapter 16 analyzes how the three formal elements of Bacon's paintings—the Figure, the contour, the structure—are all constructed by means of color: the internal variations of intensity in the structure, the "broken tones" of the Figures, the colored line of the contour. Thus, each element of Bacon's paintings converges in color, and it is modulation (the relation between colors) that explains the unity of the whole, the distribution of each element, and the way each of them acts upon the others. This is why Deleuze says that it is the "coloring sensation" that stands at the summit of Bacon's logic of sensation.

On the other hand, this use of color claims to bring out a peculiar kind of sense from sight: a *haptic* vision of color, as opposed to the optical vision of light. What Deleuze calls haptic vision is precisely this "sense" of colors. The *tactile-optical* space of representation presents a complex eye-hand relation: an ideal optical space that nonetheless maintains virtual referents to tactility (depth, contour, relief). From this, two types of subordination can occur: a subordination of the hand to the eye in *optical* space (Byzantine art), and a strict subordination of the eye to the hand in a *manual* space (Gothic art). But what Deleuze, following Riegl, terms *haptic* space (from the Greek verb *aptō*, to touch) is a space in which there is no longer a hand-eye subordination in either direction. It implies a type of seeing distinct from the optical, a close-up viewing in which "the sense of sight behaves just like the sense of touch."[53] Riegl argued that haptic space was the invention of Egyptian art and bas-relief, in which form and ground are experienced as being on the same plane, requiring a close vision. Deleuze in turn suggests that a new Egypt rises up in Bacon's work, this time composed uniquely of color and by color: the juxtaposition of pure tones arranged gradually on the flat surface produces a properly haptic space, and implies a properly haptic function of the eye (the planar character of the surface creates volumes only through the different colors that are arranged on it). In this regard, Deleuze will place Bacon in the great tradition of Turner, Monet, Cézanne, and Van Gogh—the great modern colorists who replaced relations of value with relations of tonality.

We have attempted to distinguish three conceptual trajectories in *The Logic of Sensation*, which respectively concern aspects of Bacon's paintings (isolation, deformation, coupling . . .), the nonrational logic of sensation (rhythm, chaos, force . . .), and the act of painting itself (clichés, the diagram, modulation . . .). Obviously, the three trajectories are interlinked: painting has its own manner of experimenting with the logic of sensation, and Bacon's path has a validity of its own that does not negate other paths such as abstraction or expressionism. In turn, each of these trajectories points beyond itself toward linkages with other arts such as music, cinema, and literature, such that *The Logic of Sensation* can itself be seen as an entry point into the conceptual proliferation of Deleuze's philosophy as a whole, and his other writings on the arts.

Author's Introduction to the English Edition

Francis Bacon's painting is of a very special violence. Bacon, to be sure, often traffics in the violence of a depicted scene: spectacles of horror, Crucifixions, prostheses and mutilations, monsters. But these are overly facile detours, detours that the artist himself judges severely and condemns in his work. What directly interests him is a violence that is involved only with color and line: the violence of a sensation (and not of a representation), a static or potential violence, a violence of reaction and expression. For example, a scream rent from us by a foreboding of invisible forces: "to paint the scream more than the horror…" In the long run Bacon's Figures aren't wracked bodies at all, but ordinary bodies in ordinary situations of constraint and discomfort. A man ordered to sit still for hours on a narrow stool is bound to assume contorted postures. The violence of a hiccup, of a need to vomit, but also of a hysterical, involuntary smile… Bacon's bodies, heads, Figures are of flesh, and what fascinates him are the invisible forces that model flesh or shake it. This is not the relationship of form and matter, but of materials and forces; to make these forces visible through their effects on flesh. There is, before anything else, a force of inertia that is of flesh itself: with Bacon, flesh, however firm, descends from bones; it falls or tends to fall away from them (hence those flattened sleepers who keep one arm raised, or thighs lifted from which the flesh seems to cascade). What fascinates Bacon is not movement, but its effect on an immobile body: heads whipped by wind, deformed by an aspiration—but also all the interior forces that climb through flesh. To make spasm visible. The entire body becomes plexus. If there is feeling in Bacon, it is not a taste for horror, it is pity, an intense pity: pity for flesh, including the flesh of dead animals.

There is another element in Bacon's painting: those large fields of color on which the Figure detaches itself, fields without depth or with only the kind of *shallow depth* that characterizes postcubism. These large shores are themselves divided in sections, or else crossed by tubes or very thin rails, or else sliced by a band or largish stripe. These form an armature, a bone structure. Sometimes they are like a ship's rigging, suspended in the sky of the field of color, upon which the Figure executes its taunting acrobatics.

These two pictorial elements do not remain indifferent to one another, but instead draw life from one another. It often seems that the flat fields of color curl around the Figure, together constituting a *shallow depth*, forming a hollow volume, determining a curve, an isolating track or ring at the core of which the Figure enacts its small feats (vomiting in a sink, shutting the door with the tip of its foot, twisting itself on a stool). This kind of situation finds its equivalent only in theater, or in a Beckett novel such as *Le Dépeupleur* (published in English in 1972 as *The Lost Ones*)—"inside a flattened cylinder... The light... Its yellowness"—or else it is found in visions of bodies plunging into a black tunnel. But if these fields of color press toward the Figure, the Figure in turn presses outward, trying to pass and dissolve through the Fields. Already we have here the role of the spasm or of the scream: the entire body trying to escape, to flow out of itself. And this occurs not only in Bacon's sinks but also through his famous umbrellas, which snatch part of the Figure and have a prolonged, exaggerated point, like vampires: the entire body trying to flee, to disgorge itself through a tip or a hole. Or else, on the contrary, it will flatten itself and stretch itself into a thick mirror, lodging its entirety into this width until it separates and dissipates like a lump of fat in a bowl of soup. The Figures themselves always present clean zones and foggy ones that attest to this dissipation. As of 1978–1979 we can speak of a few paintings still rare with Bacon wherein the Figure has in effect disappeared, leaving a trace or a geyser, a jet of water, of vapor, of sand, of dust, or of grass. This new period, which seems so rich to us in possibilities for the future, is an abstraction that is purely Bacon's. It consummates the double motion, of fields of color toward the Figure, and of the Figure toward the fields.

Bacon is a great colorist. And color with him relates to many different systems, two most importantly—one of which corresponds to the Figure/flesh, and the other to the color-field/section. It is as though Bacon has reassumed the entire problem of painting after Cézanne. Cézanne's "solution"—basically a modulation of color by means of distinct touches that proceed according to the order of the spectrum—in effect gave birth or rebirth to two problems: how, on the one hand, to preserve the homogeneity or unity of ground as though it were a perpendicular armature for chromatic progression, while on the other also to preserve the specificity or singularity of a form in perpetual variation? It was the new problem for Van Gogh as much as for Gauguin. A problem with two pressing dangers, since the ground could not be allowed to remain inert, nor could the form become murky or dissolve into grisaille. Van Gogh and Gauguin re-discovered the art of the portrait, "the portrait through color," by restoring to the ground vast monochrome fields that carry toward infinity, and by inventing new colors—"far from nature"—for flesh, colors that seem to have been baked in a kiln and that rival ceramics. The first aspect has not ceased to inspire experiments in modern painting: those great, brilliant monochrome fields that take life not in variations of hue but in very subtle shifts of intensity or saturation determined by zones of proximity. This would be Bacon's path: where these zones of proximity are induced either by sections of fields of color, or by virtue of a white stretched band or larger stripe that crosses the field (one finds an analogous structure in Barnett New-man). The other aspect, the colors for flesh, was to be resolved by Bacon along lines that Gauguin presaged: by producing broken tones (*tons rompus*), as though baked in a furnace and flayed by fire. Ba-con's genius as a colorist exists in both of these ideas at once, while most modern painters have concentrated on the first. These two as-pects are strict correlates in Bacon: a brilliant, pure tone for the large fields, coupled with a program of intensification; broken tones for the flesh, coupled with a procedure of rupturing or "fireblasting," a critical mixture of complementaries. It is as though painting were able to conquer time in two ways, through color: as eternity and light in the infinity of a field, where bodies fall or go through their paces; and in another way as passage, as metabolic variability in the enactment of these bodies, in their flesh and on their skin (thus three large male backs with varying chasms in value). It is a *Chronochromie*, in the spirit in which the composer Olivier Messiaen named one of his works.

The abandonment of simple figuration is the general fact of modern painting and, still more, of painting altogether, of all time. But what is interesting is the way in which Bacon, for his part, breaks with figuration: it is not impressionism, not expressionism, not symbolism, not cubism, not abstraction . . . Never (except perhaps in the case of Michelangelo) has anyone broken with figuration by elevating the Figure to such prominence. It is the confrontation of Figure and field, their solitary wrestling in *shallow depth*, that rips the painting away from all narrative as well as from all symbolization. When narrative or symbolic, figuration only obtains the bogus violence of the represented or the signified, but it expresses nothing of the violence of sensation—in other words, of the act of painting. It was natural, even necessary, that Bacon should revive the triptych: in this format he finds the conditions for painting and for color exactly as he conceives them to be. The triptych has thoroughly separate sections, truly distinct, which in advance negate any narrative that would establish itself among them. Yet Bacon also links these sections with a kind of brutal, unifying distribution that makes them interrelate free of any symbolic undercurrent. It is in the triptychs that colors become light and that light divides itself into colors. In them, one discovers rhythm as the essence of painting. For it is never a matter of this or that character, this or that object possessing rhythm. On the contrary, rhythms and rhythms alone become characters, become objects. Rhythms are the only characters, the only Figures. The triptych's function is precisely to this point—to make evident that which might otherwise risk remaining hidden. What a triptych's three panels in various ways distribute is analogous to three basic rhythms—one steady or "witness" rhythm, and two other rhythms, one of crescendo or simplification (climbing, expanding, diastolic, adding value), the other of diminuendo or elimination (descending, contracting, systolic, removing value). Let us consider every Bacon triptych: in any given case, where is the witness-Figure, where is the adjunctive or the reductive Figure? A 1972 *Triptych* shows a Figure whose back is "diminished," but whose leg is already complete, and another Figure whose torso has been completed, but who is missing one leg and whose other leg is running. These are monsters from the point of view of figuration. But from the point of view of the Figures themselves, these are rhythms and nothing else, rhythms as in a piece of music, as in the music of Messiaen which makes you hear "rhythmic characters." If one keeps the development of the triptych in mind, of this way Bacon has of effecting relationships between painting and music, then one can return to the simple paintings. No doubt one would see that each of them is organized as though a triptych, that each already encompasses a triptych, each distributes rhythms, at least three, as though so many Figures resonate in the field, and that the field separates and joins them, superposes them, of a piece.

1984

Francis Bacon

The Logic of Sensation

Preface to the 1981 Edition

Each of the following rubrics considers one aspect of Bacon's paintings, in an order that moves from the simplest to the most complex. But this order is relative and valid only from the viewpoint of a general logic of sensation.

All these aspects, of course, coexist in reality. They converge in color, in the "coloring sensation," which is the summit of this logic. Each aspect could serve as the theme of a particular sequence in the history of painting.

The cited paintings appear progressively. They are all reproduced and designated by a number that refers to their reproduction in the second volume. We thank Ms. Valerie Beston of the Marlborough Gallery for the indispensable assistance she graciously provided to us.

G. D.

CHAPTER 1

The Round Area, the Ring

The round area and its analogues — Distinction between the
Figure and the figurative — The fact — The question of
"matters of fact" — The three elements of painting:
structure, Figure, and contour — Role of the fields

A round area often delimits the place where the person—that is to say, the Figure—is seated, lying down, doubled over, or in some other position. This round or oval area takes up more or less space: it can extend beyond the edges of the painting [64, 37] or occupy the center of a triptych [60, 61]. It is often duplicated, or even replaced, by the roundness of the chair on which the person is seated, or by the oval of the bed on which the person is lying. It can be dispersed in the small disks that surround a part of the person's body, or in the gyratory spirals that encircle the bodies. Even the two peasants in *Two Men Working in a Field* [66] form a Figure only in relation to an awkward plot of land, tightly confined within the oval of a pot. In short, the painting is composed like a circus ring, a kind of amphitheater as "place." It is a very simple technique that consists in isolating the Figure. There are other techniques of isolation: putting the Figure inside a cube, or rather, inside a parallelepiped of glass or ice [6, 55]; sticking it onto a rail or a stretched-out bar, as if on the magnetic arc of an infinite circle [62]; or combining all these means—the round area, the cube, and the bar—as in Bacon's strangely flared and curved armchairs [38]. These are all "places" *[lieux]*. In any case, Bacon does not hide the fact that these techniques are rather rudimentary, despite the subtlety of their combinations. The important point is that they do not consign the Figure to immobility but, on the contrary, render sensible a kind of progression, an exploration of the Figure within the place, or upon itself. It is an operative field. The relation of the Figure to its isolating place defines a "fact": "the fact is...," "what takes place is..." Thus isolated, the Figure becomes an Image, an Icon.

Not only is the painting an isolated reality, and not only does the triptych have three isolated panels (which above all must not be united in a single frame), but the Figure itself is isolated in the painting by the round area or the parallelepiped. Why? Bacon often explains that it is to avoid the *figurative, illustrative,* and *narrative* character the Figure would necessarily have if it were not isolated. Painting has neither a model to represent nor a story to narrate. It thus has two possible ways of escaping the figurative: toward pure form, through abstraction; or toward the purely figural, through extraction or isolation. If the painter keeps to the Figure, if he or she opts for the second path, it will be to oppose the "figural" to the figurative.[1] Isolating the Figure will be the primary requirement. The figurative (representation) implies the relationship of an image to an object that it is supposed to illustrate; but it also implies the relationship of an image to other images in a composite whole that assigns a specific object to each of them. Narration is the correlate of illustration. A story always slips into, or tends to slip into, the space between two figures in order to animate the illustrated whole.[2] Isolation is thus the simplest means, necessary though not sufficient, to break with representation, to disrupt narration, to escape illustration, to liberate the Figure: to stick to the fact.

Clearly the problem is more complicated than this. Is there not another type of relationship between Figures, one that would not be narrative, and from which no figuration would follow? Diverse Figures that would spring from the same fact, that would belong to one and the same unique fact rather than telling a story or referring to different objects in a figurative whole? Nonnarrative relationships between Figures, and nonillustrative relationships between the Figures and the fact? Coupled Figures have always been a part of Bacon's work, but they do not tell a story [60, 61, 66]. Moreover, there is a relationship of great intensity between the separate panels of a triptych, although this relationship has nothing narrative about it [55, 62, 38]. Bacon modestly acknowledges that classical painting often succeeded in drawing this other type of relationship between Figures, and that this is still the task of the painting of the future: "Of course, so many of the greatest paintings have been done with a number of figures on a canvas, and of course every painter longs to do that.... But the story that is already being told between one figure and another begins to cancel out the possibilities of what can be done with the paint on its own. And this is a very great difficulty. But at any moment somebody will come along and be able to put a number of figures on a canvas."[3] What is this other type of relationship, a relationship between coupled or distinct Figures? Let us call these new relationships *matters of fact*,[4] as opposed to intelligible relations (of objects or ideas). Even if we acknowledge that, to a large degree, Bacon had already conquered this domain, he did so under more complex aspects than those we have yet considered.

We are still at the simple aspect of isolation. A figure is isolated within a ring, upon a chair, bed, or sofa, inside a circle or parallelepiped. It occupies only a part of the painting. What then fills the rest of the painting? A certain number of possibilities are already annulled, or without interest, for Bacon. What fills the rest of the painting will be neither a landscape as the correlate of the figure, nor a ground from which the form will emerge, nor a formless chiaroscuro, a thickness of color on which shadows would play, a texture on which variation would play. Yet we are moving ahead too quickly. For there are indeed, in Bacon's early works, landscape-Figures like the Van Gogh of 1957 [23]; there are extremely shaded textures, as in *Figure in a Landscape* (1945) [2] and *Figure Study I* (1945–1946) [4]; there are thicknesses and densities like those of *Head II* (1949) [5]; and above all, there is that alleged period of ten years that, according to Sylvester, was dominated by the somber, the dark, and the tonal, before Bacon returned to the "clear and precise."[5] But destiny can sometimes pass through detours that seem to contradict it. For Bacon's landscapes are a preparation for what will later appear as a set of short "involuntary free marks" lining the canvas,

asignifying traits[6] that are devoid of any illustrative or narrative function: hence the importance of grass, and the irremediably grassy
character of these landscapes (*Landscape*, 1952 [8], *Study for a Figure in
a Landscape*, 1952 [9], *Study of a Baboon*, 1953 [14], *Two Figures in the
Grass*, 1954 [17]). As for the textures, the thick, the dark, and the
blurry, they are already preparing for the great technique of local
scrubbing *[nettoyage local]* with a rag, whisk broom or brush, in which
the thickness is spread out over a nonfigurative zone. Clearly these
two techniques of local scrubbing and asignifying traits belong to an
original system which is neither that of the landscape, nor that of the
formless or the ground (although, by virtue of their autonomy, they
are apt to "make" a landscape or to "make" a ground, or even to
"make" darkness).

In fact, the rest of the painting is systematically occupied by
large fields *[aplats]* of bright, uniform, and motionless color. Thin
and hard, these fields have a structuring and spatializing function.
They are not beneath, behind, or beyond the Figure, but are strictly
to the side of it, or rather, all around it, and are thus grasped in a
close view, a tactile or "haptic" view, just as the Figure itself is.[7] At
this stage, when one moves from the Figure to the fields of color,
there is no relation of depth or distance, no incertitude of light and
shadow. Even the shadows and the blacks are not dark ("I tried to
make the shadows as present as the Figure"). If the fields function as
a background, they do so by virtue of their strict correlation with
the Figures. *It is the correlation of two sectors on a single Plane, equally
close.* This correlation, this connection, is itself provided by the place,
by the ring or round area, which is the common limit of the two,
their contour. This is what Bacon says in a very important statement
to which we will frequently recur. He distinguishes three fundamental elements in his painting, which are the material structure, the
round contour, and the raised image. If we think in sculptural terms,
we would have to say: the armature; the pedestal, which would be
mobile; and the Figure, which would move along the armature together with the pedestal. If we had to illustrate them (and to a certain degree this is necessary, as in *Man with Dog* of 1953 [15]), we

would say: a sidewalk, some pools, and the people who emerge from the pools on the way to their "daily round."[8]

We will see later what the various elements of this system have to do with Egyptian art, Byzantine art, and so forth. But what concerns us here is this absolute proximity, this coprecision, of the field that functions as a ground, and the Figure that functions as a form, on a single plane that is viewed at close range. It is this system, this coexistence of two immediately adjacent sectors, that encloses space, that constitutes an absolutely closed and revolving space, much more so than if one had proceeded with the somber, the dark, or the indistinct. This is why there is indeed a certain blurriness in Bacon; there are even two kinds of blurriness, but they both belong to this highly precise system. In the first case, the blur is obtained, not by indistinctness, but on the contrary by the operation that "consists in destroying clarity by clarity,"[9] as in the man with the pig's head in the *Self-Portrait* of 1973 [72], or the treatment of crumpled newspapers: as Leiris says, their typographic characters are clearly drawn, and it is their very mechanical precision that stands opposed to their legibility.[10] In the other case, the blur is obtained by the techniques of free marks or scrubbing, both of which are also among the precise elements of the system (we will see that there is yet a third case).

CHAPTER 2

Note on Figuration in Past Painting

Painting, religion, and photography — On two misconceptions

Painting has to extract the Figure from the figurative. But Bacon invokes two developments which seem to indicate that modern painting has a different relation to figuration or illustration than the painting of the past. First, photography has taken over the illustrative and documentary role, so that modern painting no longer needs to fulfill this function, which still burdened earlier painters. Second, painting used to be conditioned by certain "religious possibilities" that still gave a pictorial meaning to figuration, whereas modern painting is an atheistic game.[1]

Yet it is by no means certain that these two ideas, taken from Malraux, are adequate. On the one hand, such activities are in competition with each other, and one art would never be content to assume a role abandoned by another. It is hard to imagine an activity that would take over a function relinquished by a superior art. The photograph, though instantaneous, has a completely different ambition than representing, illustrating, or narrating. And when Bacon speaks of his own use of photographs, and of the relationships between photography and painting, he has much more profound things to say. On the other hand, the link between the pictorial element and religious sentiment, in past painting, in turn seems poorly defined by the hypothesis of a figurative function that was simply sanctified by faith.

Consider an extreme example: El Greco's *The Burial of the Count of Orgaz* (1586–1588) [106]. A horizontal divides the painting into two parts, upper and lower, celestial and terrestrial. In the lower half, there is indeed a figuration or narration that represents the

burial of the count, although all the coefficients of bodily deformation, and notably elongation, are already at work. But in the upper
half, where the count is received by Christ, there is a wild liberation,
a total emancipation: the Figures are lifted up and elongated, refined without measure, beyond all constraint. Despite appearances,
there is no longer a story to tell; the Figures are relieved of their
representative role, and enter directly into relation with an order of
celestial sensations. This is what Christian painting had already discovered in the religious sentiment: a properly pictorial atheism,
where one could adhere literally to the idea that God must not be
represented. With God—but also with Christ, the Virgin, and even
Hell—lines, colors, and movements are freed from the demands of
representation. The Figures are lifted up, or doubled over, or contorted, freed from all figuration. They no longer have anything to
represent or narrate, since in this domain they are content to refer
to the existing code of the church. Thus, in themselves, they no
longer have to do with anything but "sensations"—celestial, infer-
nal, or terrestrial sensations. Everything is made to pass through the
code, the religious sentiment is painted in all the colors of the world.
One must not say, "If God does not exist, everything is permitted."
It is just the opposite. For with God, everything is permitted. It is
with God that everything is permitted, not only morally, since violences and infamies always find a holy justification, but aesthetically,
in a much more important manner, because the divine Figures are
wrought by a free creative work, by a fantasy in which everything is
permitted. Christ's body is fashioned by a truly diabolical inspiration
that makes it pass through all the "areas of sensation," through all
the "levels of different feelings." Consider two further examples. In
Giotto's *Stigmatization of St. Francis* (1297–1300) [105], Christ is
transformed into a kite in the sky, a veritable airplane, which sends
the stigmata to St. Francis, while the hatched lines that trace the
path to the stigmata are like free marks, which the saint manipulates
as if they were the strings of the airplane-kite. Or Tintoretto's *Creation of the Animals* (c. 1550) [109]: God is like a referee firing the
gun at the start of a handicapped race, in which the birds and the

fish take off first, while the dog, the rabbits, the cow, and the unicorn await their turn.

Thus we cannot say that it was religious sentiment that sustained figuration in the painting of the past; on the contrary, it made possible a liberation of Figures, the emergence of Figures freed from all figuration. Nor can we say that the renunciation of figuration was easier for modern painting as a game. On the contrary, modern painting is invaded and besieged by photographs and clichés that are already lodged on the canvas before the painter even begins to work. In fact, it would be a mistake to think that the painter works on a white and virgin surface. The entire surface is already invested virtually with all kinds of clichés, which the painter will have to break with. This is exactly what Bacon says when he speaks of the photograph: it is not a figuration of what one sees, it is what modern man sees.[2] It is not dangerous simply because it is figurative, but because it claims to *reign over vision,* and thus to reign over painting. Having renounced the religious sentiment, but besieged by the photograph, modern painting finds itself in a situation that, despite appearances, makes it much more difficult to break with the figuration that would seem to be its miserable reserved domain. Abstract painting attests to this difficulty: the extraordinary work of abstract painting was necessary in order to tear modern art away from figuration. But is there not another path, more direct and more sensible?

CHAPTER 3

Athleticism

First movement: from the structure to the Figure — Isolation —
Athleticism — Second movement: from the Figure to
the structure — The body escapes from itself: abjection —
Contraction, dissipation: washbasins, umbrellas, and mirrors

Let us return to Bacon's three pictorial elements: the large fields as a spatializing material structure; the Figure, the Figures, and their fact; and the place, that is, the round area, the ring, or the contour, which is the common limit of the Figure and the field. The shape of the contour seems to be very simple, round or oval; it is rather its color that poses problems, because of the dynamic double relationship in which it is caught up. The contour, as a "place," is in fact the place of an exchange in two directions: between the material structure and the Figure, and between the Figure and the field. The contour is like a membrane through which this double exchange flows. Something happens in both directions. If painting has nothing to narrate and no story to tell, something is happening all the same, which defines the functioning of the painting.

Within the round area, the Figure is sitting on the chair, lying on the bed, and sometimes it even seems to be waiting for what is about to happen. But what is happening, or is about to happen, or has already happened, is not a spectacle or a representation. In Bacon, these waiting Figures or "attendants" are not spectators. One discovers in Bacon's paintings an attempt to eliminate every spectator, and consequently every spectacle. Thus the 1969 bullfight exists in two versions: in the first, the large field still includes an open panel through which we can glimpse a crowd, like a Roman legion at an amphitheater [56]; but the second version closes off this panel, and is no longer content merely to intertwine the two Figures of the toreador and the bull, but truly achieves their unique or common fact, while at the same time the mauve stripe disappears, which linked the spectators to what was still a spectacle [57]. *Three Studies of Isabel Rawsthorne* (1967) [43] shows the Figure closing the door on an intruder or visitor, even if this is its own double. In many cases there seems to subsist, distinct from the Figure, a kind of spectator, a voyeur, a photograph, a passerby, an "attendant": notably, but not exclusively [59], in the triptychs, where it is almost a law. However, we will see that, in his paintings and especially in his triptychs, Bacon needs the function of an *attendant*, which is not a spectator but part of the Figure. Even the simulacra of photographs, hung on a wall or a railing, can play this role of an attendant. They are attendants, not in the sense of spectators, but as a constant or point of reference in relation to which a variation is assessed. The sole spectacle is in fact the spectacle of waiting or effort, but these are produced only when there are no longer any spectators. This is where Bacon resembles Kafka: Bacon's Figure is the great Scandal, or the great Swimmer who does not know how to swim, the champion of abstinence; and the ring, the amphitheater, the platform is the theater of Oklahoma. In this respect, everything in Bacon reaches its culmination in the *Painting* of 1978 [81]: stuck onto a panel, the Figure tenses its entire body and a leg, in order to turn the key in the door with its foot from the other side of the painting. We note that the contour or the round area, a very beautiful golden orange, is no longer on the ground but has migrated and is now situated on the door itself, so that the Figure seems to be standing up on the vertical door at the extreme point of the foot, in a reorganization of the entire painting.

In this attempt to eliminate the spectator, the Figure already demonstrates a singular athleticism, all the more singular in that the source of the movement is not in itself. Instead, the movement goes from the material structure, from the field, to the Figure. In many paintings, the field is caught up in a movement that forms it into a cylinder: it curls around the contour, around the place; and it envelops and imprisons the Figure. The material structure curls around the contour in order to imprison the Figure, which accompanies the movement of all the structure's forces. It is the extreme solitude of the Figures, the extreme confinement of the bodies, which excludes every spectator: the Figure becomes a Figure only through this movement, which confines it and in which it confines itself. "Abode where lost bodies roam each searching for its lost one *[dépeupleur]*.... Inside a flattened cylinder fifty metres round and eighteen high for the sake of harmony. The light. Its dimness. Its yellowness."[1] Either the fall is suspended in the black hole of the cylinder [44]: this is the first formula for a derisory athletics, a violent comedy in which the bodily organs are prostheses. Or else the place, the contour, becomes an apparatus for the Figure's gymnastics on the fields of color [60].

But the other movement, which obviously coexists with the first, is on the contrary the movement of the Figure toward the material structure, toward the field of color. From the start, the Figure has been a body, and the body has a place within the enclosure of the round area. But the body is not simply waiting for something from the structure, it is waiting for something inside itself; it exerts an effort upon itself in order to become a Figure. Now it is inside the body that something is happening, the body is the source of movement. This is no longer the problem of the place, but rather of the event. If there is an effort, and an intense effort, it is in no way an extraordinary effort, as if it were a matter of undertaking something above and beyond the strength of the body and directed toward a separate object. The body exerts itself in a very precise manner, or waits to escape from itself in a very precise manner. It is not I who attempts to escape from my body, it is the body that attempts to escape from itself by means of . . . in short, a spasm: the body as plexus, and its effort or waiting for a spasm. Perhaps this is Bacon's approximation of horror or abjection. There is one painting that can guide us, the *Figure at a Washbasin* of 1976 [80]: clinging to the oval of the washbasin, its hands clutching the faucets, the body-figure exerts an intense motionless effort upon itself in order to escape down the blackness of the drain. Joseph Conrad describes a similar scene in which he too saw the image of abjection: in the hermetic cabin of the ship, during a wild tempest, the nigger of the *Narcissus* hears the other sailors who have succeeded in carving a small hole in the bulkhead that imprisons him. It is one of Bacon's paintings. "That infamous nigger rushed at the hole, put his lips to it, and whispered 'Help' in an almost extinct voice; he pressed his head to it, trying madly to get out through that opening one inch wide and three inches long. In our disturbed state we were absolutely paralyzed by his incredible action. It seemed impossible to drive him away."[2] The standard formula, "To pass through the eye of a needle," trivializes this abomination or Destiny. It is a scene of hysteria. The entire series of spasms in Bacon is of this type: scenes of love, of vomiting and excreting [73], in which the body attempts to escape from itself *through* one of its organs in order to rejoin the field or material structure. Bacon has often said that, in the domain of Figures, the shadow has as much presence as the body; but the shadow acquires this presence only because it escapes from the body, the shadow is the body that has escaped from itself through some localized point in the contour [63]. And the scream, Bacon's scream, is the operation through which the entire body escapes through the mouth [6]. All the pressures of the body.

The bowl of the washbasin is a place, a contour; it is a replication of the round area. But here, the new position of the body in relation to the contour shows that we have arrived at a more complex aspect (even if this aspect was there from the start). It is no longer the material structure that curls around the contour in order to envelop the Figure, it is the Figure that wants to pass through a vanishing point in the contour in order to dissipate into the material structure. This is the second direction of the exchange, and the second form of a derisory athletics. The contour thus assumes a new function, since it no longer lies flat, but outlines a hollow volume and has a vanishing point. Bacon's umbrellas, in this respect, are analogues of the washbasin. In the two versions of *Painting*, 1946 and 1971 [3, 65], the Figure is clearly lodged within the round area of a balustrade, but at the same time it lets itself be grabbed by the half-spherical umbrella, and appears to be waiting to escape in its entirety through the point of the instrument: already we can no longer see anything but its abject smile. In *Studies of the Human Body* (1970) [62] and *Triptych, May–June 1974* [75], the green umbrella is treated more like a surface, but the crouching Figure uses it all at once as a pendulum, a parachute, a vacuum cleaner, and a nozzle, through which the entire contracted body wants to pass, and which has already grabbed hold of the head. The splendor of these umbrellas as contours, with one point stretched downwards... In literature, it is William Burroughs who has best evoked this effort of the body to escape through a point or through a hole that forms a part of itself or its surroundings: "Johnny's body begins to contract, pulling up toward his chin. Each time the contraction is longer. 'Wheeeeeeee!' the boy yells, every muscle tense, his whole body strains to empty through his cock."[3] In much the same way, Bacon's *Lying Figure with Hypodermic Syringe* (1963) [31] is less a nailed-down body (though this is how Bacon describes it) than a body attempting to pass through the syringe and to escape through this hole or vanishing point functioning as a prosthesis-organ.[4]

If the ring or the round area is replicated in the washbasin and the umbrella, the cube or the parallelepiped is also replicated in the mirror. Bacon's mirrors can be anything you like—except a reflecting surface. The mirror is an opaque and sometimes black thickness [45]. Bacon does not experience the mirror in the same way as Lewis Carroll. The body enters the mirror and lodges itself inside it, itself and its shadow. Hence the fascination: nothing is behind the mirror, everything is inside it [63, 67]. The body seems to elongate, flatten, or stretch itself out in the mirror, just as it contracted itself by going through the hole. If need be, the head is split open by a large triangular crevasse, which will reappear on two sides, and disperse the head throughout the mirror like a lump of fat in a bowl of soup [51]. But in both these cases, the umbrella and the washbasin as much as the mirror, the Figure is no longer simply isolated but deformed, sometimes contracted and aspirated, sometimes stretched and dilated. This is because the movement is no longer that of the material structure curling around the Figure; it is the movement of the Figure going toward the structure and which, at the limit, tends to dissipate into the fields of color. The Figure is not simply the isolated body, but also the deformed body that escapes from itself. What makes deformation a destiny is that the body has a necessary relationship with the material structure: not only does the material structure curl around it, but the body must return to the material structure and dissipate into it, thereby passing through or into these prostheses-instruments, which constitute passages and states that are real, physical, and effective, and which are sensations and not imaginings. Thus, in many cases, the mirror or the washbasin can be localized; but even then what is happening in the mirror, or what is about to happen in the washbasin, can be immediately related to the Figure itself. What the mirror shows, or what the washbasin heralds, is exactly what happens to the Figure. The heads are all prepared to receive these deformations (hence the wiped, scrubbed, or rubbed-out zones in the portraits of heads). And to the degree that the instruments tend to occupy the whole of the material structure, they no longer even need to be specified: the entire structure can play the role of a virtual mirror, a virtual umbrella or washbasin, to the point where the instrumental deformations are immediately transferred *to* the Figure. Thus, in the 1973 *Self-Portrait* [72] of the man with the pig's head, the deformation takes place on the spot. Just as the effort of the body is exerted upon itself, so the deformation is static. An intense movement flows through the whole body, a deformed and deforming movement that at every moment transfers the real image onto the body in order to constitute the Figure.

CHAPTER 4

Body, Meat, and Spirit: Becoming-Animal

Man and animal — The zone of indiscernibility —
Flesh and bone: the meat descends from the bone —
Pity — Head, face, and meat

The body is the Figure, or rather the material of the Figure. The material of the Figure must not be confused with the spatializing material structure, which is positioned in opposition to it. The body is the Figure, not the structure. Conversely, the Figure, being a body, is not the face, and does not even have a face. It does have a head, because the head is an integral part of the body. It can even be reduced to the head. As a portraitist, Bacon is a painter of heads, not faces, and there is a great difference between the two. For the face is a structured, spatial organization that conceals the head, whereas the head is dependent on the body, even if it is the point of the body, its culmination. It is not that the head lacks spirit; but it is a spirit in bodily form, a corporeal and vital breath, an animal spirit. It is the animal spirit of man: a pig-spirit, a buffalo-spirit, a dog-spirit, a bat-spirit... Bacon thus pursues a very peculiar project as a portrait painter: *to dismantle the face*, to rediscover the head or make it emerge from beneath the face.

The deformations the body undergoes are also the *animal traits* of the head. This has nothing to do with a correspondence between animal forms and facial forms. In fact, the face lost its form by being subjected to the techniques of rubbing and brushing that disorganize it and make a head emerge in its place. The marks or traits of animality are not animal forms but rather the spirits that haunt the wiped-off parts, that pull at the head, individualizing and qualifying the head without a face.[1] Bacon's techniques of local scrubbing and

19

asignifying traits take on a particular meaning here. Sometimes the human head is replaced by an animal, but it is not the animal as a form but rather the animal as a *trait*—for example, the quivering trait of a bird spiraling over the scrubbed area, while the simulacra of portrait-faces on either side of it act as "attendants" (as in the 1976 *Triptych* [79]). Sometimes an animal, for example, a real dog, is treated as the shadow of its master [52], or conversely, the man's shadow itself assumes an autonomous and indeterminate animal existence [73]. The shadow escapes from the body like an animal we had been sheltering. In place of formal correspondences, what Bacon's painting constitutes is a *zone of indiscernibility or undecidability* between man and animal. Man becomes animal, but not without the animal becoming spirit at the same time, the spirit of man, the physical spirit of man presented in the mirror as Eumenides or Fate [77]. It is never a combination of forms, but rather the common fact: the common fact of man and animal. Bacon pushes this to the point where even his most isolated Figure is already a coupled Figure, man is coupled with his animal in a latent bullfight.

This objective zone of indiscernibility is the entire body, but the body insofar as it is flesh or meat. Of course, the body has bones as well, but bones are only its spatial structure. A distinction is often made between flesh and bone, and even between things related to them. The body is revealed only when it ceases to be supported by the bones, when the flesh ceases to cover the bones, when the two exist for each other, but each on its own terms: the bone as the material structure of the body, the flesh as the bodily material of the Figure. Bacon admires the young woman in Degas's *After the Bath* [101], whose suspended spinal column seems to protrude from her flesh, making it seem much more vulnerable and lithe, acrobatic.[2] In a completely different context, Bacon has painted such a spinal column on a Figure doubled over in contortions (*Three Figures and a Portrait*, 1975 [78]). This pictorial tension between flesh and bone is something that must be achieved. And what achieves this tension in the painting is, precisely, *meat*, through the splendor of its colors. Meat is the state of the body in which flesh and bone confront each other locally rather than being composed structurally. The same is true of the mouth and the teeth, which are little bones. In meat, the flesh seems to *descend* from the bones, while the bones rise up from the flesh. This is a feature of Bacon's that distinguishes him from Rembrandt and Soutine. If there is an "interpretation" of the body in Bacon, it lies in his taste for painting prone Figures, whose raised arm or thigh is equivalent to a bone, so that the drowsy flesh seems to descend from it. Thus, we find the two sleeping twins flanked by animal-spirit attendants in the central panel of the 1968 triptych [53]; but also the series of the sleeping man with raised arms [25], the sleeping woman with vertical legs [28], and the sleeper or addict with the hypodermic syringe [31, 58]. Well beyond the apparent sadism, the bones are like a trapeze apparatus (the carcass) upon which the flesh is the acrobat. The athleticism of the body is naturally prolonged in this acrobatics of the flesh. We can see here the importance of the *fall [chute]* in Bacon's work. Already in the crucifixions, what interests Bacon is the descent, and the inverted head that reveals the flesh. In the crucifixions of 1962 and 1965, we can see the flesh literally descending from the bones, framed by an armchair-cross and a bone-lined ring [29, 35]. For both Bacon and Kafka, the spinal column is nothing but a sword beneath the skin, slipped into the body of an innocent sleeper by an executioner.[3] Sometimes a bone will even be added only as an afterthought in a random spurt of paint.

Pity the meat! Meat is undoubtedly the chief object of Bacon's pity, his only object of pity, his Anglo-Irish pity. On this point he is like Soutine, with his immense pity for the Jew. Meat is not dead flesh; it retains all the sufferings and assumes all the colors of living flesh. It manifests such convulsive pain and vulnerability, but also such delightful invention, color, and acrobatics. Bacon does not say, "Pity the beasts," but rather that every man who suffers is a piece of meat. Meat is the common zone of man and the beast, their zone of indiscernibility; it is a "fact," a state where the painter identifies with the objects of his horror and his compassion. The painter is certainly a butcher, but he goes to the butcher shop as if it were a church, with the meat as the crucified victim (the *Painting* of 1946 [3]). Bacon is a religious painter only in butcher shops. "I've always been very moved by pictures about slaughterhouses and meat, and to me they belong very much to the whole thing of the Crucifixion.... Of course, we are meat, we are potential carcasses. If I go into a butcher shop I always think it's surprising that I wasn't there instead of the animal."[4] Near the end of the eighteenth century, the novelist K. P. Moritz described a person with "strange feelings": an extreme sense of isolation, an insignificance almost equal to nothingness; the horror of sacrifice he feels when he witnesses the execution of four men, "exterminated and torn to pieces," and when he sees the remains of these men "thrown on the wheel" or over the balustrade; his certainty that in some strange way this event concerns all of us, that this discarded meat is we ourselves, and that the spectator is already in the spectacle, a "mass of ambulating flesh"; hence his living idea that even animals are part of humanity, that we are all criminals, we are all cattle; and then, his fascination with the wounded animal, "a calf, the head, the eyes, the snout, the nostrils . . . and sometimes he lost himself in such sustained contemplation of the beast that he really believed he experienced, for an instant, the *type of existence* of such a being . . . in short, the question if he, among men, was a dog or another animal had already occupied his thoughts since childhood."[5] Moritz's passages are magnificent. This is not an arrangement of man and beast, nor a resemblance; it is a deep identity, a zone of indiscernibility more profound than any sentimental identification: the man who suffers is a beast, the beast that suffers is a man. This is the reality of becoming. What revolutionary person in art, politics, religion, or elsewhere, has not felt that extreme moment when he or she was nothing but a beast, and became responsible, not for the calves who died, but *before* the calves who died?

But can one say the same thing, exactly the same thing, about meat and the head, namely, that they are the zone of objective indecision between man and animal? Can one say objectively that the head is meat (just as meat is spirit)? Of all the parts of the body, is not the head the part that is closest to the bone? Look again at El Greco or Soutine. Yet Bacon does not seem to think of the head in this manner. The bone belongs to the face, not to the head. According to Bacon, there is no death's-head. The head is deboned rather than bony, yet it is not at all soft, but firm. The head is of the flesh, and the mask itself is not a death mask, it is a block of firm flesh that has been separated from the bone: hence the studies for a portrait of William Blake [20, 21]. Bacon's own head is a piece of flesh haunted by a very beautiful gaze emanating from eyes without sockets. And he pays tribute to Rembrandt for having known how to paint a final self-portrait as one such block of flesh without eye sockets.[6] Throughout Bacon's work, the relationship between the head and meat runs through a scale of intensity that renders it increasingly intimate. First, the meat (flesh on one side, bone on the other) is positioned on the edge of the ring or the balustrade where the Figure-head is seated [3]; but it is also the dense, fleshly rain that surrounds the head and dismantles its face beneath the umbrella [65]. The scream that comes out of the Pope's mouth, and the pity that comes out of his eyes, have meat as their object [27]. Later, the meat is given a head, through which it takes flight and descends from the cross, as in the two preceding crucifixions [29, 35]. Later still, Bacon's series of heads will assert their identity with meat, among the most beautiful of which are those painted in the colors of meat, red and blue [26]. Finally, the meat is itself the head; the head becomes the nonlocalized power of the meat, as in the 1950 *Fragment of a Crucifixion* [7], where the meat howls under the gaze of a dog-spirit perched on top of the cross. Bacon dislikes this painting because of the simplicity of its rather obvious method: it had been enough to hollow out a mouth from solid meat. Still, it is important to understand the affinity of the mouth, and the interior of the mouth, with meat, and to reach the point where the open mouth becomes nothing more than the section of a severed artery, or even a jacket sleeve that is equivalent to an artery, as in the bloodied pillow in the *Sweeney Agonistes* triptych [46]. The mouth then acquires this power of nonlocalization that turns all meat into a head without a face. It is no longer a particular organ, but the hole through which the entire body escapes, and from which the flesh descends (here the method of free, involuntary marks will be necessary). This is what Bacon calls the Scream, in the immense pity that the meat evokes.

CHAPTER 5

Recapitulative Note:
Bacon's Periods and Aspects

From the scream to the smile: dissipation —
Bacon's three successive periods — The coexistence of
all the movements — The functions of the contour

The head-meat is a becoming-animal of man. In this becoming, the entire body tends to escape from itself, and the Figure tends to return to the material structure. We have already seen this in the effort the Figure exerted upon itself in order to pass through the point or the hole; and even more so, in the state it assumed when it went into the mirror on the wall. But it has not yet dissolved into the material structure; it has not yet returned to the field in order to be truly dissipated in it, to be effaced on the wall of the closed cosmos, to melt into a molecular texture. It is this extreme point that will have to be reached, in order to allow a justice to prevail that will no longer be anything but Color or Light, a space that will no longer be anything but the Sahara.[1] Which means that, whatever its importance, becoming-animal is only one stage in a more profound becoming-imperceptible in which the Figure disappears.

The entire body escapes through the screaming mouth. The body escapes through the round mouth of the Pope or the nurse, as if through an artery [16, 24]. According to Bacon, however, this is not the last word in the series of mouths. Bacon suggests that beyond the scream there is the smile, to which, he says, he has not yet been able to gain access.[2] Bacon is certainly being modest; in fact, he has painted smiles that are among the most beautiful in painting, and which fulfill the strangest function, namely, that of securing the disappearance of the body. Bacon and Lewis Carroll meet on this single point: the smile of a cat.[3] There is already a disquieting and disappearing smile in the head of the man underneath the umbrella in the *Painting* of 1946 [3], and the face is dismantled in favor of this smile, as if there were an acid eating away at the body; and the second version of the same man accentuates and straightens the smile [65]. Furthermore, there is the scoffing, almost untenable, and insupportable smile of the 1955 *Pope* [19] or of the man sitting on the bed [11]: one senses that the smile will survive the effacement of the body. The eyes and the mouth are so completely caught up in the horizontal lines of the painting that the face is dissipated, in favor of the spatial coordinates in which only the insistent smile remains. How are we to name such a thing? Bacon suggests that this smile is "hysterical."[4] An abominable smile, an abjection of a smile. And if one dreams of introducing an order into a triptych, we believe that the 1953 triptych [13] imposes the following order, which is not to be confused with the succession of panels: the screaming mouth in the center, the hysterical smile on the left, and finally, the inclined and dissipated head on the right.[5]

At this extreme point of cosmic dissipation, in a closed but unlimited cosmos, it is clear that the Figure can no longer be isolated or put inside a limit, a ring or parallelepiped: we are faced with different coordinates. The Figure of the screaming Pope [16] is already hidden behind the thick folds (which are almost laths) of a dark, transparent curtain: the top of the body is indistinct, persisting only as if it were a mark on a striped shroud, while the bottom of the body still remains outside the curtain, which is opening out. This produces the effect of a progressive elongation, as if the body were being pulled backward by its upper half. For a rather long period of time, this technique appeared frequently in Bacon's works. The same vertical curtain strips surround and partially line the abominable smile of *Study for a Portrait* [11], while the head and the body seem to sink into the background, into the horizontal slats of the blind. It would seem that, during this entire period, conventions were required that are the opposite of those we defined at the outset. We see everywhere the reign of the blurry *[flou]* and the indeterminate, the action of a depth that pulls at the form, a thickness on which shadows play, a dark nuanced texture, effects of compression and elongation—in short, a *malerisch* treatment, as Sylvester suggests.[6] This is what justifies Sylvester in dividing Bacon's work into three periods: the first, in which the precise Figure confronts the hard and bright field of color; the second, in which the *malerisch* form is drawn against a curtained, tonal background; and finally the third, which brings together the "two opposite conventions" and returns to the vivid and thin ground, while reinventing locally the effects of blurriness by striping and brushing.[7]

Yet it is not only the third period that invents the synthesis of the two. The second period had already not so much contradicted the first period as added to it, in the unity of a style and a creation. A new position of the Figure appears, but one that coexists with the others. At its simplest, the position behind the curtains is combined perfectly with the position on the ring, bar, or parallelepiped, in a Figure that is not only isolated, stuck, and contracted, but also abandoned, escaping, evanescent, and confused, as in the 1952 *Study for a Crouching Nude* [10]. And the *Man with Dog* of 1953 [15] incorporates the three fundamental elements of painting, but within a scrambled whole where the Figure is nothing but a shadow; the puddle, an uncertain contour; and the sidewalk, a darkened surface. This is indeed the essential point: there is certainly a succession of periods, but there are also coexistent aspects that accord with the three simultaneous elements of painting, which are perpetually present. The armature or material structure, the positioned Figure, and the contour as the limit of the two—these will continue to constitute the highly precise system. It is within this system that the operations of brushing, the phenomena of blurriness, the effects of elongation and fading are produced, and which are all the stronger in that they constitute a movement within this whole that is itself precise.

There will be—or perhaps there would have been—reason to distinguish a very recent fourth period. Suppose the Figure no longer had only elements of dissipation, and that it was no longer even content to privilege or return to this element. Suppose the Figure had effectively disappeared, leaving behind only a vague trace of its former presence. The field will then open up like a vertical sky, and at the same time will increasingly take over the structuring functions: the elements of the contour will establish more and more divisions within the field, creating flat sections and regions in space that form a free armature. But at the same time, the scrambled or wiped-off zone, which used to make the Figure emerge, will now stand on its own, independent of every definite form, appearing as a pure Force without an object: the wind of the tempest, the jet of water or vapor, the eye of the hurricane, which reminds one of Turner living in a world that had turned into a steamship [110]. Everything (particularly the black section) is organized around the confrontation of the two adjacent blues, the jet of water and the field of color [82]. The fact that we are familiar with only a few instances of this new organization in Bacon's work [86, 88, 97] must not make us rule out the possibility that this is a nascent period, which would be characterized by an "abstraction" that no longer has any need of the Figure. The Figure is dissipated by realizing the prophecy: you will no longer be anything but sand, grass, dust, or a drop of water...[8] The landscape flows on its own outside of the polygon of presentation, retaining the disfigured elements of a sphinx that already seemed to be made of sand. But now the sand no longer retains any Figure, nor does the grass, earth, or water. And a radiant use of pastels lies at the transition between the Figures and these new empty spaces. The sand might even reconstitute the sphinx [83], but it is so fragile and pastelized that we sense the world of Figures is profoundly threatened by the new power.

If we confine ourselves to the three attested periods, it is difficult to comprehend the coexistence of all these movements. And yet the painting *is* this coexistence. Given the three basic elements— Structure, Figure, and Contour—a first movement ("tension") goes from the structure to the Figure. The structure then appears as a field of color, but one that will curl around the contour like a cylinder; the contour appears as an isolator—a round area, an oval, a bar or system of bars; and the Figure is isolated within the contour, in a completely closed world. But it is here that a second movement, a second tension, is brought into play, one that goes from the Figure to the material structure: the contour changes, it turns into the half-sphere of the washbasin or umbrella, the thickness of the mirror, acting as a deformer; the Figure is contracted or dilated in order to pass through a hole or into the mirror; it experiences an extraordinary becoming-animal in a series of screaming transformations; and it itself tends to return to the field of color, to dissipate into the structure with a final smile, through the intermediary of the contour that no longer acts as a deformer, but as a curtain where the Figure shades off into infinity. Thus, this most closed of worlds was also the most unlimited. If we confine ourselves to the simplest element, the contour (which begins as a simple circle or round area), we can see the variety of its functions at the same time as the development of its form: it is first of all isolating, the final territory of the Figure; but it is thus already the "depopulator" or the "deterritorializer," since it forces the structure to curl around the Figure, cutting it off from any natural milieu; it is still a vehicle, since it guides the little stroll of the Figure in its remaining territory; and it is a trapeze apparatus or prosthesis, because it sustains the athleticism of the Figure confined inside it; it then acts as a deformer, when the Figure passes into it through a hole or a point; and it again becomes a trapeze apparatus or prosthesis in a new sense, for the acrobatics of the flesh; and finally, it is the curtain behind which the Figure is dissolved by joining with the structure. In short, it is a membrane, it has never ceased to be a membrane that assures the communication in both directions between the Figure and the material structure. In the 1978 *Painting* [81], we can see that the golden orange contour that strikes the door has all these functions and is ready to assume all these forms. Everything is divided into diastole and systole, with repercussions at each level. The systole, which contracts the body, goes from the structure to the Figure, whereas the diastole, which extends and dissipates it, goes from the Figure to the structure. But there is already a diastole in the first movement, when the body extends itself in order to better close in on itself; and there is a systole in the second movement, when the body is contracted in order to escape from itself; and even when the body is dissipated, it still remains contracted by the forces that seize hold of it in order to return it to its surroundings. The coexistence of all these movements in the painting . . . is rhythm.

CHAPTER 6

Painting and Sensation

*Cézanne and sensation — The levels of sensation —
Figuration and violence — The movement of translation,
the stroll — The phenomenological unity of the senses:
sensation and rhythm*

There are two ways of going beyond figuration (that is, beyond both the illustrative and the figurative): either toward abstract form or toward the Figure. Cézanne gave a simple name to this way of the Figure: sensation. The Figure is the sensible form related to a sensation; it acts immediately upon the nervous system, which is of the flesh, whereas abstract form is addressed to the head and acts through the intermediary of the brain, which is closer to the bone. Certainly Cézanne did not invent this way of sensation in painting, but he gave it an unprecedented status. Sensation is the opposite of the facile and the ready-made, the cliché, but also of the "sensational," the spontaneous, etc. Sensation has one face turned toward the subject (the nervous system, vital movement, "instinct," "temperament"—a whole vocabulary common to both Naturalism and Cézanne), and one face turned toward the object (the "fact," the place, the event). Or rather, it has no faces at all, it is both things indissolubly, it is Being-in-the-World, as the phenomenologists say: at one and the same time I *become* in the sensation and something *happens* through the sensation, one through the other, one in the other.[1] And at the limit, it is the same body that, being both subject and object, gives and receives the sensation. As a spectator, I experience the sensation only by entering the painting, by reaching the unity of the sensing and the sensed. This was Cézanne's lesson against the impressionists: sensation is not in the "free" or disembodied play of light and

31

color (impressions); on the contrary, it is in the body, even the body of an apple. Color is in the body, sensation is in the body, and not in the air. Sensation is what is painted. What is painted on the canvas is. the body, not insofar as it is represented as an object, but insofar as it is experienced as sustaining *this* sensation (what Lawrence, speaking of Cézanne, called "the appleyness of the apple").[2]

This is the very general thread that links Bacon to Cézanne: *paint the sensation*, or, as Bacon will say in words very close to Cézanne's, *record the fact.*[3] "It is a very, very close and difficult thing to know why some paint comes across directly onto the nervous system and other paint tells you the story in a long diatribe through the brain."[4] There would seem to be only obvious differences between these two painters: Cézanne's world as landscape and still life (even before the portraits, which are treated as landscapes) versus Bacon's inverted hierarchy that dismisses still lifes and landscapes;[5] the world as Nature in Cézanne versus the world as artifact in Bacon. But precisely, are not these obvious differences in the service of "sensation" and "temperament"? In other words, are they not inscribed in what links Bacon to Cézanne, in what they have in common? When Bacon speaks of sensation, he says two things, which are very similar to Cézanne. Negatively, he says that the form related to the sensation (the Figure) is the opposite of the form related to an object that it is supposed to represent (figuration). As Valéry put it, sensation is that which is transmitted directly, and avoids the detour and boredom of conveying a story.[6] And positively, Bacon constantly says that sensation is what passes from one "order" to another, from one "level" to another, from one "area" to another. This is why sensation is the master of deformations, the agent of bodily deformations. In this regard, the same criticism can be made against both figurative painting and abstract painting: they pass through the brain, they do not act directly upon the nervous system, they do not attain the sensation, they do not liberate the Figure—all because they remain at *one and the same level.*[7] They can implement transformations of form, but they cannot attain deformations of bodies. In what sense Bacon is Cézannian, even more so than if he were a disciple of Cézanne, we will have occasion to consider later.

What does Bacon mean when, throughout the interviews, he speaks of "orders of sensation," "levels of feeling," "areas of sensation," or "shifting sequences"?[8] At first, one might think that each order, level, or area corresponds to a specific sensation: each sensation would thus be a term in a sequence or a series. For example, the series of Rembrandt's self-portraits involves us in different areas of feeling.[9] And it is true that painting, and especially Bacon's painting, proceeds through series: series of crucifixions, series of Popes, series of self-portraits, series of the mouth, of the mouth that screams, the mouth that smiles...Moreover, there can be series of simultaneity, as in the triptychs, which make at least three levels or orders coexist. And the series can be closed, when it has a contrasting composition, but it can be open, when it is continued or continuable beyond the three.[10] All this is true. But it would not be true were there not something else as well, something that is already at work in each painting, each Figure, each sensation. It is each painting, each Figure, that is itself a shifting sequence or series (and not simply a term in a series); it is each sensation that exists at diverse levels, in different orders, or in different domains. This means that there are not sensations of different orders, but different orders of one and the same sensation. It is the nature of sensation to envelop a constitutive difference of level, a plurality of constituting domains. Every sensation, and every Figure, is already an "accumulated" or "coagulated" sensation, as in a limestone figure.[11] Hence the irreducibly synthetic character of sensation. What then, we must ask, is the source of this synthetic character, through which each material sensation has several levels, several orders or domains. What are these levels, and what makes up their sensing or sensed unity?

A first response must obviously be rejected. What makes up the material synthetic unity of a sensation would be the represented object, the figured thing. This is theoretically impossible, since the Figure is opposed to figuration. But even if we observe practically, as

Bacon does, that something is nonetheless figured (for instance, a screaming Pope), this secondary figuration depends on the neutralization of all primary figuration. Bacon himself formulates this problem, which concerns the inevitable preservation of a practical figuration at the very moment when the Figure asserts its intention to break away from the figurative. We will see how he resolves the problem. In any case, Bacon has always tried to eliminate the "sensational," that is, the primary figuration of that which provokes a violent sensation. This is the meaning of the formula, "I wanted to paint the scream more than the horror."[12] When he paints the screaming Pope, there is nothing that might cause horror, and the curtain in front of the Pope is not only a way of isolating him, of shielding him from view; it is rather the way in which the Pope himself sees nothing, and screams *before the invisible*. Thus neutralized, the horror is multiplied because it is inferred from the scream, and not the reverse. And certainly it is not easy to renounce the horror, or the primary figuration. Sometimes he has to turn against his own instincts, renounce his own experience. Bacon harbors within himself all the violence of Ireland, and the violence of Nazism, the violence of war. He passes through the horror of the crucifixions, and especially the fragment of the crucifixion, or the head of meat, or the bloody suitcase. But when he passes judgment on his own paintings, he rejects all those that are still too "sensational," because the figuration that subsists in them reconstitutes a scene of horror, even if only secondarily, thereby reintroducing a story to be told: even the bullfights are too dramatic. As soon as there is horror, a story is reintroduced, and the scream is botched. In the end, the maximum violence will be found in the seated or crouching Figures, which are subjected to neither torture nor brutality, to which nothing visible happens, and yet which manifest the power of the paint all the more. This is because violence has two very different meanings: "When talking about the violence of paint, it's nothing to do with the violence of war."[13] The violence of sensation is opposed to the violence of the represented (the sensational, the cliché). The former is inseparable from its direct action on the nervous system, the levels through which it passes, the domains it traverses: being itself a Figure, it must have nothing of the nature of a represented object. It is the same with Artaud: cruelty is not what one believes it to be, and depends less and less on what is represented.

A second interpretation must also be rejected, which would confuse the levels of sensation, that is, the valencies of the sensation, with an ambivalence of feeling. At one point, Sylvester suggests, "Since you talk about recording different levels of feeling in one image... you may be expressing at one and the same time a love of the person and a hostility towards them... both a caress and an assault?" To which Bacon responds, "That is too logical. I don't think that's the way things work. I think it goes to a deeper thing: how do I feel I can make this image more immediately real to myself? That's all."[14] In fact, the psychoanalytic hypothesis of ambivalence not only has the disadvantage of localizing the ambivalence on the side of the spectator who looks at the painting; for even if we presuppose an ambivalence in the Figure itself, it would refer to feelings that the Figure would experience in relation to represented things, in relation to a narrated story. But there are no feelings in Bacon: there are nothing but affects, that is, "sensations" and "instincts," according to the formula of Naturalism. Sensation is what determines instinct at a particular moment, just as instinct is the passage from one sensation to another, the search for the "best" sensation (not the most agreeable sensation, but the one that fills the flesh at a particular moment of its descent, contraction, or dilation).

There is a third, more interesting, hypothesis. This would be the motor hypothesis. The levels of sensation would be like arrests or snapshots of motion, which would recompose the movement synthetically in all its continuity, speed, and violence, as in synthetic cubism, futurism, or Duchamp's *Nude* [102]. It is true that Bacon is fascinated by the decomposition of movement in Muybridge, which he has used as a subject matter. It is also true that he obtains very intense and violent movements of his own [39], such as George Dyer's 180-degree turn of the head toward Lucian Freud [42]. More generally, Bacon's Figures are often frozen in the middle of a strange stroll

[68], as in *Man Carrying a Child* [22] or the Van Gogh [23]. The round area or the parallelepiped that isolates the Figure itself becomes a motor, and Bacon has not abandoned the project that a mobile sculpture could achieve more easily: in this case, the contour or pedestal would slide along the length of the armature so that the Figure could make its "daily round."[15] But it is precisely the nature of this daily round that can inform us of the status of movement in Bacon. Beckett and Bacon have never been so close, and this daily round is the kind of stroll typical of Beckett's characters: they too trundle about fitfully without ever leaving their circle or parallelepiped. It is the stroll of the paralytic child and its mother clinging to the edge of the balustrade in a curious handicapped race [36]. It is the about-face in *Figure Turning* [30]. It is George Dyer's bicycle ride [40], which closely resembles that of Moritz's hero: "his vision was limited to the small piece of land he could see about him. . . . To him, the end of all things seemed to lead, at the end of his journey, *to just such a point*."[16] Therefore, even when the contour is displaced, the movement consists less of this displacement than the amoeba-like exploration that the Figure is engaged in inside the contour. Movement does not explain sensation; on the contrary, it is explained by the elasticity of the sensation, its *vis elastica*. According to Beckett's or Kafka's law, there is immobility beyond movement: beyond standing up, there is sitting down, and beyond sitting down, lying down, beyond which one finally dissipates. The true acrobat is one who is consigned to immobility inside the circle. The large feet of the Figures often do not lend themselves to walking: they are almost clubfeet (and the large armchairs often seem to resemble shoes for clubfeet). In short, it is not movement that explains the levels of sensation, it is the levels of sensation that explain what remains of movement. And in fact, what interests Bacon is not exactly movement, although his painting makes movement very intense and violent. But in the end, it is a movement "in-place," a spasm, which reveals a completely different problem characteristic of Bacon: *the action of invisible forces on the body* (hence the bodily deformations, which are due to this more profound cause). In the 1973 triptych

[73], the movement of translation occurs between two spasms, between the two movements of a contraction in one place.

Then there would be yet another hypothesis, more "phenomenological." The levels of sensation would really be domains of sensation that refer to the different sense organs; but precisely each level, each domain, would have a way of referring to the others, independently of the represented object they have in common. Between a color, a taste, a touch, a smell, a noise, a weight, there would be an existential communication that would constitute the "pathic" (non-representative) moment of *the* sensation. In Bacon's bullfights, for example, we hear the noise of the beast's hooves [56, 57]; in the 1976 triptych, we touch the quivering of the bird plunging into the place where the head should be [79], and each time meat is represented, we touch it, smell it, eat it, weigh it, as in Soutine's work; and the portrait of Isabel Rawsthorne [41] causes a head to appear to which ovals and traits have been added in order to widen the eyes, flair the nostrils, lengthen the mouth, and mobilize the skin in a common exercise of all the organs at once. The painter would thus *make visible* a kind of original unity of the senses, and would make a multisensible Figure appear visually.

But this operation is possible only if the sensation of a particular domain (here, the visual sensation) is in direct contact with a vital power that exceeds every domain and traverses them all. This power is Rhythm, which is more profound than vision, hearing, etc. Rhythm appears as music when it invests the auditory level, and as painting when it invests the visual level. This is a "logic of the senses," as Cézanne said, which is neither rational nor cerebral. What is ultimate is thus the relation between sensation and rhythm, which places in each sensation the levels and domains through which it passes. This rhythm runs through a painting just as it runs through a piece of music. It is diastole-systole: the world that seizes me by closing in around me, the self that opens to the world and opens the world itself.[17] Cézanne, it is said, is the painter who put a vital rhythm into the visual sensation. Must we say the same thing of Bacon, with his co-existent movements, when the flat field closes in around the Figure and when the Figure contracts or, on the contrary, expands in order to rejoin the field, to the point where the figure merges with the field? Could it be that Bacon's closed and artificial world reveals the same vital movement as Cézanne's Nature? Bacon is not using empty words when he declares that he is cerebrally pessimistic but nervously optimistic, with an optimism that believes only in life.[18] The same "temperament" as Cézanne? Bacon's formula would be: figuratively pessimistic, but figurally optimistic.

Hysteria

This ground, this rhythmic unity of the senses, can be discovered only by going beyond the organism. The phenomenological hypothesis is perhaps insufficient because it merely invokes the lived body. But the lived body is still a paltry thing in comparison with a more profound and almost unlivable Power *[Puissance]*. We can seek the unity of rhythm only at the point where rhythm itself plunges into chaos, into the night, at the point where the differences of level are perpetually and violently mixed.

Beyond the organism, but also at the limit of the lived body, there lies what Artaud discovered and named: the body without organs. "The body is the body / it stands alone / it has no need of organs / the body is never an organism / organisms are the enemies of bodies."[1] The body without organs is opposed less to organs than to that organization of organs we call an organism. It is an intense and intensive body. It is traversed by a wave that traces levels or thresholds in the body according to the variations of its amplitude. Thus the body does not have organs, but thresholds or levels. Sensation is not qualitative and qualified, but has only an intensive reality, which no longer determines within itself representative elements, but allotropic variations. Sensation is vibration. We know that the egg reveals just this state of the body "before" organic representation: axes and vectors, gradients, zones, kinematic movements, and dynamic tendencies, in relation to which forms are contingent or accessory. "No mouth.

No tongue. No teeth. No larynx. No esophagus. No belly. No anus." It is a whole nonorganic life, for the organism is not life, it is what imprisons life. The body is completely living, and yet nonorganic. Likewise sensation, when it acquires a body through the organism, takes on an excessive and spasmodic appearance, exceeding the bounds of organic activity. It is immediately conveyed in the flesh through the nervous wave or vital emotion. Bacon and Artaud meet on many points: the Figure is the body without organs (dismantle the organism in favor of the body, the face in favor of the head); the body without organs is flesh and nerve; a wave flows through it and traces levels upon it; a sensation is produced when the wave encounters the Forces acting on the body, an "affective athleticism," a scream-breath. When sensation is linked to the body in this way, it ceases to be representative and becomes real; and *cruelty* will be linked less and less to the representation of something horrible, and will become nothing other than the action of forces upon the body, or sensation (the opposite of the sensational). As opposed to a *misérabiliste* painter who paints parts of organs, Bacon has not ceased to paint bodies without organs, the intensive fact of the body. The scrubbed and brushed parts of the canvas are, in Bacon, parts of a neutralized organism, restored to their state of zones or levels: "the human visage has not yet found its face."

A powerful nonorganic life: this is how Worringer defined Gothic art, "the northern Gothic line."[2] It is opposed in principle to the organic representation of classical art. Classical art can be figurative, insofar as it refers to something represented, but it can also be abstract, when it extricates a geometric form from the representation. But the pictorial line in Gothic painting is completely different, as are its geometry and figure. First of all, this line is decorative; it lies at the surface, but it is a material decoration that does not outline a form. It is a geometry no longer in the service of the essential and eternal, but a geometry in the service of "problems" or "accidents": ablation, adjunction, projection, intersection. It is thus a line that never ceases to change direction, that is broken, split, diverted, turned in on itself, coiled up, or even extended beyond its natural limits, dying away in a "disordered convulsion": there are *free marks* that extend or arrest the line, acting beneath or beyond representation. It is thus a geometry or a decoration that has become vital and profound, on the condition that it is no longer organic: it elevates mechanical forces to sensible intuition, it works through violent movements. If it encounters the animal, if it becomes *animalized*, it is not by outlining a form but, on the contrary, by imposing, through its clarity and nonorganic precision, a zone where forms become indiscernible. It also attests to a high *spirituality*, since what leads it to seek the elementary forces beyond the organic is a spiritual will. But this spirituality is a spirituality of the body; the spirit is the body itself, the body without organs... (The first Figure of Bacon would be that of a Gothic decorator.)

Life provides many ambiguous approaches to the body without organs (alcohol, drugs, schizophrenia, sadomasochism, and so on). But can the living reality of this body be named "hysteria," and if so, in what sense? A wave with a variable amplitude flows through the body without organs; it traces zones and levels on this body according to the variations of its amplitude. When the wave encounters external forces at a particular level, a sensation appears. An organ will be determined by this encounter, but it is a provisional organ that endures only as long as the passage of the wave and the action of the force, and which will be displaced in order to be posited elsewhere. "No organ is constant as regards either function or position... sex organs sprout anywhere... rectums open, defecate and close... the entire organism changes color and consistency in split-second adjustments."[3] In fact, the body without organs does not lack organs, it simply lacks the organism, that is, this particular organization of organs. The body without organs is thus defined by *an indeterminate organ*, whereas the organism is defined by determinate organs: "Instead of a mouth and an anus to get out of order why not have one all-purpose hole to eat *and* eliminate? We could seal up nose and mouth, fill in the stomach, make an air hole direct into the lungs where it should have been in the first place."[4] But what does it mean to speak of a polyvalent orifice or an indeterminate organ?

Are not a mouth and an anus very distinct, and is not a passage of time needed to get from one to the other? Even in the meat, is there not a very distinct mouth, recognizable through its teeth, which cannot be confused with other organs? This is what must be understood: the wave flows through the body; at a certain level, an organ will be determined depending on the force it encounters; and this organ will change if the force itself changes, or if it moves to another level. In short, the body without organs is not defined by the absence of organs, nor is it defined solely by the existence of an indeterminate organ; it is finally defined by the *temporary and provisional presence* of determinate organs. This is one way of introducing time into the painting, and there is a great force of time in Bacon; time itself is being painted. The variation of texture and color on a body, a head, or a back (as in *Three Studies of the Male Back* of 1970 [63]) is actually a temporal variation regulated down to a tenth of a second. Hence the chromatic treatment of the body, which is very different from the treatment of the fields of color: the chronochromatism of the body is opposed to the monochromatism of the flat fields. To put time inside the Figure—this is the force of bodies in Bacon: the large male back as variation.

We can see from this how every sensation implies a difference of level (of order, of domain), and moves from one level to another. Even the phenomenological unity did not give an account of it. But the body without organs does give an account of it, if we look at the complete series: without organs—to the indeterminate polyvalent organ—to temporary and transitory organs. What is a mouth at one level becomes an anus at another level, or at the same level under the action of different forces. Now this complete series constitutes the hysterical reality of the body. If we look at the "picture" of hysteria that was formed in the nineteenth-century, in psychiatry and elsewhere, we find a number of features that have continually animated Bacon's bodies. First of all, there are the famous spastics and paralytics, the hyperesthetics or anesthetics, associated or alternating, sometimes fixed and sometimes migrant, depending on the passage of the nervous wave and the zones it invests or withdraws from.

Then, there are the phenomena of precipitation and anticipation or, on the contrary, of delay (hysteresis), of the afterward, which depend on the accelerations and delays of the wave's oscillations. Next, there is the transitory character of the organ's determination, which depends on the forces that are exerted upon it. Next, there is the direct action of these forces on the nervous system, as if the hysteric were a sleepwalker, a somnambulist in the waking state, a "Vigilambulist." Finally, there is a very peculiar feeling that arises from within the body, precisely because the body is felt *under* the body, the transitory organs are felt under the organization of the fixed organs. Furthermore, this body without organs and these transitory organs are themselves *seen*, in phenomena known as internal or external "autoscopia": it is no longer *my* head, but I feel myself inside *a* head, I see and I see myself inside a head; or else I do not see myself in the mirror, but I feel myself in the body that I see, and I see myself in this naked body when I am dressed . . . and so forth.[5] Is there a psychosis in the world that might include this hysterical condition? "A kind of incomprehensible *stopping place* in the spirit, right in the middle of everything . . . ?"[6]

Beckett's Characters and Bacon's Figures share a common setting, the same Ireland: the round area, the isolator, the Depopulator; the series of spastics and paralytics inside the round area; the stroll of the Vigilambulator; the presence of the attendant, who still feels, sees, and speaks; the way the body escapes from itself, that is, the way it escapes from the organism . . . It escapes from itself through the open mouth, through the anus or the stomach, or through the throat, or through the circle of the washbasin, or through the point of the umbrella.[7] The presence of a body without organs under the organism, the presence of transitory organs under organic representation. A clothed Figure of Bacon's is seen nude in the mirror or on the canvas (*Two Studies for a Portrait of George Dyer,* 1968 [50]). The spastics and the hyperesthetics are often indicated by wiped or scrubbed zones [71], and the anesthetics and paralytics, by missing zones (as in the very detailed 1972 triptych [70]). Above all, we will see that Bacon's whole "style" takes place in a beforehand and an afterward: what takes place before the painting has even begun, but also what takes place afterward, a hysteresis that will break off the work each time, interrupt its figurative course, and yet give it back afterward . . .

Presence, presence . . . this is the first word that comes to mind in front of one of Bacon's paintings.[8] Could this presence be hysterical? The hysteric is at the same time someone who imposes his or her presence, but also someone for whom things and beings are present, *too* present, and who attributes to every thing and communicates to every being this excessive presence. There is therefore little difference between the hysteric, the "hystericized," and the "hystericizor." Bacon explains rather testily that the hysterical smile he painted on the 1953 portrait [11], on the human head of 1953 [13], and on the 1955 Pope [19], came from a "model" who was "very neurotic and almost hysterical."[9] But in fact it is the whole painting that is hystericized. Bacon himself hystericizes when, beforehand, he abandons himself completely to the image, abandons his entire head to the camera of a photobooth, or rather, sees himself in a head that belongs to the camera, that has disappeared into the camera. What is this hysterical smile? Where is the abomination or abjection of this smile? Presence or insistence. Interminable presence. The insistence of the smile beyond the face and beneath the face. The insistence of a scream that survives the mouth, the insistence of a body that survives the organism, the insistence of transitory organs that survive the qualified organs. And in this excessive presence, the identity of an already-there and an always-delayed. Everywhere there is a presence acting directly on the nervous system, which makes representation, whether in place or at a distance, impossible. Sartre meant nothing less when he called himself a hysteric, and spoke of Flaubert's hysteria.[10]

What kind of hysteria are we speaking of here? Is it the hysteria of Bacon himself, or of the painter, or of the painting itself, or of painting in general? It is true that there are numerous dangers in constructing a clinical aesthetic (which nonetheless has the advantage of *not* being a psychoanalysis). And why refer specifically to painting, when we could invoke so many writers or even musicians (Schumann and the contraction of the finger, the audition of the voice...)? What we are suggesting, in effect, is that there is a special relation between painting and hysteria. It is very simple. Painting directly attempts to release the presences beneath representation, beyond representation. The color system itself is a system of direct action on the nervous system. This is not a hysteria of the painter, but a hysteria of painting. With painting, hysteria becomes art. Or rather, with the painter, hysteria becomes painting. What the hysteric is incapable of doing—a little art—is accomplished in painting. It must also be said that the painter *is not* hysterical, in the sense of a negation in negative theology. Abjection becomes splendor; the horror of life becomes a very pure and very intense life. "Life is frightening," said Cézanne, but in this cry he had already given voice to all the joys of line and color. Painting transmutes this cerebral pessimism into nervous optimism. Painting is hysteria, or converts hysteria, because it makes presence immediately visible. It invests the eye through color and line. But *it does not treat the eye as a fixed organ*. It liberates lines and colors from their representative function, but at the same time it also liberates the eye from its adherence to the organism, from its character as a fixed and qualified organ: the eye becomes virtually the polyvalent indeterminate organ that sees the body without organs (the Figure) as a pure presence. Painting gives us eyes all over: in the ear, in the stomach, in the lungs (the painting breathes...). This is the double definition of painting: subjectively, it invests the eye, which ceases to be organic in order to become a polyvalent and transitory organ; objectively, it brings before us the reality of a body, of lines and colors freed from organic representation. And each is produced by the other: the pure presence of the body becomes visible at the same time that the eye becomes the destined organ of this presence.

Painting has two ways of avoiding this fundamental hysteria: either by conserving the figurative coordinates of organic representation, even if that means using them in very subtle ways or making these liberated presences or unorganized bodies pass beneath or between these coordinates; or else by turning toward abstract form, and inventing a properly pictorial cerebrality ("reviving" painting in this direction). Velázquez was undoubtedly the wisest of the classical painters, possessing an immense wisdom: he created his extraordinary audacities by holding firmly to the coordinates of representation, by assuming completely the role of a documentarian . . .[11] What is Bacon's relation to Velázquez, and why does he claim him as his master? Why, when he speaks of his versions of the portrait of Pope Innocent X, does he express his doubt and discontent? In a way, Bacon has hystericized all the elements of Velázquez's painting. We cannot simply compare the two portraits of Innocent X, that of Velázquez and that of Bacon, who transforms it into the screaming Pope. We must compare Velázquez's portrait with all of Bacon's paintings. In Velázquez, the armchair already delineates the prison of the parallelepiped; the heavy curtain in back is already tending to move up front, and the mantelet has aspects of a side of beef; an unreadable yet clear parchment is in the hand, and the attentive, fixed eye of the Pope already sees something invisible looming up [112]. But all of this is strangely restrained, it is something that is going to happen, but has not yet acquired the ineluctable, irrepressible presence of Bacon's newspapers, the almost animal-like armchairs, the curtain up front, the brute meat, and the screaming mouth. Should these presences have been let loose? asks Bacon. Were not things better, infinitely better, in Velázquez? In refusing both the figurative path and the abstract path, was it necessary to display this relationship between hysteria and painting in full view? While our eye is enchanted with the two Innocent X's, Bacon questions himself.[12]

But in the end, why should all this be peculiar to painting? Can we speak of a hysterical essence of painting, under the rubric of a purely aesthetic clinic, independent of any psychiatry and psychoanalysis? Why could not music also extricate pure presences, but through an ear that has become the polyvalent organ for sonorous bodies? And why not poetry or theater, when it is those of Artaud or Beckett? This problem concerning the essence of each art, and possibly their clinical essence, is less difficult than it seems to be. Certainly music traverses our bodies in profound ways, putting an ear in the stomach, in the lungs, and so on. It knows all about waves and nervousness. But it involves our body, and bodies in general, in another element. It strips bodies of their inertia, of the materiality of their presence: it *disembodies* bodies. We can thus speak with exactitude of a sonorous body and even of a bodily combat in music—for example, in a motif—but as Proust said, it is an immaterial and disembodied combat "in which there subsists not one scrap of inert matter refractory to the mind."[13] In a sense, music begins where painting ends, and this is what is meant when one speaks of the superiority of music. It is lodged on lines of flight that pass through bodies, but which find their consistency elsewhere, whereas painting is lodged farther up, where the body escapes from itself. But in escaping, the body discovers the materiality of which it is composed, the pure presence of which it is made, and which it would not discover otherwise. Painting, in short, discovers the material reality of bodies with its line-color systems and its polyvalent organ, the eye. "Our eye," said Gauguin, "insatiable and in heat." The adventure of painting is that it is the eye alone that can attend to material existence or material presence—even that of an apple. When music sets up its sonorous system and its polyvalent organ, the ear, it addresses itself to something very different from the material reality of bodies. It gives a disembodied and dematerialized body to the most spiritual of entities: "The beats of the timpani in the Requiem are sharp, majestic, and divine, and they can only announce to our surprised ears the coming of a being who, to use Stendhal's words, surely has relations with another world."[14] This is why music does not have hysteria as its clinical essence, but is confronted more and more with a galloping schizophrenia. To hystericize music we would have to reintroduce colors, passing through a rudimentary or refined system of correspondence between sounds and colors.

CHAPTER 8

Painting Forces

From another point of view, the question concerning the separation of the arts, their respective autonomy, and their possible hierarchy loses all importance. For there is a community of the arts, a common problem. In art, and in painting as in music, it is not a matter of reproducing or inventing forms, but of capturing forces. For this reason no art is figurative. Paul Klee's famous formula—"Not to render the visible, but to render visible"—means nothing else. The task of painting is defined as the attempt to render visible forces that are not themselves visible. Likewise, music attempts to render sonorous forces that are not themselves sonorous. That much is clear. Force is closely related to sensation: for a sensation to exist, a force must be exerted on a body, on a point of the wave. But if force is the condition of sensation, it is nonetheless not the force that is sensed, since the sensation "gives" something completely different from the forces that condition it. How will sensation be able to sufficiently turn in on itself, relax or contract itself, so as to capture these non-given forces in what it gives us, to make us sense these insensible forces, and raise itself to its own conditions? It is in this way that music must render nonsonorous forces sonorous, and painting must render invisible forces visible. Sometimes these are the same thing: time, which is nonsonorous and invisible—how can time be painted, how can time be heard? And elementary forces such as pressure, inertia, weight, attraction, gravitation, germination—how can they be rendered? Sometimes, on the contrary, the insensible force of one art instead seems to take part in the "givens" of another art: for example, how to paint sound, or even the scream? (And conversely, how to make colors audible?)

This is a problem of which painters are very conscious. When pious critics criticized Millet for painting peasants who were carrying an offertory like a sack of potatoes, Millet responded by saying that the weight common to the two objects was more profound than their figurative distinction. As a painter, he was striving to paint the force of that weight, and not the offertory *or* the sack of potatoes. And was it not Cézanne's genius to have subordinated all the techniques of painting to this task: rendering visible the folding force of mountains, the germinative force of a seed, the thermic force of a landscape, and so on? And Van Gogh: Van Gogh even invented unknown forces, the unheard-of force of a sunflower seed. For many painters, however, the problem of *capturing forces,* no matter how conscious it may have been, was mixed with another problem, equally important but less pure. This other problem was *the decomposition and recomposition of effects:* for example, the decomposition and recomposition of depth in the Renaissance, the decomposition and recomposition of colors in impressionism, the decomposition and recomposition of movement in cubism. We can see how one problem leads to the other, since movement, for example, is an effect that refers both to a unique force that produces it, and to a multiplicity of decomposable and recomposable elements beneath this force.

Bacon's Figures seem to be one of the most marvelous responses in the history of painting to the question, How can one make invisible forces visible? This is the primary function of the Figures. In this respect, we will see that Bacon remains relatively indifferent to the problem of effects. Not that he despises them, but he thinks that in the whole history of painting, they have been adequately mastered by the painters he admires, particularly the problem of movement, of "rendering" movement.[1] But if this is the case, it is reason enough to confront even more directly the problem of "rendering" invisible forces visible. This is true of all Bacon's series of heads and the series of self-portraits, and it is even the reason he made these series [34, 48, 49, 54]: the extraordinary agitation of these heads is not derived from a movement that the series would supposedly reconstitute, but rather from the forces of pressure, dilation, contraction, flattening, and elongation that are exerted on the immobile head. They are like the forces of the cosmos confronting an intergalactic traveler immobile in his capsule. It is as if invisible forces were striking the head from many different angles. The wiped and swept parts of the face here take on a new meaning, because they mark the zone where the force is in the process of striking. This is why the problems Bacon faces are indeed those of deformation and not transformation. These are two very different categories. The transformation of form can be abstract or dynamic. But deformation is always bodily, and it is static, it happens at one place; it subordinates movement to force, but it also subordinates the abstract to the Figure. When a force is exerted on a scrubbed part, it does not give birth to an abstract form, nor does it combine sensible forms dynamically: on the contrary, it turns this zone into a zone of indiscernibility that is common to several forms, irreducible to any of them; and the lines of force that it creates escape every form through their very clarity, through their deforming precision (we saw this in the becoming-animal of the Figures). Cézanne was perhaps the first to have made deformations without transformation, thereby making truth fall back on the body. Here again Bacon is Cézannian: for both Bacon and Cézanne, the deformation is obtained in the *form at rest;* and at the same time, the whole material environment, the structure, begins to stir, "walls twitch and slide, chairs bend or rear up a little, cloths curl like burning paper..."[2] Everything is now related to forces, everything is force. It is force that constitutes deformation as an act of painting: it lends itself neither to a transformation of form nor to a decomposition of elements. And Bacon's deformations are rarely constrained or forced, they are not tortures, despite appearances: on the contrary, they are the most natural postures of a body that has been reorganized by the simple force being exerted upon it: the desire to sleep, to vomit, to turn over, to remain seated as long as possible...

We must consider the special case of the scream. Why does Bacon think of the scream as one of the highest objects of painting? "Paint the scream..." [16, 24]. It is not at all a matter of giving color to a particularly intense sound. Music, for its part, is faced with the same task, which is certainly not to render the scream harmonious, but to establish a relationship between the sound of the scream and the forces that sustain it. In the same manner, painting will establish a relationship between these forces and the visible scream (the mouth that screams). But the forces that produce the scream, that convulse the body until they emerge at the mouth as a scrubbed zone, must not be confused with the visible spectacle before which one screams, nor even with the perceptible and sensible objects whose action decomposes and recomposes our pain. If we scream, it is always as victims of invisible and insensible forces that scramble every spectacle, and that even lie beyond pain and feeling. This is what Bacon means when he says he wanted "to paint the scream more than the horror."[3] If we could express this as a dilemma, it would be: either I paint the horror and I do not paint the scream, because I make a figuration of the horrible; or else I paint the scream, and I do not paint the visible horror, I will paint the visible horror less and less, since the scream captures or detects an invisible force.[4] Alban Berg knew how to make music out of the scream in the scream of Marie, and then in the very different scream of Lulu. But in both cases, he established a relationship between the sound of the scream and inaudible forces, those of the Earth in the horizontal scream of Marie, and those of Heaven in the vertical scream of Lulu. Bacon creates the painting of the scream because he establishes a relationship between the visibility of the scream (the open mouth as a shadowy abyss) and invisible forces, which are nothing other than the forces of the future. It was Kafka who spoke of detecting the diabolical powers of the future knocking at the door.[5] Every scream contains them potentially. Innocent X screams, but he screams behind the curtain, not only as someone who can no longer be seen, but as someone who cannot see, who has nothing left to see, whose only remaining function is to render visible these invisible forces that are making him scream, these powers of the future. This is what is expressed in the phrase "to scream at"—not to scream *before* or *about*, but to scream *at* death—which suggests this coupling of forces, the perceptible force of the scream and the imperceptible force that makes one scream.

This is all very curious, but it is a source of extraordinary vitality. When Bacon distinguishes between two violences, that of the spectacle and that of sensation, and declares that the first must be renounced to reach the second, it is a kind of declaration of faith in life. The interviews contain many statements of this sort. Bacon says that he himself is cerebrally pessimistic; that is, he can scarcely see anything *but* horrors to paint, the horrors of the world. But he is nervously optimistic, because visible figuration is secondary in painting, and will have less and less importance: Bacon will reproach himself for painting too much horror, as if that were enough to leave the figurative behind; he moves more and more toward a Figure without horror. But why is it an act of vital faith to choose "the scream more than the horror," the violence of sensation more than the violence of the spectacle? The invisible forces, the powers of the future—are they not already upon us, and much more insurmountable than the worst spectacle and even the worst pain? Yes, in a certain sense—every piece of meat testifies to this. But in another sense, no. When, like a wrestler, the visible body confronts the powers of the invisible, it gives them no other visibility than its own. It is within this visibility that the body actively struggles, affirming the possibility of triumphing, which was beyond its reach as long as these powers remained invisible, hidden in a spectacle that sapped our strength and diverted us. It is as if combat had now become possible. The struggle with the shadow is the only real struggle. When the visual sensation confronts the invisible force that conditions it, it releases a force that is capable of vanquishing the invisible force, or even befriending it. Life screams *at* death, but death is no longer this all-too-visible thing that makes us faint; it is this invisible force that life detects, flushes out, and makes visible through the scream. Death is judged from the point of view of life, and not the reverse, as we like to believe.[6] Bacon, no less than Beckett, is one of those artists who, in the name of a very intense life, can call for an even more intense life. He is not a painter who "believes" in death. His is indeed a figurative *misérabilisme*, but one that serves an increasingly powerful Figure of life. The same homage should be paid to Bacon that can be paid to Beckett or Kafka. In the very act of "representing" horror, mutilation, prosthesis, fall, or failure, they have erected indomitable Figures, indomitable through both their insistence and their presence. They have given life a new and extremely direct power of laughter.

Since the visible movements of the Figures are subordinated to the invisible forces exerted upon them, we can go behind the movements to these forces, and make an empirical list of the forces Bacon detects and captures. Although Bacon likens himself to a "pulverizer" or a "grinder," he is really more like a detective. The first invisible forces are those of isolation: they are supported by the fields, and become visible when they wrap themselves around the contour and wrap the fields around the Figure. The second are the forces of deformation, which seize the Figure's body and head, and become visible whenever the head shakes off its face, or the body its organism. (Bacon knows how to "render" intensely, for example, the flattening force of sleep [53, 76].) The third are the forces of dissipation, when the Figure fades away and returns to the field: what then renders these forces visible is a strange smile. But there are still many other forces. What can be said, first of all, about that invisible force of coupling that sweeps over two bodies with an extraordinary energy, but which they render visible by extracting from it a kind of polygon or diagram? And beyond that, what is the mysterious force that can only be captured or detected by triptychs? It is at the same time a force (characteristic of light) that unites the whole, but also a force that separates the Figures and panels, a luminous separation that should not be confused with the preceding isolation. Can Life, can Time, be rendered sensible, rendered visible? To render time visible, to render the force of time visible—Bacon seems to have done this twice. There is the force of changing time, through the allotropic variation of bodies, "down to a tenth of a second," which involves deformation; and then there is the force of eternal time, the eternity of time, through the uniting-separating that reigns in the triptychs, a pure light. To render Time sensible in itself is a task common to the painter, the musician, and sometimes the writer. It is a task beyond all measure or cadence.

CHAPTER 9

Couples and Triptychs

Coupled Figures — The battle and the coupling of sensation —
Resonance — Rhythmic Figures — Amplitude and the three
rhythms — Two types of "matters of fact"

It is a characteristic of sensation to pass through different levels due
to the action of forces. But two sensations, each having its own level
or zone, can also confront each other and make their respective levels
communicate. Here we are no longer in the domain of simple vibration, but that of resonance. There are thus two Figures coupled
together. Or rather, what is decisive is the coupling of sensations:
there is one and the same *matter of fact* for two Figures, or even a
single coupled Figure for two bodies. From the start, we have seen
that, according to Bacon, the painter could not give up the idea of
putting several Figures in the painting at the same time, although
there was always the danger of reintroducing a "story" or falling
back into narrative painting. The question thus concerns the possibility that there may exist relations between simultaneous Figures
that are nonillustrative and nonnarrative (and not even logical), and
which could be called, precisely, "matters of fact." Such is indeed
the case here, where the coupling of sensations from different levels
creates the coupled Figure (and not the reverse). What is painted is
the sensation. There is a beauty to these entangled Figures [69].
They do not merge with each other, but are rendered indiscernible
by the extreme precision of the lines, which acquire a kind of autonomy in relation to the body, like a *diagram* whose lines would bring
together nothing but sensations.[1] There is one Figure common to two
bodies, or one "fact" common to two Figures, without the slightest
story being narrated [12, 17, 60, 61]. Bacon never stopped painting

coupled Figures, either during his *malerisch* period or in the later works of clarity: crushed bodies, included in a single Figure, under a single force of coupling. Far from contradicting the principle of isolation, the coupled Figure seems to make the isolated Figures simple particular cases. For even in cases where there is a single body or a simple sensation, the different levels through which this sensation passes already necessarily constitute couplings of sensation. Vibration already produces resonance. For example, the man under the umbrella of 1946 [3] is a simple Figure, corresponding to the passage of sensations from top to bottom (the meat above the umbrella) and from bottom to top (the head seized by the umbrella). But it is also a coupled Figure, corresponding to the confrontation of the sensations in the head and in the meat, to which the horrible falling smile bears witness. In the end, there are only coupled Figures in Bacon (the *Lying Figure in a Mirror* of 1971 [67] has to be unique, it counts as two Figures, it is a veritable diagram of sensation). Even the simple Figure is often coupled with its animal.

At the beginning of his book on Bacon, John Russell invokes Proust and involuntary memory.[2] Although Proust's world seems to have little in common with Bacon's (though Bacon often invokes the involuntary), one still has the impression that Russell is correct. This is perhaps because Bacon, when he refuses the double way of a figurative painting and an abstract painting, is put in a situation analogous to that of Proust in literature. Proust did not want an abstract literature that was too voluntary (philosophy), any more than he wanted a figurative, illustrative, or narrative literature that merely told a story. What he was striving for, what he wanted to bring to light, was a kind of Figure, torn away from figuration and stripped of every figurative function: a Figure-in-itself, for example, the Figure-in-itself of Combray. He himself spoke of "truths written with the help of figures."[3] And if, in many cases, he resorted to involuntary memory, it was because it succeeded in making this pure Figure appear, as opposed to voluntary memory, which was content to illustrate or narrate the past.

How, according to Proust, did involuntary memory operate? It coupled together two sensations that existed at different levels of the body and that seized each other like two wrestlers, the present sensation and the past sensation, in order to make something appear that was irreducible to either of them, irreducible to the past as well as to the present: this Figure. And in the end, the fact that the two sensations were divided into present and past, and thus that it was an instance of memory, was of little importance. There were cases where the coupling of sensation, the imprint of sensations, made no appeal to memory; for instance, desire, or still more profoundly, art (Elstir's painting or Vinteuil's music). What mattered was the resonance of the two sensations when they seized each other, like the sensation of the violin and the sensation of the piano in the sonata. "It was like the beginning of the world, as if there had been, as yet, only the two of them on Earth, or rather *in this world closed to all the rest*, constructed by the logic of a creator in such a way that in it no one else would ever exist except the two of them: this sonata."[4] This is the Figure of the sonata, or the emergence of this sonata *as* a Figure. The same thing happens in the septet, where two motifs confront each other violently, each defined by a sensation, the one as a spiritual "calling," the other as a bodily "pain" or a "neuralgia." We are no longer concerned with the difference between music and painting. The important point is that the two sensations are coupled together like "wrestlers" and form a "combat of energies," even if it is a disembodied combat, from which is extracted an ineffable essence, a resonance, an epiphany erected within the closed world.[5] Proust knew very well how to imprison things and people: he did so, he said, in order to capture their colors (Combray in a cup of tea, Albertine in a bedroom).

In a curious passage, Bacon the portraitist says that he does not like to paint the dead, nor people that he does not know (since they have no flesh); and those he knows he does not like to have in front of his eyes. He prefers a current photograph and a recent memory, or rather the sensation of a current photograph and that of a recent impression: this is what makes the act of painting a kind of "recall."[6] But in fact it is not a question of memory (even less so than it was for Proust). What matters is the confrontation of the two sensations, and the resonance that is derived from it. It is like the wrestlers whose movement was decomposed by Muybridge's photographs. It is not that everything is at war, embattled, as one might think from the viewpoint of a figurative pessimist. What produces the struggle or confrontation is the coupling of diverse sensations in two bodies, and not the reverse. So that the struggle is also the variable Figure of two bodies sleeping intertwined, or which desire mixes together, or which painting makes resonate. Sleeping, desire, art: these are places of confrontation and resonance, places of a struggle.

Coupling or resonance is not the only development of the complex sensation. Coupled Figures frequently appear in the triptychs, particularly in the central panel. Yet we quickly realize that the coupling of sensation, important as it is, gives us no means of discovering the nature of a triptych, its function, and above all the relations that exist between its three parts. The triptych is undoubtedly the form in which the following demand is posed most precisely: there must be a relationship between the separated parts, but this relationship must be neither narrative nor logical. The triptych does not imply a progression, and it does not tell a story. Thus it too, in turn, has to incarnate a common fact for diverse Figures. It has to produce a "matter of fact." But the previous solution of coupling is of no use here, for the Figures are and remain separated in the triptych. They must remain separated, and do not resonate. There are therefore two types of nonnarrative relations, two types of "matters of fact" or common facts: the coupled Figure and the separated Figures as parts of a triptych. But how can these latter Figures have a common fact?

The same question could be asked apart from the triptychs. Bacon admires Cézanne's *The Bathers* [98] because several Figures are put together on the canvas, and yet they are not caught up in a "story."[7] These Figures are separated, and not at all coupled: their inclusion on a single canvas must thus imply a common fact of a different type than the coupling of sensation. Consider a painting of Bacon's like the 1963 *Man and Child* [32]: the two Figures, the contorted man sitting on the chair and the little girl standing stiffly, are separated by a whole region of the field that cuts an angle between the two. Russell comments: "Is the girl standing in disgrace before her unforgiving father? Is she the man's jailor, outfacing him with folded arms as he writhes in his chair and looks the other way? Is she an abnormality, a physical freak returned to haunt him, or is he a man set on high, a judge who shall shortly pass sentence?" And he refuses each hypothesis in turn, for they would all introduce a narration into the painting. "We shall never know, and we shouldn't even ask to know."[8] Doubtless one could say that the painting is the possibility of all these hypotheses or narrations at the same time. But this is because the painting itself is beyond all narration. This is thus one case in which the "matter of fact" cannot be a coupling of sensation, and must take into account the separation of Figures that are nonetheless united in the painting. The little girl seems to function as an "attendant." But this attendant, as we have seen, does not signify an observer or a spectator-voyeur (although it might also be one from the point of view of a figuration that remains, despite everything). More profoundly, the attendant only indicates a constant, a measure or cadence, in relation to which we can appraise a variation. This is why the girl is stiff like a stake, and seems to beat time with her clubfoot, while the man is seated in a double variation, as if he were seated on a barber's chair that raises and lowers him through the levels of sensation, which he travels through in both directions. Even Beckett's characters require attendants that measure the intimate allotropic variations of their bodies, and that *look inside their heads* ("Can you hear me?" "Can anyone see me?" "Can anyone hear me?" "Does anyone care about me at all?"). In both Bacon and Beckett, the attendant can be reduced to the circle of the circus ring, to a photographic apparatus or camera, to a photo-memory. But there must be an attendant-Figure for the variation-Figure. And doubtless the double variation, moving in two directions, can affect a single Figure, but obviously it can also be divided between two Figures. And the attendant, for its part, can be two attendants or several attendants (but in any case the interpretation of the attendant as a voyeur or spectator is insufficient and merely figurative).

Thus the problem already exists quite apart from the triptychs, but it is in the triptychs, with their separate panels, that it is posed in the pure state. We would then have three rhythms: first, an "active" rhythm, with an increasing variation or amplification; then, a "passive" rhythm, with a decreasing variation or elimination; and finally, the "attendant" rhythm. Rhythm would cease to be attached to and dependent on a Figure: *it is rhythm itself that would become the Figure, that would constitute the Figure.* This is exactly what Olivier Messiaen said about music, when he distinguished between active rhythm, passive rhythm, and attendant rhythm, and demonstrated that they no longer referred to characters that have rhythm, but themselves constitute rhythmic characters. "Imagine a scene in a play between three characters: the first acts in a brutal manner by hitting the second; the second character suffers this act, since his actions are dominated by those of the first; lastly, the third character is present at the conflict but remains inactive."[9] We can thus formulate a hypothesis about the nature of the triptych, about its law or its order. That the triptych was traditionally a mobile painting or piece of furniture, that the wings of the triptych often included observers, priors, or tutelaries—all of this suits Bacon, who thinks of his paintings as movable objects, and likes to paint constant attendants on them. But how does he restore such a topicality to the triptych, how does he implement this total re-creation of the triptych? He makes the triptych equivalent to the movements or parts of a piece of music more than a piece of furniture. The triptych would be the distribution of the three basic rhythms. There is a circular organization in the triptych, rather than a linear one.

This hypothesis allows us to assign the triptychs a privileged place in Bacon's oeuvre. Paint the sensation, which is essentially rhythm . . . But in the simple sensation, rhythm is still dependent on the Figure, it appears as the *vibration* that flows through the body without organs, it is the vector of the sensation, it is what makes the sensation pass from one level to another. In the coupling of sensation, rhythm is already liberated, because it confronts and unites the diverse levels of different sensations: it is now *resonance*, but it is still merged together with the melodic lines, the points and counterpoints, of a coupled Figure; it is the diagram of the coupled Figure. With the triptych, finally, rhythm takes on an extraordinary amplitude in a *forced movement* that gives it an autonomy and produces in us the impression of Time: the limits of sensation are broken, exceeded in all directions; the Figures are lifted up, or thrown in the air, placed upon aerial riggings from which they suddenly fall. But at the same time, in this immobile fall, the strangest phenomenon of recomposition or redistribution is produced, for it is the rhythm itself that becomes sensation; it is rhythm that becomes Figure, according to its own separated directions, the active, the passive, and the attendant... Messiaen looked to Stravinsky and Beethoven as his precursors, and Bacon could look to Rembrandt for his own (and Soutine, with very different means). For in Rembrandt's still lifes or genre paintings, but also in his portraits, there is first of all a disturbance or vibration: the contour is in the service of vibration. But there are also resonances that are derived from the layers of superimposed sensations. And even more, there is what Claudel described, this amplitude of light, an immense "stable and motionless background," that will have a strange effect, assuring the extreme division of Figures, their distribution into active, passive, and attendant Figures, as in Rembrandt's *Nightwatch* [108] (or in those still lifes where the glasses at a constant level are "half-aerial attendants," while the two spirals of the peeled lemon and the mother-of-pearl are set against each other).[10]

CHAPTER 10

Note: What Is a Triptych?

The attendant — The active and the passive —
The fall: the active reality of the difference in level —
Light, union, and separation

The hypothesis must be verified: is there an order in the triptychs, and does this order consist in distributing the three fundamental rhythms, one of which would be the attendant or the measure of the two others? But since this order, if it exists, combines many variables, we must expect it to present very diverse aspects. We can only respond to this question through an empirical study of the triptychs.

First, we can see that there are many explicit attendants in the triptychs: 1962, the two disquieting characters in the left panel [29]; 1965, the two small old men seated at a table in the right panel and the nude woman in the left panel [35]; 1968, the two "attendants," one nude and the other clothed, on the left and right panels [53]; 1970, the observer on the left and the photographer on the right [61]; 1974, the photographer on the right [74]; 1976, the two simulacra of portraits on the right and left [79], and so on. But we can also see that things are much more complicated. For the attendant-function can refer to these characters figuratively, since there is always a figuration that persists, even if only secondarily. Yet this same attendant-function can suddenly refer figuratively to a completely different character. The attendant in this second sense will not be the same as the attendant in the first sense. Moreover, this more profound attendant (in the second sense) will not be one who observes or sees, but on the contrary one who sees the superficial attendant (in the first sense): there will thus have been a genuine exchange of the attendant-function in the triptych. The more profound attendant, the figural attendant, will be one who does not see, who is not in a position to see. It will be defined as an attendant because of a completely different feature, namely, its horizontality, its almost constant level. The horizontal defines a rhythm that is retrogradable in itself, thus without increase or decrease, without augmentation or diminution: it is the attendant-rhythm, whereas the two others, which are vertical, are only retrogradable in relation to each other, each being the retrogradation of the other.[1]

In the triptychs, it is thus on the horizontal that we must seek the attendant-rhythm with a constant value. This horizontal can be presented in several Figures. First, there is the flat hysterical smile, which not only appears, as we have seen, in the 1953 triptych of the head (left panel) [13], but already in the 1944 triptych of monsters (central panel) [1], where the head with bandaged eyes is not a head preparing to die, but an abominable head that smiles along the horizontal deformation of the mouth. The horizontal can also be executed in a movement of translation, as in the 1973 triptych [73]: a horizontal translation in the center panel makes us move from the spasm on the right to the spasm on the left (here again we see that the order of succession, when there is one, does not necessarily go from left to right). Again, the horizontal can be executed in a prone body, as in the central panel of 1962 [29], the central panel of 1964 [33], the left panel of 1965 [35], and the central panel of 1966 [38], where a flattening force is exerted on the sleepers. Or again, it can be executed in several prone or coupled bodies, following a horizontal diagram, as in the two pairs of sleepers in the right and left panels of *Sweeney Agonistes* [46], or in the two sleepers in the central panels of the 1970 triptychs [60, 61]. The triptychs thus use coupled Figures in their own way. Here then is the first element of complexity, one that, by its very complexity, testifies to a law of the triptychs: an attendant-function is first imposed upon the visible characters, but it abandons them to affect more profoundly a rhythm that has itself become a character, a retrogradable rhythm or attendant that follows the horizontal. (Bacon occasionally puts the two attendants, the visible character and the rhythmic character, together on the same panel, as in the left panel of the 1965 triptych [35], or the right panel of *Sweeney Agonistes* [46].)

At this point, a second element of complexity appears. To the extent that the attendant-function circulates throughout the painting, to the extent that the visible attendant gives way to the rhythmic attendant, two things take place. On the one hand, the rhythmic attendant does not appear as such immediately; it comes into existence only when the function is passed on to it; until then it still has an active or passive rhythm. This is why the sleeping characters in the triptychs often have a disturbing trace of activity or passivity; although they are aligned on the horizontal, they still retain a heaviness or vivacity, a relaxation or contraction that comes from elsewhere. Thus, in *Sweeney Agonistes* [46], the coupled Figure in the left panel is lying passively on its back, while the one on the right is still animated, almost whirling. Or again, even more frequently, the same coupled Figure will be composed of an active body and a passive body, with one part of the Figure pointing below the horizon (the head, the buttocks . . .). But on the other hand, conversely, the visible attendant, which now ceases to be one, is free to assume other functions; it thus turns into an active rhythm or a passive rhythm, it links itself to one or the other at the very moment it ceases to be an attendant. For example, the visible attendants of the 1962 triptych [29] seem to raise themselves up like vampires, but one is passive and supporting his back so as not to fall, while the other is active and ready to fly away; or again, in a triptych of 1970 [61], we can compare the visible attendant on the left and the one on the right. There is thus a great mobility within the triptych, a great circulation. The rhythmic attendants are active or passive Figures that have just discovered their constant level or are still seeking it, whereas the visible attendants are on the verge of springing up or falling down, becoming active or passive.

A third element of complexity concerns these two other rhythms, active and passive. What do these two directions of vertical variation consist of? How are these two opposable rhythms distributed? There are simple cases in which it is a matter of a *descending-rising* opposition. In the 1944 triptych of monsters [1], a descending head whose hair is falling downward, and an inverted head whose screaming mouth is aimed upward, are placed on either side of the head with the horizontal smile; or again, in the 1970 *Studies of the Human Body* [62], the two recumbent Figures in the middle panel are flanked, on the left, by a form that seems to rise up from its shadow and, on the right, by a form that seems to descend into itself and into a puddle. But this is already a particular case of another opposition, a *diastolic-systolic* opposition. Here, it is the contraction that is opposed to a kind of extension, expansion, or descent-flow. The 1965 *Crucifixion* [35] opposes the descent-flow of the crucified meat on the central panel, to the extreme contraction of the Nazi executioner; the 1964 *Three Figures in a Room* [33] opposes the dilatation of the man on the toilet, on the left, to the contortion of the man on the stool, on the right. And perhaps it is the *Three Studies of the Male Back* of 1970 [63] that displays most subtly, through lines and colors, the opposition between a large, relaxed, rose-colored back on the left, and a tense, red-and-blue-colored back on the right, while the blue in the center seems to remain at a constant level, even covering the dark mirror so as to emphasize its attendant-function. But sometimes the opposition is completely different and surprising: it is the opposition of *the naked and the clothed*, which we find on the right and left panels of a 1970 triptych [60], but which we had also found on the right and left panels of the 1968 triptych [53] in the two visible attendants. More subtly, in the 1966 triptych of Lucian Freud [38] the exposed shoulder with the contracted head, on the left, is opposed to the covered shoulder with the relaxed and sunken head, on the right. Finally, is there not another opposition that would even account for the naked and the clothed? This would be the *augmentation-diminution* opposition. There can be an extraordinary subtlety in what one chooses to add or take away: here we enter into a more profound domain of values and rhythm, since what is added or subtracted is not a quantity, a multiple or submultiple, but values defined by their precision or "brevity." In particular, an added value can sometimes be produced by random spurts of paint, which Bacon likes to utilize.

But perhaps the most striking and most moving example is in the triptych of August 1972 [70]. If the attendant in the center is furnished with elongations and a well-defined mauve oval, we find a diminished torso in the Figure on the left, since a whole portion of it is missing, while the torso on the right is in the process of being built up, half of it having already been added. But then everything changes with the legs. In the left panel, one leg is already finished, while the other is in the process of being defined; in the right panel, it is just the opposite: one leg is already amputated, while the other is flowing away. Correlatively, the mauve oval in the center changes status, turning into a pink pool lying next to the chair, in the left panel, and a red discharge from the leg, in the right panel. In this way, Bacon uses mutilations and prostheses in a game of added and subtracted values. It is like a collection of hysterical "sleepings" and "awakenings" affecting the diverse parts of a body. But it is above all one of Bacon's most profoundly musical paintings.

If we reach such a great degree of complexity here, it is because these diverse oppositions are not equivalent, and their terms do not coincide. The result is a combinatorial freedom, and no list can ever be complete. The rising-descending, contraction-dilatation, and systolic-diastolic oppositions cannot be identified with each other. A discharge, for example, is indeed a descent, as well as a dilatation and expansion, but there is also a contraction in the discharge, as in the man at the washbasin [80] and the man on the toilet in the 1973 triptych [73]. But must we still maintain an opposition between the local dilatation of the anus and the local contraction of the throat? Or is the opposition between two distinct contractions, with a passage from one to the other in the triptych? Everything can coexist, and the opposition can vary or even be reversed depending on the viewpoint one adopts, that is, depending on the value one considers. Sometimes, especially in the so-called closed series, the opposition is almost reduced to its direction in space. In the end, what matters in the two opposable rhythms is that each is the "retrogradation" of the other, while a common and constant value appears in the attendant-rhythm, retrogradable in itself. This relativity of the triptych, however, is not sufficient. For if we have the impression that one of the opposable rhythms is "active" and the other "passive," what is it that justifies this impression, even if we assign these two terms extremely variable points of view that can change for a single painting, depending on the part one considers?

What presides over the assignation in each case this time seems to be rather simple. In Bacon, primacy is given to the descent. Strangely, it is the active that descends, that plunges. *The active is the fall*, but it is not necessarily a descent in space, in extension. It is the descent as the passage of sensation, as the difference in level contained in the sensation. Most artists, when confronted with this problem of intensity in the sensation, seem to have encountered the same response: the difference in intensity is experienced in a fall. Hence the idea of a fight *for* the fall: "Over their heads their hands touched 'accidentally.' And as they touched they pulled them down abruptly and violently. For some time they both gazed attentively at their joined hands. Then they suddenly fell down—it was impossible to tell who had been pushed by whom—it looked as though it was their hands that had pushed them down."[2] It is like this in Bacon: the flesh descends from the bones, the body descends from the arms and the raised thighs. Sensation develops through the fall, by falling from one level to another. The idea of a positive and active reality of the fall is essential here.

Why is the difference in level not experienced in the other direction, as a rise? Because the fall must not be interpreted in a thermodynamic manner, as if it produced an entropy, a tendency to equalize at the lowest level. On the contrary, the fall exists to affirm the difference in level as such. All *tension* is experienced in a fall. Kant laid down the principle of intensity when he defined it as an instantaneously apprehended magnitude: he concluded that the plurality apprehended in this magnitude could only be represented by its approximation to negation = 0.[3] Consequently, even when sensation tends toward a superior or higher level, it can only make us experience it by the approximation of this superior level to zero, that is, by a fall. Whatever the sensation may be, its intensive reality is a descent in depth that has a greater or lesser "magnitude," and not a rise. Sensation is inseparable from the fall that constitutes its most inward movement or "clinamen." This idea of the fall implies no context of misery, failure, or suffering, though it might be illustrated more easily in such a context. But just as the violence of a sensation must not be confused with the violence of a represented scene, the ever deeper fall of a sensation must not be confused with a fall represented in space, except for convenience and humor. The fall is what is most alive in the sensation, that through which the sensation is experienced as living. The intensive fall can thus coincide with a spatial descent, but also with a rise. It can coincide with a diastole, a dilatation or a dissipation, but equally with a contraction or systole. It can coincide with a diminution, but equally with an augmentation. In short, everything that develops is a fall (there are developments by diminutions). The fall is precisely the active rhythm.[4] Consequently, it becomes possible in each painting to determine (through the sensation) what counts as the fall. It is in this way that we determine the active rhythm, which varies from one painting to the other. And the opposable character, present in the painting, will assume the role of the passive rhythm.

We can thus summarize these laws of the triptych, whose necessity is grounded in the coexistence of the three panels: (1) the distinction between the three rhythms or the three rhythmic Figures; (2) the existence of a attendant-rhythm, along with the circulation of this attendant throughout the painting (visible attendant and rhythmic attendant); (3) the determination of an active rhythm and a passive rhythm, with all the variations that depend on the character chosen to represent the active rhythm. These laws have nothing to do with a conscious formula that would simply need to be applied; they are a part of this irrational logic, or this logic of sensation, that constitutes painting. They are neither simple nor voluntary. They must not be confused with the order of succession from left to right. They do not assign a univocal role to the center panel. The constants they imply change depending on the case at hand.

They govern extremely variable terms, from the viewpoint of both their nature and their relations. There are so many movements in Bacon's paintings that the law of the triptychs can only be a movement of movements, or a state of complex forces, inasmuch as movement is always derived from the forces exerted upon the body. But the final question that remains is to know which forces correspond to the triptych. If its laws are those that we have just laid out, what forces are they responding to?

In the first place, in the simple paintings, there was a double movement, from the structure to the Figure, and from the Figure to the structure: forces of isolation, deformation, and dissipation. But in the second place, there is a movement between the Figures themselves: forces of coupling that incorporate the phenomena of isolation, deformation, and dissipation in their own levels. Finally, there is a third type of movement and force, and it is here that the triptych intervenes: it can, in turn, incorporate coupling as a phenomenon, but it operates with other forces and implies other movements. On the one hand, it is no longer the Figure that returns to the structure or field; rather, it is the relations between Figures that are violently projected onto the field and are now governed by the uniform color or the naked light; so that, in many cases [60, 62], the Figures look like trapeze artists whose milieu is no longer anything but light and color. We at once realize that the triptychs have need of this luminous or colored vivacity, and are rarely susceptible to a global *malerisch* treatment; the 1953 triptych of the head [13] would be one of the rare exceptions. But on the other hand, if the unity of light or color immediately incorporates the relationships between the Figures and the field, the result is that the Figures also attain their maximum separation in light and color: a force of separation or division sweeps over them, very different from the preceding force of isolation.

This then is the principle of the triptychs: the maximum unity of light and color for the maximum division of Figures. Such was the lesson of Rembrandt: it is light that engenders rhythmic characters.[5] This is why the body of the Figure passes through three levels of force, which culminate in the triptych. First, there is the fact of the Figure, when the body is submitted to forces of isolation, deformation, and dissipation. Then, a first "matter of fact," when two Figures are included in a single fact, that is, when the body submits to a force of coupling, a melodic force. Finally, the triptych: it is the separation of bodies in universal light and universal color, which becomes the common fact of the Figures, their rhythmic being, the second "matter of fact" or the union that separates. A joining-together separates the Figures and separates the colors—such is light. The Figure-beings separate while falling into the black light. The color-fields separate while falling into the white light. Everything becomes aerial in these triptychs of light; the separation itself is in the air. Time is no longer in the chromatism of bodies, it has become a monochromatic eternity. An immense space-time unites all things, *but only by introducing between them the distances of a Sahara, the centuries of an Aion:* the triptych and its separated panels. The triptych, in this sense, is indeed one way of going beyond "easel" painting; the three canvasses remain separated, but they are no longer isolated; and the frame or borders of a painting no longer refer to the limitative unity of each, but to the distributive unity of the three. And in the end, there are nothing but triptychs in Bacon: even the isolated paintings are, more or less visibly, composed like triptychs.

CHAPTER 11

The Painting before Painting

Cézanne and the fight against the cliché — Bacon and photographs — Bacon and probabilities — Theory of chance: accidental marks — The visual and the manual — The status of the figurative

It is a mistake to think that the painter works on a white surface. The figurative belief follows from this mistake. If the painter were before a white surface, he could reproduce on it an external object functioning as a model, but such is not the case. The painter has many things in his head, or around him, or in his studio. Now everything he has in his head or around him is already in the canvas, more or less virtually, more or less actually, before he begins his work. They are all present in the canvas as so many images, actual or virtual, so that the painter does not have to cover a blank surface but rather would have to empty it out, clear it, clean it. He does not paint in order to reproduce on the canvas an object functioning as a model; he paints on images that are already there, in order to produce a canvas whose functioning will reverse the relations between model and copy. In short, what we have to define are all these "givens" *[données]* that are on the canvas before the painter's work begins, and determine, among these givens, which are obstacles, which are helps, or even the effects of a preparatory work.

In the first place, there are *figurative givens*. Figuration exists, it is a fact, and it is even a prerequisite of painting. We are besieged by photographs that are illustrations, by newspapers that are narrations, by cinema images, by television images. There are psychic clichés just as there are physical clichés—ready-made perceptions, memories, phantasms. There is a very important experience here for the painter: a whole category of things that could be termed clichés already fills the canvas, before the beginning. It is dramatic. Cézanne seems to have effectively passed through this dramatic experience at its highest point. Clichés are always-already on the canvas, and if the painter is content to transform the cliché, to deform or mutilate it, to manipulate it in every possible way, this reaction is still too intellectual, too abstract: it allows the cliché to rise again from its ashes; it leaves the painter within the milieu of the cliché, or else gives him or her no other consolation than parody. D. H. Lawrence wrote some superb passages on this ever-renewed experience of Cézanne's: "After a fight tooth-and-nail for forty years, he did succeed in knowing an apple, fully; and, not quite as fully, a jug or two. That was all he achieved. It seems little, and he died embittered. But it is the first step that counts, and Cézanne's apple is a great deal, more than Plato's Idea....If Cézanne had been willing to accept his own baroque cliché, his drawing would have been perfectly conventionally 'all right,' and not a critic would have had a word to say about it. But when his drawing was conventionally all right, to Cézanne himself it was mockingly all wrong, it was cliché. So he flew at it and knocked all the shape and stuffing out of it, and when it was so mauled that it was all wrong, and he was exhausted with it, he let it go; bitterly, because it was still not what he wanted. And here comes in the comic element in Cézanne's pictures. His rage with the cliché made him distort the cliché sometimes into parody, as we see in pictures like *The Pasha* [99] and *La Femme* [100]....He wanted to express something, and *before* he could do it he had to fight the hydra-headed cliché, whose last head he could never lop off. The fight with the cliché is the most obvious thing in his pictures. The dust of battle rises thick, and the splinters fly wildly. And it is this dust of battle and flying of splinters which his imitators still so fervently imitate.... I am convinced that what Cézanne himself wanted *was* representation. He *wanted* true-to-life representation. Only he wanted it *more* true-to-life. And once you have got photography, it is a very, very difficult thing to get representation *more* true-to-life....Try as he might, women remained a known, ready-made cliché object for him, and he *could not* break through the concept obsession to get at the intuitive awareness of her. Except with his wife—and in his wife he did at least know the appleyness.... With men Cézanne often dodged it by insisting on the clothes, those stiff cloth jackets bent into thick folds, those hats, those blouses, those curtains.... Where Cézanne did sometimes escape the cliché altogether and really give a complete intuitive interpretation of actual objects is in some of the still-life compositions.... Here he is inimitable. His imitators imitate his accessories of tablecloths folded like tin, etc.—the unreal parts of his pictures—but they don't imitate the pots and apples, because they can't. It's the real appleyness, and you can't imitate it. Every man must create it new and different out of himself: new and different. The moment it looks 'like' Cézanne, it is nothing."[1]

Clichés, clichés! The situation has hardly improved since Cézanne. Not only has there been a multiplication of images of every kind, around us and in our heads, but even the reactions against clichés are creating clichés. Even abstract painting has not been the last to produce its own clichés: "all these tubes and corrugated vibrations are stupid enough for anything and pretty sentimental."[2] Every imitator has always made the cliché rise up again, even from what had been freed from the cliché. The fight against clichés is a terrible thing. As Lawrence says, it is already something to have succeeded, to have gotten somewhere, with regard to an apple, or a jug or two. The Japanese know that a whole life barely suffices for a single blade of grass. This is why great painters are so severe with their own work. Too many people mistake a photograph for a work of art, a plagiarism for an audacity, a parody for a laugh, or worse yet, a miserable stroke of inspiration for a creation. But great painters know that it is not enough to mutilate, maul, or parody the cliché in order to obtain a true laugh, a true deformation. Bacon is as severe with himself as was Cézanne, and like Cézanne, he ruined many of his paintings, or renounced them, threw them away, as soon as the enemy reappeared. He passes judgment: the series of Crucifixions? Too sensational, too sensational to be felt. Even the Bullfights, too dramatic. The series of Popes? "I have tried very, very unsuccessfully to do certain records—distorted records" of Vélazquez's Pope, and "I regret them, because I think they're very silly... because I think that this thing was an absolute thing."[3] What then, according to Bacon himself, should remain of Bacon's work? Some of the series of heads, perhaps, one or two aerial triptychs, and a large back of a man. Nothing more than an apple, or one or two jugs.

We can see how Bacon's problem arises in relation to photography. He is truly fascinated by photographs (he surrounds himself with photographs; he paints his portraits from photographs of the model, while also making use of completely different photographs; he studies photographs of past paintings; and he has an extraordinary abandon for photographs of himself...) At the same time, he ascribes no aesthetic value to the photograph (he says he prefers photographs that have no ambition in this regard, like those of Muybridge; above all, he likes X rays and medical plates or, for the series of heads, pictures from photo booths; and he senses a certain abjection in his own love of the photograph, his effusion for the photograph...) How are we to explain this attitude? It is due to the fact that the figurative givens are much more complex than they appear to be at first. No doubt they are ways of seeing, and as such, they are illustrative and narrative reproductions or representations (photographs, newspapers). But we can already see that they can work in two ways: by resemblance or by convention, through analogy or through a code. And no matter how they work, they themselves are something, they exist in themselves: they are not only ways of seeing, *they are what is seen, until finally one sees nothing else.*[4] The photograph "creates" the person or the landscape in the sense that we say the newspaper creates the event (and is not content to narrate it). What we see, what we perceive, are photographs. The most significant thing about the photograph is that it forces upon us the "truth" of implausible and doctored images. Bacon has no intention of reacting against this movement; on the contrary, he abandons himself to it, and not without delight. Like Lucretius's simulacrum, photographs seem to him to cut across ages and temperaments, to come from afar, in order to fill every room or every brain. He therefore does not simply criticize photographs for being figurative or for representing something, since he is very sensitive to the fact that they *are* something, that they impose themselves upon sight and rule over the eye completely. They can thus lay claim to aesthetic pretensions and compete with painting. Bacon does not believe they succeed at this, because he thinks the photograph tends to reduce sensation to a single level, and is unable to include within the sensation the difference between constitutive levels.[5] But even if it could happen, as in Eisenstein's cinema-images or Muybridge's photo-images, it would only be by means of a transformation of the cliché or, as Lawrence said, by mauling the image. It would not create the kind of deformation that art produces (except in miracles like those of Eisenstein). In short, even when the photograph ceases to be merely figurative, it remains figurative as a given, as a "perceived thing"—the opposite of painting.

This is why, despite all his abandon, Bacon has a radical hostility toward the photograph. Many modern or contemporary painters have integrated the photograph into the creative process of painting. They did this directly or indirectly, sometimes because they recognized a certain artistic power in photography, and sometimes, more simply, because they thought they could avoid the cliché by using the photograph to transform the picture.[6] Now what is striking is that Bacon, for his part, sees nothing but imperfect solutions in all these methods: at no point does he ever integrate the photograph into the creative process. Occasionally he is content to paint something that functions as a photograph in relation to the Figure, and thus plays the role of an attendant; or else, twice, to paint a camera that sometimes resembles a prehistoric beast, sometimes a heavy rifle (like Marey's rifle, which decomposed movement) [61, 74]. Bacon's whole attitude, after all his reckless abandon, is one that rejects the photograph. This is because the photograph was much more fascinating, especially for him, when it already filled the entire painting, before the painter set to work. Consequently, one cannot leave the photograph behind or escape from clichés simply by transforming the cliché. The greatest transformation of the cliché will not be an act of painting, it will not produce the slightest pictorial deformation. It would be much better to abandon oneself to clichés, to collect them, accumulate them, multiply them, as so many prepictorial givens: "the will to lose the will" comes first.[7] Only when one leaves them behind, through rejection, can the work begin.

Bacon does not claim to dictate universal solutions. This is simply the particular path he follows with regard to the photograph. But what appear to be very different givens also seem to manifest themselves on the canvas, and inspire a practically analogous attitude in Bacon. For example, the interviews address the question of chance as often as the question of the photograph. And when Bacon speaks of chance, he does so in much the same way that he speaks of the photograph: he has a very complex sentimental attitude (here again, with abandon) but from which he draws rules for rejection and very precise action. He often speaks of chance with his friends, but he seems to have had a hard time making himself understood. For he divides this domain into two parts, one of which is still rejected in the prepictorial stage, while the other belongs to the act of painting itself. If we consider a canvas before the painter begins working, all the places on it seem to be equivalent, they are all equally "probable." And if they are not equivalent, it is because the canvas is a well-defined surface, with limits and a center. But even more so, it depends on what the painter wants to do, and what he has in his head: this or that place becomes privileged in relation to this or that project. The painter has a more or less precise idea of what he wants to do, and this prepictorial idea is enough to make the probabilities unequal. There is thus an entire order of *equal and unequal probabilities* on the canvas. And it is when the unequal probability becomes almost a certitude that I can begin to paint. But at that very moment, once I have begun, how do I proceed so that what I paint does not become a cliché? "Free marks" will have to be made rather quickly on the image being painted so as to destroy the nascent figuration in it and to give the Figure a chance, which is the *improbable itself.* These marks are accidental, "by chance"; but clearly the same word, "chance," no longer designates probabilities, but now designates a type of choice or action without probability.[8] These marks can be called "nonrepresentative," precisely because they depend on the act of chance and express nothing regarding the visual image: they only concern the hand of the painter. In themselves, they serve no other purpose than to be utilized and reutilized by the hand of the painter, who will use them to wrench the visual image away from the nascent cliché, to wrench himself away from the nascent illustration and narration. He will use the manual marks to make the visual image of the Figure emerge. From start to finish, accident and chance (in this second sense) will have been an act or a choice, a certain type of act or choice. Chance, according to Bacon, is inseparable from a possibility of utilization. It is *manipulated chance*, as opposed to *conceived or seen probabilities*.

Puis Servien proposed a very interesting theory in which he claimed to dissociate two domains that were usually confused: probabilities, which are givens, the objects of a possible science, and which concern the dice before they are thrown; and chance, which designates, on the contrary, a type of choice, nonscientific and not yet aesthetic.[9] Here is an original conception that seems to be spontaneously close to Bacon's, and which distinguishes him from other recent painters who have invoked chance or, more generally, art as play. For first of all, everything changes depending on whether the game invoked is of a combinatorial type (chess) or a "throw-by-throw" type (roulette without a Martingale). For Bacon, it is a matter of roulette, and he plays several tables at the same time—for example, three tables, exactly as if he were in front of the three panels of a triptych.[10] But what this constitutes is precisely a set of probabilistic visual givens, to which Bacon can abandon himself all the more insofar as they are *prepictorial*; they express a prepictorial state of the painting, and will not be integrated into the act of painting. On the other hand, the chance choice made at each move is, rather, nonpictorial or apictorial: *it will become pictorial*, it will be integrated into the act of painting, to the extent that it consists of manual marks that will reorient the visual whole, and will *extract the improbable Figure from the set of figurative probabilities*. We believe that this felt distinction between chance and probabilities is very important for Bacon. It ex-plains the mass of misunderstandings that set Bacon against those who speak with him about chance, or who compare him with other painters. For example, he has been compared with Duchamp, who let three threads fall on the painted canvas, and fixed them exactly where they fell [103]; but for Bacon, this is nothing more than a set of probabilistic, prepictorial givens, which are not part of the act of painting. To take another example, Bacon is asked if anyone at all, such as his cleaning woman, would be capable of making random marks or not. And this time, the complex response is that, yes, the cleaning woman could do it in principle, abstractly; but she could not do it in fact, because she would not know how to utilize this chance or how to manipulate it.[11] It is in the manipulation, in the re-action of the manual marks on the visual whole, that chance becomes pictorial or is integrated into the act of painting. Hence Bacon's ob-stinate insistence, despite the incomprehension of his interlocutors, that there is no chance except "manipulated" chance, no accident except a "utilized" accident.[12]

In short, Bacon can have the same attitude toward both clichés and probabilities: a reckless, almost hysterical, abandon, since he turns this abandon into a ruse, a snare. Clichés and probabilities are on the canvas; they fill it, they must fill it, before the painter's work begins. And the reckless abandon comes down to this: the painter himself must enter into the canvas before beginning. The canvas is already so full that the painter must enter into the canvas. In this way, he enters into the cliché, and into probability. He enters into it precisely because he *knows what he wants to do*, but what saves him is the fact that he *does not know how to get there*, he does not know how to do what he wants to do.[13] He will only get there by getting out of the canvas. The painter's problem is not how to enter into the can-vas, since he is already there (the prepictorial task), but how to get out of it, thereby getting out of the cliché, getting out of probability (the pictorial task). It is the chance manual marks that will give him a chance, though not a certitude, which would still imply a maxi-mum probability. In fact, the manual marks could easily add nothing and definitively botch the painting. But if there is a chance, it is because they work by extracting the visual whole from its figurative state, in order to constitute a Figure that has finally become pictorial.

One can only fight against the cliché with much ruse, perseverance, and prudence: it is a task perpetually renewed with every painting, with every moment of every painting. It is the way of the Figure. For it is easy to oppose the figural to the figurative in an abstract manner, but we never cease to trip over the objection of fact: the Figure is still figurative; it still represents someone (a screaming man, a smiling man, a seated man), it still narrates something, even if it is a surrealistic tale (head-umbrella-meat, howling meat...). We can now say that the opposition of the Figure to the figurative exists in a very complex inner relationship, and yet is not practically compromised or even attenuated by this relationship. There is a first, prepictorial figuration: it is on the canvas and in the painter's head, in what the painter wants to do, before the painter begins, in the form of clichés and probabilities. This first figuration cannot be completely eliminated; something of it is always conserved.[14] But there is a second figuration: the one that the painter obtains, this time as a result of the Figure, as an effect of the pictorial act. For the pure presence of the Figure is indeed the reconstitution of a representation, the re-creation of a figuration ("this is a seated man, a Pope that screams or smiles..."). As Lawrence said, the first figuration (the photograph) should be criticized, not for being too faithful or "true-to-life," but for not being faithful enough. And these two figurations—the figuration conserved despite everything and the recovered figuration, the false fidelity and the true—do not have the same nature. Between the two a leap in place is produced, a deformation in place, the emergence-in-place of the Figure: the pictorial act. Between what the painter wants to do and what he does there was necessarily a know-how, a "how-to." *A probable visual whole (first figuration) has been disorganized and deformed by free manual traits that, by being reinjected into the whole, will produce the improbable visual Figure (second figuration).* The act of painting is the unity of these free manual traits and their effect upon and reinjection into the visual whole. By passing through these traits, figuration recovers and re-creates, but does not resemble, the figuration from which it came. Hence Bacon's constant formula: create resemblance, but through accidental and nonresembling means.[15]

So the act of painting is always shifting, it is constantly oscillating between a beforehand and an afterward: the hysteria of painting ... Everything is already on the canvas, and in the painter himself, before the act of painting begins. Hence the work of the painter is shifted back and only comes later, afterward: manual labor, out of which the Figure will emerge into view...

CHAPTER 12

The Diagram

The diagram in Bacon (traits and color-patches)[1] —
Its manual character — Painting and the experience
of catastrophe — Abstract painting, code, and optical space —
Action Painting, diagram, and manual space —
What Bacon dislikes about both these ways

We do not listen closely enough to what painters have to say. They say that the painter is *already* in the canvas, where he or she encounters all the figurative and probabilistic givens that occupy and preoccupy the canvas. An entire battle takes place on the canvas between the painter and these givens. There is thus a preparatory work that belongs to painting fully, and yet precedes the act of painting. This preparatory work can be done in sketches, though it need not be, and in any case sketches do not replace it (like many contemporary painters, Bacon does not make sketches).[2] This preparatory work is invisible and silent, yet extremely intense, and the act of painting itself appears as an afterward, an *après-coup* ("hysteresis") in relation to this work.

What does this act of painting consist of? Bacon defines it in this way: make random marks (lines-traits); scrub, sweep, or wipe the canvas in order to clear out locales or zones (color-patches); throw the paint, from various angles and at various speeds. Now this act, or these acts, presupposes that there were already figurative givens on the canvas (and in the painter's head), more or less virtual, more or less actual. It is precisely these givens that will be removed by the act of painting, either by being wiped, brushed, or rubbed, or else covered over. For example, a mouth: it will be elongated, stretched from one side of the head to the other. For example, the head: part of it will be cleared away with a brush, broom, sponge, or rag. This is what Bacon calls a "graph" or a *Diagram*: it is as if a Sahara, a zone of the Sahara, were suddenly inserted into the head; it is as if a piece of rhinoceros skin, viewed under a microscope, were stretched over it; it is as if the two halves of the head were split open by an ocean; it is as if the unit of measure were changed, and micrometric, or even cosmic, units were substituted for the figurative unit.[3] A Sahara, a rhinoceros skin: such is the suddenly outstretched diagram. It is as if, in the midst of the figurative and probabilistic givens, a *catastrophe* overcame the canvas.

It is like the emergence of another world. For these marks, these traits, are irrational, involuntary, accidental, free, random. They are nonrepresentative, nonillustrative, nonnarrative. They are no longer either significant or signifiers: they are a-signifying traits. They are traits of sensation, but of confused sensations (the confused sensations, as Cézanne said, that we bring with us at birth). And above all, they are manual traits. It is here that the painter works with a rag, stick, brush, or sponge; it is here that he throws the paint with his hands.[4] It is as if the hand assumed an independence, and began to be guided by other forces, making marks that no longer depend on either our will or our sight. These almost blind manual marks attest to the intrusion of another world into the visual world of figuration. To a certain extent, they remove the painting from the optical organization that was already reigning over it and rendering it figurative in advance. The painter's hand intervenes in order to shake its own dependence and break up the sovereign optical organization: one can no longer see anything, as if in a catastrophe, a chaos.

This is the act of painting, or the turning point of the painting. There are two ways in which the painting can fail, once visually and once manually. One can remain entangled in the figurative givens and the optical organization of representation; but one can also spoil the diagram, botch it, so overload it that it is rendered inoperative (which is another way of remaining in the figurative: one will have simply mutilated or mauled the cliché . . .).[5] The diagram is thus the operative set of asignifying and nonrepresentative lines and zones, line-strokes and color-patches. And the operation of the diagram, its function, says Bacon, is to be "suggestive." Or, more rigorously, to use language similar to Wittgenstein's, it is to introduce "possibilities of fact."[6] Because they are destined to give us the Figure, it is all the more important for the traits and color-patches to break with figuration. This is why they are not sufficient in themselves, but must be "utilized." They mark out possibilities of fact, but do not yet constitute a fact (the pictorial fact). In order to be converted into a fact, in order to evolve into a Figure, they must be reinjected into the visual whole; but it is precisely through the action of these marks that the visual whole will cease to be an optical organization; it will give the eye another power, as well as an object that will no longer be figurative.

The diagram is the operative set of traits and color-patches, of lines and zones. Van Gogh's diagram, for example, is the set of straight and curved hatch marks that raise and lower the ground, twist the trees, make the sky palpitate, and which assume a particular intensity from 1888 onward. We can not only differentiate diagrams, we can also date the diagram of a painter, because there is always a moment when the painter confronts it most directly. The diagram is indeed a chaos, a catastrophe, but it is also a germ of order or rhythm. It is a violent chaos in relation to the figurative givens, but it is a germ of rhythm in relation to the new order of the painting. As Bacon says, it "unlocks areas of sensation."[7] The diagram ends the preparatory work and begins the act of painting. There is no painter who has not had this experience of the chaos-germ, where he or she no longer sees anything and risks foundering: the collapse of visual coordinates. This is not a psychological experience, but a properly pictorial experience, although it can have an immense influence on the psychic life of the painter. Painters here confront the greatest of dangers both for their work and for themselves. It is a kind of experience that is constantly renewed by the most diverse painters: Cézanne's "abyss" or "catastrophe," and the chance that this abyss will give way to rhythm; Paul Klee's "chaos," the vanishing "gray point," and the chance that this gray point will "leap over itself" and unlock dimensions of sensation ...[8] Of all the arts, painting is undoubtedly the only one that necessarily, "hysterically," integrates its own catastrophe and consequently is constituted as a flight in advance. In the other arts, the catastrophe is only associated. But painters pass through the catastrophe themselves, embrace the chaos, and attempt to emerge from it. Where painters differ is in their manner of embracing this nonfigurative chaos, and in their evaluation of the pictorial order to come, and the relation of this order with this chaos. In this respect, we might perhaps distinguish three great paths, each of which groups together very different painters, but each of which designates a "modern" function of painting, or expresses what painting claims to bring to "modern man" (why still paint today?).

Abstraction would be one of these paths, but it is a path that reduces the abyss or chaos (as well as the manual) to a minimum: it offers us an asceticism, a spiritual salvation. Through an intense spiritual effort, it raises itself above the figurative givens, but it also turns chaos into a simple stream we must cross in order to discover the abstract and signifying Forms. Mondrian's square leaves the figurative (landscape) and leaps over chaos. It retains a kind of oscillation from this leap. Such an abstraction is essentially seen. One is tempted to say of abstract painting what Péguy said of Kantian morality: it has pure hands, but it has no hands. This is because the abstract forms are part of a new and purely optical space that no longer even needs to be subordinate to manual or tactile elements. In fact, they are distinguished from simple geometrical forms by "tension": tension is what internalizes in the visual the manual movement that describes the form and the invisible forces that determine it. It is what makes the form a properly visual transformation. Abstract optical space has no need of the tactile connections that classical representation was still organizing. But it follows that what abstract painting elaborates is less a diagram than a symbolic *code*, on the basis of great formal oppositions. It replaced the diagram with a code. This code is "digital," not in the sense of the manual, but in the sense of a finger that counts. "Digits" are the units that group together visually the terms in opposition. Thus, according to Kandinsky, vertical-white-activity, horizontal-black-inertia, and so on. From this is derived a conception of binary choice that is opposed to random choice. Abstract painting took the elaboration of such a properly pictorial code very far (as in Auguste Herbin's "plastic alphabet," in which the distribution of forms and colors can be done according to the letters of a word).[9] It is the code that is responsible for answering the question of painting today: what can save man from "the abyss," from external tumult and manual chaos? Open up a spiritual state for the man of the future, a man without hands. Restore to man a pure and internal optical space, which will perhaps be made up exclusively of the horizontal and the vertical. "Modern man seeks rest because he is deafened by the external."[10] The hand is reduced to a finger that presses on an internal optical keyboard.

A second path, often named abstract expressionism or *art informel*, offers an entirely different response, at the opposite extreme of abstraction. This time the abyss or chaos is deployed to the maximum. Somewhat like a map that is as large as the country, the diagram merges with the totality of the painting, the entire painting is diagrammatic. Optical geometry disappears in favor of a manual line, exclusively manual. The eye has difficulty following it. The incomparable discovery of this kind of painting is that of a line (and a patch of color) that does not form a contour, that delimits nothing, neither inside nor outside, neither concave nor convex: Pollock's line, Morris Louis's stain. It is the northern stain, the "Gothic line": the line does not go from one point to another, but passes *between* points, continually changing direction, and attains a power greater than 1, becoming adequate to the entire surface. From this point of view, we can see how abstract painting remained figurative, since its line still delimited an outline. If we seek the precursors of this new path, of this radical manner of escaping the figurative, we will find them every time a great painter of the past stopped painting things in order "to paint between things."[11] Turner's late watercolors conquer not only all the forces of impressionism, but also the power of an explosive line without outline or contour, which makes the painting itself an unparalleled catastrophe (rather than illustrating the catastrophe romantically). Moreover, is this not one of the most prodigious constants of painting that is here being selected and isolated? In Kandinsky, there were nomadic lines without contour next to abstract geometric lines; and in Mondrian, the unequal thickness of the two sides of the square opened up a virtual diagonal without contours. But with Pollock, this line-trait and this color-patch will be pushed to their functional limit: no longer the transformation of the form but a decomposition of matter, which abandons us to its lineaments and granulations. The painting thus becomes a catastrophe-painting and a diagram-painting at one and the same time. This time, it is at the point closest to catastrophe, in absolute proximity, that modern man discovers rhythm: we can easily see how this response to the question of a "modern" function of painting is different from that given by abstraction. Here it is no longer an inner vision that gives us the infinite, but a manual power that is spread out "all over,"[12] from one edge of the painting to the other.

In the unity of the catastrophe and the diagram, man discovers rhythm as matter and material. The painter's instruments are no longer the paintbrush and the easel, which still conveyed the subordination of the hand to the requirements of an optical organization. The hand is liberated, and makes use of sticks, sponges, rags, syringes: Action Painting, the "frenetic dance" of the painter around the painting, or rather in the painting, which is no longer stretched on an easel but nailed, unstretched, to the ground. There has been a conversion from the horizon to the ground: the optical horizon reverts completely to the tactile ground. The diagram expresses the entire painting at once, that is, the optical catastrophe and the manual rhythm. The current evolution of abstract expressionism is completing this process by realizing what was still little more than a metaphor in Pollock: (1) the extension of the diagram to the spatial and temporal whole of the painting (displacement of the "beforehand" and the "afterward"); (2) the abandonment of any visual sovereignty, and even any visual control, over the painting in the process of being executed (the blindness of the painter); (3) the elaboration of lines that are "more" than lines, surfaces that are "more" than surfaces, or, conversely, volumes that are "less" than volumes (Carl André's planar sculptures, Robert Ryman's fibers, Martin Barré's laminated works, Christian Bonnefoi's strata).[13]

It is all the more curious that the American critics, who took the analysis of abstract expressionism very far, could have defined it as the creation of a purely optical space, exclusively optical, peculiar to "modern man." This seems to us to be a quarrel over words, an ambiguity of words. In effect, what they meant was that the pictorial space lost all the imaginary tactile referents that, in classical three-dimensional representation, made it possible to see depths and contours, forms and grounds. But these tactile referents of classical representation expressed a relative subordination of the hand to the eye, of the manual to the visual. By liberating a space that is (wrongly) claimed to be purely optical, the abstract expressionists in fact did nothing other than to make visible an exclusively manual space, defined by the "planarity" of the canvas, the "impenetrability" of the painting, and the "gesturality" of the color—a space that is imposed upon the eye as an absolutely foreign power in which the eye can find no rest.[14] These are no longer the tactile referents of vision, but precisely because it is the manual space of what is seen, a violence done to the eye. In the end, it was abstract painting that produced a purely optical space and suppressed tactile referents in favor of an eye of the mind: it suppressed the task of controlling the hand that the eye still had in classical representation. But Action Painting does something completely different: it reverses the classical subordination, it subordinates the eye to the hand, it imposes the hand on the eye, and it replaces the horizon with a ground.

One of the most profound tendencies of modern painting is the tendency to abandon the easel. For the easel was a decisive element not only in the maintenance of a figurative appearance, and not only in the relationship between the painter and Nature (the search for a motif), but also in the delimitation (frame and borders) and internal organization of the painting (depth, perspective . . .). What matters today is less the fact—does the painter still have an easel?—than the tendency, and the diverse ways this tendency is realized. In an abstraction of Mondrian's type, the painting ceases to be an organism or an isolated organization in order to become a division of its own surface, which must create its own relations with the divisions of the "room" in which it will be hung. In this sense, Mondrian's painting is not decorative but architectonic, and abandons the easel in order to become mural painting. Pollock and others explicitly reject the easel in a completely different manner, namely, by making "all-over" paintings, by rediscovering the secret of the "Gothic line" (in Worringer's sense), by restoring an entire world of equal probabilities, by tracing lines that cross the entire painting and that start and continue off the frame, and by opposing to the organic notions of symmetry and center the power of a mechanical repetition elevated to intuition. This is no longer an easel painting but a ground painting (true easels have no other horizon than the ground).[15] But in truth there are many ways of breaking with the easel. Bacon's triptych form is one of these ways, very different from the two preceding ways. In Bacon, what is true of the triptychs is also true of each independent painting, which is always, in one way or another, composed like a triptych. In the triptych, as we have seen, the borders of each of the three panels cease to isolate, though they continue to separate and divide. This uniting-separating is Bacon's technical solution, which brings his entire set of techniques into play, and distinguishes them from the techniques of abstract and informal painting. Are these three ways of once again becoming "Gothic"?

The important question is, Why did Bacon not become involved in either of the two preceding paths? The severity of his reactions, rather than claiming to pass judgment, simply indicates what was not right for him and explains why Bacon personally took neither of these paths. On the one hand, he is not attracted to paintings that tend to substitute a visual and spiritual code for the involuntary diagram (even if there is an exemplary attitude on the part of the artist). The code is inevitably cerebral and lacks sensation, the essential reality of the fall, that is, the direct action upon the nervous system. Kandinsky defined abstract painting by "tension," but according to

Bacon, tension is what abstract painting lacks the most. By internalizing tension in the optical form, abstract painting neutralized it. Finally, because it is abstract, the code can easily become a simple symbolic coding of the figurative.[16] On the other hand, Bacon is not drawn to abstract expressionism, or to the power and mystery of the line without contour. This is because the diagram covers the entire painting, he says, and because its proliferation creates a veritable "mess." All the violent methods of Action Painting—stick, brush, broom, rag, and even pastry bag—are let loose in a catastrophe-painting. This time sensation is indeed attained, but it remains in an irremediably confused state. Bacon will never stop speaking of the absolute necessity of preventing the diagram from proliferating, the necessity of confining it to certain areas of the painting and certain moments of the act of painting. He thinks that, in this domain of the irrational trait and the line without contour, Michaux went further than Pollock, precisely because he remained a master of the diagram.[17]

Save the contour—nothing is more important for Bacon than this. A line that delimits nothing still has a contour or outline itself. Blake at least understood this.[18] The diagram must not eat away at the entire painting; it must remain limited in space and time. It must remain operative and controlled. The violent methods must not be given free rein, and the necessary catastrophe must not submerge the whole. The diagram is a possibility of fact—it is not the Fact itself. Not all the figurative givens have to disappear; and above all, a new figuration, that of the Figure, should emerge from the diagram and make the sensation clear and precise. To emerge from the catastrophe ... Even if, as an afterthought, one finishes a painting with a spurt of paint, it functions like a local "whiplash" that makes us emerge from the catastrophe rather than submerging us further.[19] Could we at least say that during the *malerisch* period the diagram covered the whole painting? Had not the entire surface of the painting been lined with traits of grass, or variations of a dark color-patch functioning as a curtain? But even then, the precision of the sensation, the clarity of the Figure, and the rigor of the contour continued to act beneath the color-patch or the traits—which did not efface the former, but instead gave them a power of vibration and nonlocalization (the mouth that smiles or screams). And in his subsequent period, Bacon returns to a localization of random traits and scrubbed zones. Bacon thus follows a third path, which is neither optical like abstract painting, nor manual like Action Painting.

CHAPTER 13

Analogy

*Cézanne: the motif as diagram — The analogical and
the digital — Painting and analogy — The paradoxical
status of abstract painting — The analogical
language of Cézanne, of Bacon: plane, color, and mass —
Modulation — Resemblance recovered*

There would thus be a tempered use of the diagram, a kind of middle way in which the diagram is not reduced to the state of a code, and yet does not cover the entire painting, avoiding both the code and its scrambling...Must we then speak of wisdom or classicism? It is hard to believe, however, that Cézanne followed a middle way. Rather, he invented a specific way, distinct from the two preceding ones. Few painters have produced the experience of chaos and catastrophe as intensely, while fighting to limit and control it at any price. Chaos and catastrophe imply the collapse of all the figurative givens, and thus they already entail a fight, the fight against the cliché, the preparatory work (all the more necessary in that we are no longer "innocent"). It is out of chaos that the "stubborn geometry" or "geologic lines" first emerge; and this geometry or geology must in turn pass through the catastrophe in order for colors to arise, for the earth to rise toward the sun.[1] It is thus a temporal diagram, with two moments. But the diagram connects these two moments indissolubly: the geometry is its "frame" and color is the sensation, the "coloring sensation." The diagram is exactly what Cézanne called the motif. In effect, the motif is made up of two things, the sensation and the frame. It is their intertwining. A sensation, or a point of view, is not enough to make a motif: the sensation, even a coloring sensation, is ephemeral and confused, lacking duration and clarity (hence the critique of impressionism). But the frame suffices even less: it is abstract. The geometry must be made concrete or felt, and at the same time the sensation must be given duration and clarity.[2] Only then will something emerge from the motif or diagram. Or rather, this operation that relates geometry to the sensible, and sensation to duration and clarity, is already just that: it is the outcome, the result. Two questions follow from this: What makes this relation within the motif or diagram possible (possibility of fact)? And how is this relation constituted when it emerges from the diagram (the fact itself)?

The first question concerns use. For if geometry is not a part of painting, there are nonetheless properly pictorial uses of geometry. We called one of these uses "digital," not in direct reference to the hand, but in reference to the basic units of a code. Once again, these basic units or elementary visual forms are indeed aesthetic and not mathematic, inasmuch as they have completely internalized the manual movement that produces them. They still form a code of painting, however, and turn painting into a code. It is in this sense, close to abstract painting, that we must understand Paul Sérusier's saying: "synthesis consists in reducing all forms to the smallest number of forms of which we are capable of thinking—straight lines, some angles, arcs of the circle and the ellipse." Synthesis is thus an Analytic of elements. When Cézanne, on the contrary, urges the painter to "treat nature through the cylinder, the sphere, the cone, putting the whole in perspective," one has the impression that abstract painters would be wrong to see this as a blessing—not only because Cézanne puts the emphasis on volumes, except the cube, but above all because he suggests a completely different use of geometry than that of a code of painting.[3] The cylinder is this stovepipe (emerging from the tinsmith's hands) or this man (whose arms do not matter...). Following current terminology, we could say that Cézanne creates an analogical use of geometry, and not a digital use. The diagram or motif would be analogical, whereas the code is digital.

"Analogical language," it is said, belongs to the right hemisphere of the brain or, better, to the nervous system, whereas "digital language" belongs to the left hemisphere. Analogical language would be a language of relations, which consists of expressive movements, paralinguistic signs, breaths and screams, and so on. One can question whether or not this is a language properly speaking. But there is no doubt, for example, that Artaud's theater elevated scream-breaths to the state of language. More generally, painting elevates colors and lines to the state of language, and it is an analogical language. One might even wonder if painting has not always been the analogical language par excellence. When we speak of analogical language in animals, we do not consider their possible songs, which belong to a different domain; rather we are essentially concerned with cries, variable colors, and lines (attitudes, postures). Now our first temptation, which would be to define the digital by convention, and the analogical by similitude or resemblance, is obviously ill-founded. A scream no more resembles what it signals than a word resembles what it designates. One could then define the analogical by a certain obviousness or "evidence," by a certain presence that makes itself felt immediately, whereas the digital needs to be learned. But this is no better, for the analogical requires an apprenticeship as well, even in animals, although it is a different type of apprenticeship than the acquisition of the digital. The very existence of painting would be enough to confirm the necessity of a lengthy apprenticeship for the analogical to become language. The question therefore cannot be decided by appealing to a clear-cut theory, but must be made the object of practical studies (on which the status of painting depends).

Thus we cannot be content with saying that analogical language proceeds by resemblance, whereas the digital operates through code, convention, and combinations of conventional units. For one can do at least three things with a code. One can make an intrinsic combination of abstract elements. One can also make a combination which will yield a "message" or a "narrative," that is, which will have an isomorphic relation to a referential set. Finally, one can code the extrinsic elements in such a way that they would be reproduced in an autonomous manner by the intrinsic elements of the code (in portraits produced by a computer, for instance, and in every instance where one could speak of "making a shorthand of figuration").[4] It seems, then, that a digital code covers certain forms of similitude or analogy: analogy by isomorphism, or analogy by produced resemblance.

But conversely, even when analogy is independent of every code, one can still distinguish two forms of it, depending on whether the resemblance is the producer or the product. Resemblance is the producer when the relations between the elements of one thing pass directly into the elements of another thing, which then becomes the image of the first—for example, the photograph, which captures relations of light. The fact that these relations play within a margin of error great enough for the image to present significant differences from the original object does not negate the fact that these differences are attained by a loose resemblance, sometimes decomposed in its operation, sometimes transformed in its result. In this case, analogy is figurative, and resemblance remains primary in principle. The photograph can rarely escape this limit, despite all its ambitions. On the contrary, one says that resemblance is the product when it appears abruptly as the result of relations that are completely different from those it is supposed to reproduce: resemblance then emerges as the brutal product of nonresembling means. We have already seen an instance of this in one of the analogies of the code, in which the code reconstituted a resemblance as a function of its own internal elements. But in that case, it was only because the relations to be reproduced had themselves already been coded, whereas now, in the absence of any code, the relations to be reproduced are instead produced directly by completely different relations, creating a resemblance through nonresembling means. In this last type of analogy, a sensible resemblance is produced, but instead of being produced symbolically, through the detour of the code, it is produced "sensually," through sensation. The name "aesthetic Analogy" must be reserved for this last eminent type, in which there is neither primary resemblance nor prior code, and which is both nonfigurative and noncodified.

In his great semiological theory, Peirce first defined icons by similitude and symbols by a conventional rule. But he acknowledged that conventional symbols are composed of icons (by virtue of phenomena of isomorphism), and that pure icons range far beyond qualitative similitude and consist of "diagrams."[5] But it is still difficult to explain what an analogical diagram is, as opposed to a digital or symbolic code. Today we can relate it to the sonorous example of synthesizers. *Analogical* synthesizers are "modular": they establish an immediate connection between heterogeneous elements; they introduce a literally unlimited possibility of connection between these elements, on a field of presence or finite plane whose moments are all actual and sensible. *Digital* synthesizers, however, are "integral": their operation passes through a codification, through a homogenization and binarization of the data, which is produced on a separate plane, infinite in principle, and whose sound will be produced only as the result of a conversion-translation. A second difference appears at the level of filters. The primary function of the filter is to modify the basic color of a sound, to constitute or vary its timbre. But digital filters proceed by an additive synthesis of elementary codified formants, whereas the analogical filter usually acts through the subtraction of frequencies ("high-pass," "low-pass," . . .). What is added from one filter to the next are intensive subtractions, and it is thus an addition of subtractions that constitutes modulation and sensible movement as a fall.[6] In short, *it is perhaps the notion of modulation in general (and not similitude)* that will enable us to understand the nature of analogical language or the diagram.

Painting is the analogical art par excellence. It is even the form through which analogy becomes a language, or finds its own language: by passing through a diagram. Abstract painting consequently poses a very particular problem. Abstract painting obviously proceeds by code and program, implying operations of homogenization and binarization that are constitutive of a digital code. But the abstractionists often happen to be great painters, which means that they do not simply apply to painting a code that would be external to it; on the contrary, they elaborate an intrinsically pictorial code. It is thus a paradoxical code since, instead of being opposed to analogy, it takes analogy as its object; it is the digital expression of the analogical as such.[7] Analogy will pass through a code rather than passing through a diagram. It has a status that borders on the impossible. And in another way, perhaps *art informel* also borders on the impossible, for by extending the diagram to the entire painting, it takes the diagram for the analogical flux itself, rather than making the flux pass through the diagram. This time, it is as if the diagram were directed toward itself, rather than being used or treated. It no longer goes beyond itself in a code, but grounds itself in a scrambling.

The "middle" way, on the contrary, is one that makes use of the diagram in order to constitute an analogical language. It assumes its complete independence with Cézanne. It is called a "middle" way only from a very external point of view, since it implies just as much radical invention and destruction of figurative coordinates as the other ways. As an analogical language, painting has three dimensions: the *planes*, the connection or junction of planes (primarily of the vertical plane and the horizontal plane), which replaces perspective; *color*, the modulation of color, which tends to suppress relations of value, chiaroscuro, and the contrast of shadow and light; and the *body*, the mass and declination of the body, which exceeds the organism and destroys the form-background relationship. There is a triple liberation here—of the body, of the planes, and of color (for what enslaves color is not only the contour but also the contrast of values). Now this liberation can only occur by passing through the catastrophe, that is, through the diagram and its involuntary irruption: bodies are thrown off balance, they are in a state of perpetual fall; the planes collide with each other; colors become confused and no longer delimit an object. In order for the rupture with figurative resemblance to avoid perpetuating the catastrophe, in order for it to succeed in producing a more profound resemblance, the planes, starting with the diagram, must maintain their junction; the body's mass must integrate the imbalance in a deformation (neither transformation nor decomposition, but the "place" of a force); and above all, modulation must find its true meaning and technical formula as the law of Analogy. It must act as a variable and continuous mold, which is not simply opposed to relief in chiaroscuro, but invents a new type of relief

Analogy - 97

through color. And perhaps this modulation *of* color is Cézanne's principal operation. By substituting for relations of value a juxtaposition of tints brought together in the order of the spectrum, modulation will define a double movement of expansion and contraction: an expansion in which the planes, and especially the horizontal and the vertical planes, are connected and even merged in depth; and at the same time, a contraction through which everything is restored to the body, to the mass, as a function of a point of imbalance or a fall.[8] It is through such a system that geometry becomes sensible, and sensations become clear and durable: one has "realized" the sensation, says Cézanne. Or, following Bacon's formula, one has passed from the possibility of fact to the Fact, from the diagram to the painting.

In what sense is Bacon Cézannian, and in what sense does he have nothing to do with Cézanne? The enormity of their differences is obvious. The depth where the planes are joined is no longer the strong depth of Cézanne but a "shallow" or "superficial" depth, inherited from the postcubism of Picasso and Braque (and which one finds elsewhere in abstract expressionism).[9] It is this type of depth that Bacon achieves, sometimes by joining the vertical and horizontal planes, as in his works of radical precision, and sometimes by merging them, as in the *malerisch* period, where, for example, the verticals of the curtain cut through the horizontals of the blinds. In the same way, the treatment of color not only passes through the modulated flat patches of color (smooth planes *[méplats]*) that envelop the bodies, but also through the large surfaces or fields that imply axes, structures, or armatures that are perpendicular to the bodies: it is the whole modulation that changes nature.[10] Finally, the deformation of bodies is very different, as we have seen, insofar as the forces that are exerted upon bodies, in the open world of Cézanne (Nature) and in the closed world of Bacon, are not the same.

But where Bacon does remain Cézannian is in the extreme elaboration of painting as analogical language. To be sure, even the distribution of rhythms in the triptychs has nothing to do with a code. The conic scream that combines with the verticals, and the extended triangular smile that merges with the horizontals, are the true "motifs" of this painting. But it is this kind of painting in its entirety which is a scream and a smile, that is to say, analogical. Analogy finds its highest law in the treatment of colors. This treatment is opposed to relations of value, of light and shadow, of chiaroscuro. One consequence of this is that even black and white are liberated, they are turned into colors, so that black shadows acquire a real presence and white light acquires an intense clarity, which is diffused throughout all the ranges of color. But "colorism" is not opposed to relief nor even to a drawn contour. The contour or outline can even have a separate existence, becoming the common limit of the armature and the body-mass, because the latter are no longer in a relationship of form to ground, but a relation of coexistence or proximity modulated by color. And through the membrane of the contour, a double movement is produced—a flat extension toward the armature and a voluminous contraction toward the body. This is why Bacon's three elements were the structure or armature, the Figure, and the contour, which find their effective convergence in color. The diagram, the agent of analogical language, acts not as a code but *as a modulator*. The diagram and its involuntary manual order will have been used to break all the figurative coordinates; but it is through this very action (when it is operative) that it defines possibilities of fact, by liberating lines for the armature and colors for modulation. Lines and colors are then able to constitute the Figure or the Fact, that is, to produce the new resemblance inside the visual whole, where the diagram must operate and be realized.

Painters Recapitulate the History of Painting in Their Own Way

*Egypt and haptic presentation — Essence and accident —
Organic representation and the tactile-optical world —
Byzantine art: a pure optical world? — Gothic art and the
manual — Light and color, the optical and the haptic*

Glory to the Egyptians. "I could never dissociate myself from the
great European images of the past—and by 'European' I mean to
include Egyptian, even if the geographers wouldn't agree with me."[1]
Can the Egyptian assemblage be taken as the point of departure for
Western painting? It is an assemblage of bas-relief even more than
of painting. Aloïs Riegl defined it as follows: (1) Bas-relief brings
about the most rigid link between the eye and the hand because its
element is *the flat surface*, which allows the eye to function like the
sense of touch; furthermore, it confers, and indeed imposes, upon
the eye a tactile, or rather *haptic*, function; it thereby ensures, in the
Egyptian "will to art," the joining together of the two senses of touch
and sight, like the soil and the horizon. (2) It is a frontal and close
view that assumes this haptic function, since the form and the ground
lie on the *same plane* of the surface, equally close to each other and
to ourselves. (3) What separates and unites both the form and the
ground is the *contour* as their common limit. (4) It is the rectilinear
contour, or regular curve, that isolates the form as an *essence*, a closed
unity that is shielded from all accident, change, deformation, and
corruption; essence acquires a formal and linear presence that dom-
inates the flux of existence and representation. (5) It is thus a geometry
of the plane, of the line, and of essence that inspires Egyptian bas-
relief; but it will also incorporate volume by covering the funerary
cube with a *pyramid*, that is, by erecting a Figure that only reveals to

us the unitary surface of isosceles triangles on clearly limited sides. (6) It is not only man and the world that in this way receive their planar or linear essence; it is also the animal and the vegetal, the sphinx and the lotus, which are raised to their perfect geometrical form, whose very mystery is the mystery of essence.[2]

Through the centuries, there are many things that make Bacon an Egyptian: the fields, the contour, the form and the ground as two equally close sectors lying on the same plane, the extreme proximity of the Figure (presence), the system of clarity [netteté]. Bacon renders to Egypt the homage of the Sphinx [18] and declares his love for Egyptian sculpture: like Rodin, he thinks that durability, essence, or eternity are the primary characteristics of the work of art (which even the photograph lacks). And when he considers his own painting, he says something curious, namely, that sculpture had tempted him a great deal, but also that he realized what he expected from sculpture was exactly what he had succeeded in doing in painting.[3] What kind of sculpture was he thinking of? A sculpture that would have included the three pictorial elements: the armature-ground, the Figure-form, and the contour-limit. He specifies that the Figure, along with its contour, should be able to slide along the armature. But even taking this mobility into account, we can see that Bacon is thinking of a bas-relief type of sculpture, something in between sculpture and painting. Yet as close as Bacon may be to Egypt, how can we explain the fact that his sphinx is scrambled, treated in a *malerisch* manner?

What is at stake here is no longer just Bacon, but undoubtedly the entire history of Western painting. If we attempted to define this Western painting, we could take Christianity as our first point of reference. For Christianity subjected the form, or rather the Figure, to a fundamental deformation. Insofar as God was incarnated, crucified, descended, ascended to heaven, and so on, the form or the Figure was no longer rigorously linked to essence, but to what, in principle, is its opposite: the event, or even the changeable, the accident. Christianity contains a germ of tranquil atheism that will nurture painting; the painter can easily be indifferent to the religious subject he is asked to represent. Nothing prevents him from realizing that, because of its now-essential relation with the accident, the form can become, not a God on the cross, but more simply a "napkin or a rug on the point of unrolling, the handle of a knife ready to become detached, a little loaf of bread falling into slices as if of its own volition, an overturned cup, all sorts of vases or fruits tumbled into a heap, and overhanging plates."[4] All of this can be put on Christ himself, or close by him: Christ is besieged, and even replaced, by accidents. Modern painting begins when man no longer experiences himself as an essence, but as an accident. There is always a fall, a risk of the fall; the form begins to express the accident, and no longer the essence. Claudel is correct to see one summit of this movement in Rembrandt and Dutch painting, but it thereby belongs eminently to Western painting. It is because Egypt put the form in the service of essence that Western painting could make this conversion (the problem was posed very differently in the Orient, which did not "begin" with essence).

We only took Christianity as a first point of reference that it would be necessary to look beyond. For Greek art had already freed the cube from its pyramidal covering: it *distinguished the planes*, invented a perspective, and put into play light and shadow, hollows and reliefs. If we can speak of a classical representation, it is because it implies the conquest of an optical space, a distant viewing that is never frontal: the form and the ground are no longer on the same plane, the planes are distinguished from each other, and a perspective traverses them in depth, uniting the background-plane to the foreground-plane; objects overlap each other, light and shadow fill up space and make it rhythmic, the contour ceases to be the common limit on a single plane and becomes the self-limitation of the form or the *primacy of the foreground*. Classical representation thus takes the accident as its object, but it incorporates the accident into an optical *organization* that makes it something well founded (a phenomenon) or a "manifestation" of essence. There are laws of the accident, and certainly painting, for example, does not simply apply laws that come from elsewhere. What painting discovers are properly aesthetic laws, which make classical representation a form of representation that is organic and organized, plastic. Art can indeed be figurative, although we have seen that it was not so at first, and that figuration is only a result. If the representation is related to an object, this relation is derived from the form of representation; if this object is the organism and organization, it is because the representation is first of all organic in itself, it is because the form of representation first of all expresses the organic life of man as subject.[5] And doubtless it is at this point that we must specify the complex nature of this optical space. For while it breaks with "haptic" vision and close viewing, it is not merely visual but refers to tactile values, even though it still subordinates them to vision. In fact, what replaces haptic space is *a tactile-optical space*, in which what is expressed is no longer essence but connection, that is, the organic activity of man. "Despite all the talk about Greek light, the space of classical Greek art is a tactile-optical space. In it, the energy of light is given a rhythm in accordance with the order of the forms. . . . The forms refer to themselves, from themselves, in the space between the planes which they themselves sustain. Increasingly freed from the background, they are increasingly freed up for space, where the gaze receives them and gathers them together. But this space is never the free space that invests and traverses the spectator."[6] The contour has ceased to be geometric in order to become organic, but the organic contour acts as a mold, in which contact is made to work toward the perfection of the optical form. Somewhat like a stick whose straightness in the water I can verify, the hand is only a servant, but it is an absolutely necessary servant, laden with a receptive passivity. Hence, the organic contour remains unchanging and is not affected by the plays of shadow and light, no matter how complex they may be, because it is a tangible contour, which must guarantee the individuation of the optical form through visual variations and diverse points of view.[7] In short, the eye, having abandoned its haptic function and become optical, subordinated itself to the tactile as a secondary power (here again, this "organization" entails an extraordinary set of properly pictorial inventions).

But if an evolution is produced—or rather interruptions that destabilize organic representation—it can only move in one of the following two directions. *Either toward the exposition of a purely optical space*, which is freed from its references to even a subordinate tactility (it is in this sense that Wölfflin speaks, in the evolution of art, of a tendency "to abandon itself to the pure optical vision").[8] *Or, on the contrary, toward the imposition of a violent manual space*, which rebels against and suppresses the subordination, as in automatic writing, where the hand seems to be guided by a "foreign, imperious will" in order to express itself in an independent way. These two opposed directions seem to be incarnated in Byzantine art and in Gothic or "barbarian" art. This is because Byzantine art reverses Greek art by giving such a degree of activity to the background that we no longer know where the background ends and the forms begin. The plane—enclosed in a dome, vault, or arch, and having become the *background plane*, owing to the distance it creates between itself and the spectator—is the active support of impalpable forms that depend increasingly on the alternation of light and dark, on the purely optical play of light and shadows. The tactile referents are annulled, and even the contour ceases to be a limit and is now the result of shadow and light, of black shores and white surfaces. It is in accordance with an analogous principle that painting, much later, in the seventeenth century, will develop rhythms of light and shadow that will no longer respect the integrity of a plastic form, but will instead make an optical form emerge out of the background. As opposed to classical representation, distant viewing no longer has to vary its distance according to this or that part, nor does it have to be confirmed by a close viewing that picks out the tactile connections, but is established directly by the whole of the painting. The eye no longer appeals to the tactile; and not only do indistinct zones become essential, but even if the object's form is in the light, its clarity communicates directly with shadows, darkness, and the background through an inner relationship that is specifically optical. The accident thereby changes status, and rather than finding laws in the "natural" organic, it finds a spiritual assumption, a "grace" or "miracle," in the independence of light (and color): it is as if the classical *organization* has given way to a *composition*. It is no longer even essence that appears, it is rather the apparition itself that creates essence and law: things rise up and ascend into the light. The form is no longer separable from a transformation or transfiguration that, from the dark to the bright, from shadow to light, establishes "a kind of love affair kindled by a decent life," a unique tonality. But what is a composition, and how does it differ from an organization? A composition is itself an organization, but one that is in the process of disintegrating (Claudel suggested just this with regard to light). Beings disintegrate while ascending into the light, and the emperor of Byzantium was not wrong when he set about persecuting and dispersing his artists. Even abstract painting, in its radical attempt to institute an optical space of transformation, will rely on disintegrating factors, on relations of value, of light and shadow, of clarity and obscurity, rediscovering a pure Byzantine inspiration beyond the seventeenth century: an optical code ...

Barbarian or Gothic art (in Worringer's broad sense of the term) also dismantles organic representation, but in a completely different manner. We are no longer directed toward the purely optical; on the contrary, the tactile once again assumes its pure activity, it is restored to the hand and given a speed, a violence, and a life that the eye can barely follow. Worringer has described this "northern line," which goes to infinity either by continually changing direction, perpetually twisting, splitting, and breaking off from itself; or else by turning back on itself in a violent peripheral or whirling movement. Barbarian art goes beyond organic representation in two ways, either through the mass of the body in movement, or through the speed and changing direction of the flat line. Worringer discovered the formula of this frenetic line: it is a life, but the most bizarre and intense kind of life, a *nonorganic* vitality. It is an abstraction, but an expressionistic abstraction.[9] It is thus opposed to the organic life of classical representation, but also to the geometric line of Egyptian essence, and the optical space of luminous apparition. Neither form nor ground exists any longer, in any sense, because the powers of the line and the plane tend to be equalized: by constantly being broken, the line becomes more than a line, while at the same time the plane becomes less than a surface. As for the contour, the line does not delimit one; it is never the outline of anything, either because the line is swept along by the infinite movement, or else because it alone possesses an outline, like a ribbon, as the limit of the movement of the inner mass. If this Gothic line is also animalistic, or even anthropomorphic, it is not in the sense that it would rediscover forms, but because it is composed of strokes [*traits*] that confer on it an intense realism—traits of the body or the head, traits of animality or humanity. It is a realism of deformation, as opposed to the idealism of transformation; and the strokes do not constitute zones of indistinctness in the form, as in chiaroscuro, but zones of indiscernibility in the line, insofar as it is common to different animals, to the human and the animal, and to pure abstraction (serpent, beard, ribbon). If there is a geometry here, it is a very different geometry from that of Egypt or Greece; it is an operative geometry of the trait or the accident. The accident is everywhere, and the line never ceases to encounter obstacles that force it to change direction and to intensify itself through these changes. It is a manual space, a space of active, manual strokes, which works through *manual aggregates* rather than through *luminous disaggregation*. One also finds in Michelangelo a power that stems directly from this manual space, namely, the manner in which the body exceeds the organism or makes it fall apart. It is as if the organisms were caught up in a whirling or serpentine movement that gives them a single "body" or unites them in a single "fact," apart from any figurative or narrative connection. Claudel can speak of a *peinture à la truelle*, a "trowel painting" in which the manipulated body is placed in a vault or a cornice, as if it were on a rug, garland, or ribbon, within which it executes its "little feats of strength."[10] It is as if a purely manual space were taking its revenge, for if the eyes that judge still maintain their accuracy, the hand that manipulates has discovered how to free itself from them.[11]

It would be wrong, however, to oppose these two tendencies—toward a purely optical space and toward a purely manual space—as if they were incompatible. At the very least, what they have in common is the dismantling of the tactile-optical space of so-called classic representation, and as such they can enter into new and complex combinations and correlations. For example, when light is liberated and becomes independent of forms, the curved form, for its part, tends to be decomposed into flat strokes that change direction, or even into strokes dispersed inside the mass.[12] One no longer knows if the accidents of the form are determined by the optical light, or if the accidents of light are determined by the manual line. It is enough to look at a Rembrandt painting upside down and close up to discover the manual line as the reverse of optical light. One could say that the optical space has itself liberated new tactile values (and also the reverse). And things become even more complicated if one considers the problem of color.

First of all, color, like light, seems to belong to a purely optical world, and at the same time seems to maintain its independence in relation to the form. Color, like light, begins to take control of the form, rather than simply to be related to it. This is what Wölfflin means when he says that, in an optical space where colors are more or less indifferent, it matters little "whether we speak of colors or only light or dark spaces."[13] But things are not so simple. For color itself is capable of two very different kinds of relation: *relations of value*, based on the contrast of black and white, in which a tone is defined as either dark or light, saturated or rarefied; and *relations of tonality*, based on the spectrum, on the opposition of yellow and blue, or green and red, in which this or that pure tone is defined as warm or cool.[14] It is obvious that these two scales of color continually mix with one another, and that their combinations constitute powerful acts of painting. Byzantine mosaic, for example, was not satisfied with making black shores and white surfaces (or the saturated tone of blue enamel and the same transparent tone of marble) resonate together in a modulation of light; it also made its four pure tones (gold, red, blue, and green) play together in a modulation of color: it invented colorism as well as luminism.[15] Seventeenth-century painting pursued both the liberation of light and the emancipation of color in relation to the tangible form. And Cézanne often made the two systems coexist, the first through a local tone, shadow and light, shaped by chiaroscuro, the second through a sequence of tones in the order of the spectrum, a pure modulation of color that tends to be self-sufficient.[16] But even when the two kinds of relation work together, we cannot conclude that, being addressed to sight, they thereby serve one and the same optical space. If it is true that relations of value, modeling in chiaroscuro, or the modulation of light appeal to a purely optical function of distant vision, the modulation of color, on the contrary, re-creates a properly *haptic* function, in which the juxtaposition of pure tones arranged gradually on the flat surface forms a progression and a regression that culminates in a close vision. Thus, it is through very different means that color is conquered in light, or that light attains color ("it is through the oppositions of warm and cool tones that the colors used by the painter—without any absolute luminous quality in themselves—come to represent light and shadow").[17]

Was this not already the great difference between Newton and Goethe from the point of view of a theory of colors? We will be able to speak of optical space only when the eye fulfills a function that is itself optical, depending on the prevailing or even exclusive relations of value. On the contrary, when relations of tonality tend to eliminate relations of value, as in Turner, Monet, or Cézanne, we will speak of a haptic space and a haptic function of the eye, in which the planar character of the surface creates volumes only through the different colors that are arranged on it. Are there not two very different kinds of gray, the optical gray of black-white and the haptic gray of green-red? It is no longer a manual space that is opposed to the optical space of sight, nor is it a tactile space that is connected to the optical. Now, within sight itself, there is a haptic space that competes with optical space. The latter was defined by the opposition of bright and dark, light and shadow; but the former, by the relative opposition of warm and cool, and the corresponding eccentric or concentric movement of expansion or contraction (whereas the bright and dark instead attest to an "aspiration" to movement).[18] Still other oppositions follow from this: as different as it may be from an external tactile mold, optical modeling in chiaroscuro still acts like a mold that has been internalized, in which the light penetrates the mass unequally. There is even an intimacy linked to the optical, which is precisely what colorists cannot tolerate in chiaroscuro, the idea of an intimacy or even a "homely atmosphere," even if it could be extended to the whole world.[19] So while the painting of light or value indeed broke with the figuration that resulted from a tactile-optical space, it still conserves a menacing relation with a possible narration (we represent what we think we can touch, but we narrate what we see, what seems to be happening in the light or what we presume is happening in the shadows). And the way luminism escapes from this danger of storytelling is by taking refuge in a pure code of black and white, which raises inner space to an abstraction. By contrast, colorism is the analogical language of painting: if there is still molding by color, it is no longer even an interior mold, but a temporal, variable, and continuous mold, to which alone the name of *modulation* belongs, strictly speaking.[20] There is neither an inside nor an outside, but only a continuous creation of space, the spatializing energy of color. By avoiding abstraction, colorism avoids both figuration and narration, and moves infinitely closer to the pure state of a pictorial "fact" that has nothing left to narrate. This fact is the constitution or reconstitution of a haptic function of sight. One might say that a new Egypt rises up, composed uniquely of color and by color, an Egypt of the accident, the accident that has itself become durable.

CHAPTER 15

Bacon's Trajectory

The haptic world and its avatars — Colorism —
A new modulation — From Van Gogh and Gauguin to Bacon —
The two aspects of color: bright tone and broken tone,
field and Figure, shores and flows . . .

A great painter never recapitulates the history of painting in his own work in an eclectic manner. Nor does this history correspond directly to the painter's periods, though the periods may have an indirect relation to it. It does not even correspond to the separate aspects of a given painting. Rather, it would be like the space covered by the unity of a single simple gesture. The historical recapitulation consists of stopping points and passages, which are extracted from or reconstitute an open sequence.

Bacon first of all seems to be an Egyptian. This is his first stopping point. A painting by Bacon first of all has an Egyptian look to it: the form and the ground, connected to each other by the contour, lie on a single plane of a close, haptic vision. But we can already discern an important difference creeping into the Egyptian world like a first catastrophe—the form collapses; it is inseparable from a fall. The form is no longer essence but becomes accident; man is an accident. The accident opens up a space between the two planes, which is where the fall occurs. It is as if the ground has receded a little into a background plane, and the form moved up a little into a foreground plane. This qualitative difference, however, is not quantitatively large, for what separates the background from the foreground is not perspective but a "shallow" depth.

This is enough to make the beautiful unity of the haptic world seem doubly broken. The contour ceases to be the common limit of the form and the ground on a single plane (the round area, the ring). It becomes the cube, or its analogues; and in so doing, the cube becomes the organic contour of the form—the mold. This marks the birth of the tactile-optical world. In the foreground plane, the form appears to be tangible, and owes its very clarity to this tangibility (figuration follows from this, as a consequence). This form of representation also affects the ground insofar as, in the background-plane, it curls around the form, producing a connection that is itself tactile. But in the other direction, the ground of the background-plane attracts the form. And here it is a pure optical world that tends to free itself, at the very moment when the form loses its tactile character. Sometimes it is light that gives the form a clarity which is purely optical and aerial, disaggregating; sometimes, on the contrary, it is the *malerisch* shadow, the darkening of color, which overcomes the form and dissolves it, severing it from all its tactile connections. The danger now is no longer simply that of figuration but that of narration (What is happening? What is going to happen? or What happened?).

Figuration and narration are only effects, but for that reason they are all the more intrusive in painting. They are what must be eliminated. But neither the tactile-optical world nor the purely optical world is a stopping point for Bacon. On the contrary, he cuts through them, subverting and scrambling them. The manual diagram produces an irruption like a scrambled or cleaned zone, which overturns the optical coordinates as well as the tactile connections. Yet one might think that the diagram is essentially optical, either because it tends toward white or, with all the more reason, because it tends toward black and works with shadows or dark colors, as in the *malerisch* period. But Bacon continually denounces the annoying "intimacy" or "homely atmosphere" of chiaroscuro, and calls for a painting that will take the image "away from the interior and the home."[1] If Bacon renounces the *malerisch* treatment, it is because of this ambiguous association. For even when darkened or tending toward black, the diagram does not form a relative zone of indistinction that is still optical, but an absolute zone of indiscernibility or objective indetermination that is opposed to the optical, and that forces the eye to confront this manual power as if it were a foreign power. The diagram is never an optical effect, but an unbridled manual power. It is a frenetic zone in which the hand is no longer guided by the eye and is forced upon sight like another will, which appears as chance, accident, automatism, or the involuntary. It is a catastrophe, and a much more profound catastrophe than the preceding one. The optical world, and the tactile-optical world, is swept out, wiped away. If there is still an eye, it is the "eye" of a hurricane, as in Turner, which more often tends to the bright than the dark, and which designates a rest or stopping point that is always linked to an immense agitation of matter. The diagram is indeed a stopping or resting point in Bacon's paintings, but it is a stop closer to green and red than black and white, that is, a rest surrounded by an immense agitation, or, on the contrary, one that surrounds the most agitated kind of life.

To say that the diagram, in turn, is a stopping point in the painting is not to say that it completes or constitutes the painting; indeed, on the contrary. It acts as a relay. We have seen that the diagram must remain localized, rather than covering the entire painting (as in expressionism), and that something must *emerge* from the diagram. Even in the *malerisch* period, the diagram covers everything in appearance only. It does in fact remain localized, no longer in surface, but in depth. When the curtain striates the entire surface, it seems to be in front of the Figure, but if we look closely, we can see that in fact it falls *between* the two planes, in the interval between the planes. It occupies or fills the shallow depth, and in this sense remains localized. The diagram always has effects that go beyond it. As an unbridled manual power, the diagram dismantles the optical world, but at the same time, it must be reinjected into the visual whole, where it introduces a properly haptic world and gives the eye a haptic function. It is color, and the relations between colors, that form this haptic world and haptic sense, in accordance with relations of warm and cool, expansion and contraction. Certainly the color that shapes the Figure and fills the fields does not depend on the diagram, but it does pass through the diagram and emerge from it.

The diagram acts as a modulator, and as the common locus of warm and cool colors, of expansions and contractions. In every part of the painting, the haptic sense of color will have been made possible by the diagram and its manual intrusion.

Light is time, but space is color. Painters we call "colorists" are those who tend to substitute relations of tonality for relations of value, and who "render" not only the form but also shadow and light, and time, through these pure relations of color. Certainly it is not a question of a better solution, but of a tendency that runs through painting and leaves behind characteristic masterpieces, distinct from those that characterize other tendencies. Colorists can indeed make use of black and white, light and dark; but this is because they treat light and dark, black and white, as colors, and establish tonal relations between them.[2] "Colorism" means not only that relations are established between colors (as in every painting worthy of this name), but that color itself is discovered to be the variable relation, the differential relation, on which everything else depends. The formula of the colorists is, If you push color to its pure internal relations (hot-cold, expansion-contraction), then you have everything. If the color is perfect, if the relations of color are developed for their own sake, then you have everything, form and ground, light and shadow, bright and dark. *Clarity* no longer resides in the tangible form or the optical light, but in the incomparable flash produced by complementary colors.[3] Colorism claims to bring out a peculiar kind of sense from sight: a haptic sight of color-space, as opposed to the optical sight of light-time. Against the Newtonian conception of optical color, it was Goethe who laid down the first principles of such a haptic vision. The practical rules of colorism are the following: the abandonment of local tone; the juxtaposition of unblended touches; the aspiration of each color to totality by appealing to its complementary color; the contrasting of colors with their intermediaries or transitions; the prohibition of mixtures except to obtain a "broken" tone; the juxtaposition of two complementary or similar colors, one of which is broken and the other pure; the production of light and even time through the unlimited activity of color; the production of clarity through color...[4] Painting not only creates its masterpieces by combining its own tendencies (linear-tactile, luminist, colorist), but also by differentiating and opposing them. Everything is visual in painting, but vision has at least two senses. Colorism, with its own means, merely claims to give this haptic sense back to sight, which it was forced to abandon when the planes of ancient Egypt separated and diverged. The vocabulary of colorism—not only hot and cold, but "touch" *[touche]*, "vividness" *[vif]*, "seizing hold of life" *[saisir sur le vif]*, "achieving clarity" *[tirer au clair]*—attests to this haptic sense of the eye (as Van Gogh says, a vision such that "everyone who has eyes could see clearly").

Modulation by pure and distinct tints following the order of the spectrum—this was the properly Cézannian invention for attaining the haptic sense of color. But in addition to the danger of reconstituting a code, modulation had to take into account *two demands:* the demand for a homogeneous ground and an aerial armature, perpendicular to the chromatic progression; and the demand for a singular or specific form, which the size of the color patches seemed to put in question.[5] This is why colorism found itself faced with this double problem: how to erect large sections of homogeneous color, creating fields that would make up the armature, while at the same time inventing singular, disconcerting, and unknown forms in variation, forms that truly have the volume of a body? Georges Duthuit, despite his reservations, has profoundly demonstrated this complementarity of a "unitive vision" and a singularized perception as they appear in Gauguin and Van Gogh.[6] The bright field and the encircled Figure, "partitioned off," reviving a Japanese art, or even a Byzantine or primitive art, Gauguin's *La Belle Angèle*... [104]. One might say that by splitting into these two directions, modulation is lost, color loses all its modulation—hence Cézanne's severe judgments against Gauguin. But this is true only when the ground and the form, the field and the Figure, do not succeed in communicating, as if the singularity of the body were let loose on a flat, uniform, indifferent, and abstract surface.[7] In fact, we believe that modulation, which is strictly inseparable from colorism, takes on a completely new meaning and function, distinct from Cézannian modulation. One attempts to avoid any possible codification, as Van Gogh said when he boasted of being an "arbitrary colorist."[8] On the one hand, no matter how uniform it may be, the *bright tone* of the fields seizes upon color as a passage or tendency, with very fine differences of saturation rather than of value (for example, the way in which blue or yellow tends toward red; and even if there is perfect homogeneity, there is still a virtual or "identical passage"). On the other hand, the body's volume will be rendered by one or more *broken tones*, which form another type of passage in which the color seems to have been fired and baked in a kiln. By mixing complementary colors in critical proportion, the broken tone subjects color to a heating or a firing that rivals ceramics. One of Van Gogh's Roulin postmen [111] exhibits a blue that shades into white, while the flesh of the face is treated by broken tones, "yellows, greens, violets, roses, reds."[9] (As for the possibility of treating the body with a single broken tone—this would perhaps be one of Gauguin's inventions, a revelation of Martinique or Tahiti.) The problem of modulation thus concerns the passage of bright color in the flat field, the passage of the broken tones, and the nonindifferent relation between these two passages or movements of color. Cézanne is reproached for lacking an armature as much as the flesh. What is misunderstood is not the Cézannian modulation, but rather this other modulation that colorism discovers. It entails a change in the Cézannean hierarchy: whereas modulation in Cézanne belonged particularly to landscapes and still lifes, in this new viewpoint the primacy now moves to the portrait—the painter once again becomes a portraitist.[10] This is because the flesh calls for broken tones, and the portrait is able to make the broken tones and the bright tones resonate, as the voluminous body of the head and the uniform background of the flat field. The "modern portrait" would be done in color and broken tones, as opposed to past portraits, which were done in light and blended tones.

Bacon is one of the greatest colorists since Van Gogh and Gauguin. His insistent appeal to "flesh" as a property of color, in the interviews, is worthy of a manifesto. In Bacon, the broken tones produce the body of the Figure, and the bright or pure tones, the armature of the fields. "Flesh-colored whitewash" and "highly-polished steel," says Bacon.[11] The whole problem of modulation lies in the relation between the two, between the fleshly matter and the large uniform panels. The colors are not blended, but have two modes of clarity: the shores of vivid color and the flows of broken colors. Shores and flows: the latter produces the body or the Figure, the former, the armature or the field. Time itself seems to result from color in two ways: as time that passes, in the chromatic variation of the broken tones that compose the flesh; and as the eternity of time, that is, as the eternity of the passage in itself, in the monochromy of the field. This treatment of color, in turn, undoubtedly has its own dangers and its possible catastrophe, without which there would be no painting. The first danger, as we have seen, is that the ground would remain indifferent and inert, with an abstract and coagulated brightness. But there is yet another danger, namely, that the broken tones of the Figure would be allowed to blend together and become scrambled, losing their clarity and lapsing into a monotonous gray.[12] This ambiguity, from which Gauguin suffered so much, can be seen in Bacon's *malerisch* period: the broken tones only seem to form a mixture or a blending that ends up darkening the entire painting. But in fact, such was not the case. The dark curtain falls, but in so doing it occupies the shallow depth that separates the two planes, the foreground-plane of the Figure and the background-plane of the field, thereby introducing the harmonious relation between the two that, in principle, preserves their clarity throughout. But the fact remains that the *malerisch* period flirts with the danger, at least in terms of the optical effect it reintroduced. This is why Bacon will leave this period behind and, in a manner again reminiscent of Gauguin (was it not Gauguin who invented this new type of depth?), will leave the validity of the shallow depth intact, introducing all the possible relations between the two planes in the haptic space that is thereby constituted.

CHAPTER 16

Note on Color

Color and the three elements of painting — Color-structure:
the fields and their divisions — The role of black —
Color-force: Figures, flows, and broken tones —
Heads and shadows — Color-contour —
Painting and taste: good and bad taste

We have seen that the three fundamental elements of Bacon's painting were the armature or structure, the Figure, and the contour. Doubtless there are some traits, rectilinear or curvilinear, that already delineate a contour that belongs to the armature or the Figure, thereby seeming to reintroduce a kind of tactile mold (Gauguin and Van Gogh were already criticized for this). But these lines, on the one hand, simply serve to establish the different modalities of color; for on the other hand, there is a third contour, which no longer belongs to either the armature or the Figure, but is raised to the status of an autonomous element, as much a surface or volume as it is a line: this is the round area, the ring, the puddle or the pedestal, the bed, the mattress, the armchair, which delineate the common limit of the Figure and the armature on what is supposed to be a single plane (or almost) viewed at close range. Thus there are indeed three distinct elements. Now *all three of these converge on color, in color.* And it is modulation, that is, the relations between colors, which at the same time explains the unity of the whole, the distribution of each element, and the way each of them acts upon the others.

Consider an example analyzed by Marc Le Bot. The 1976 *Figure at a Washbasin* [80] "is like a piece of wreckage washed downstream by a river of ocher color with circular eddies and a red reef, which prevent the unlimited expansion of color through a double spatial effect that confines the color locally and fixes it, in such a way that it is enhanced and accelerated. Broad flows of color in this way cross the space of Francis Bacon's pictures. If their space is comparable to a homogeneous and fluid mass in its monochromatism, but disrupted by breakwaters, their regime of signs cannot be derived from a geometry of stable measure. It is derived, in this painting, from a dynamic that makes the gaze glide from the bright ocher to the red. This is why a directional arrow can be inscribed on it."[1] This distribution can be clearly seen. There is the large, monochrome ocher *shore* as the background, which provides the armature. There is the contour as an autonomous power (the reef)—it is the crimson of the mattress or cushion on which the Figure is standing, a crimson that is combined with the black of the disk and contrasted with the white of the crumpled newspaper. Finally, there is the Figure, like a *flow* of broken tones—ochers, reds, and blues. But there are still other elements. First, there is the black blind that seems to cut across the field of ocher; then the washbasin, itself a bluish broken tone; and the long curved pipe, a white marked with manual daubs of ocher, which surrounds the mattress, the Figure, and the washbasin, and which also cuts across the field. We can see the function of these secondary yet indispensable elements. The washbasin is like a second autonomous contour, which surrounds the Figure's head, just as the first surrounded its foot. And the pipe is itself a third autonomous contour, whose upper half divides the field of color in half. As for the blind, its role is all the more important insofar as, in keeping with a technique dear to Bacon, it falls between the field and the Figure, in such a way that it occupies the shallow depth that separates them and relates the entire painting to one and the same plane. It is a rich communication of colors. The Figure's broken tones incorporate not only the pure tone of the field but also the pure tone of the red cushion, adding to it bluish tones that resonate with the tone of the washbasin, a broken blue that contrasts with the pure red.

Hence a first question: what is the mode of the shore or the field, what is the modality of color in the field, and how does the field provide the armature or structure? If we consider the particularly significant example of the triptychs, we see the large, brilliant fields of monochrome colors spread out before us—oranges, reds, ochers, golden yellows, greens, violets, pinks. Now if, in the beginning, modulation could still be obtained through differences of value (as in the 1944 *Three Studies for Figures at the Base of a Crucifixion* [1]), it quickly becomes apparent that modulation must simply consist of internal variations of intensity or saturation, and that these variations themselves change depending on relations of proximity to this or that zone of the field. These relations of proximity are determined in several ways. *Sometimes* the field itself has clear-cut sections of another intensity or even another color. This technique, it is true, is rare in the triptychs, but it often appears in the simple paintings, as in the 1946 *Painting* [3] or the *Pope No. II* of 1960 [27] (violet sections in the green field). *Sometimes*, by means of a technique frequently employed in the triptychs, the field is limited and contained, pushed back on itself, by a large curvilinear contour that takes up at least the bottom half of the painting, forming a horizontal plane that joins the vertical field in the shallow depth. In a way, this large contour still belongs to the field, precisely because it is itself only the outer limit of other, more concise contours. Thus, in the 1962 *Three Studies for a Crucifixion* [29], we see the large orange contour pushing back the red field; and in *Two Figures Lying on a Bed with Attendants* [53], the violet field is contained by the large red contour. *Sometimes* again, the field is interrupted only by a thin white bar that crosses it completely, as in the three faces of the beautiful rose-colored *Triptych* of 1970 [62]; and this is also the case, partially, in the *Figure at a Washbasin* [80], where the field is crossed by a white bar, subordinating it to the contour. *Sometimes*, finally, the field rather frequently includes a band or ribbon of another color. Such is the case in the right panel of the 1962 triptych (*Three Studies for a Crucifixion* [29], which displays a vertical green ribbon, but also in the first bullfight (*Study for Bullfight No. 1*, 1969 [56]), where the orange field is accentuated by a violet ribbon (which is replaced by a white bar in the second bullfight [57]), and the two outer panels of a 1974 triptych [75], where a blue ribbon crosses the green field horizontally.

The purest pictorial situation doubtless appears when the field is neither sectioned off, nor limited, nor even interrupted, but covers the entire painting, sometimes encompassing a midsize contour (for example, the orange field that encompasses a green bed in the 1970 *Studies of the Human Body* [62], sometimes even surrounding a small contour on all sides (the center panel of the 1970 triptych [61]. Under these conditions, the painting becomes truly aerial and attains a maximum of light like the eternity of a monochrome time, "Chronochromie."[2] But the cases in which the ribbon crosses the field are no less interesting and important, for they manifest directly the way a homogeneous, colored field introduces subtle internal variations that depend on relations of proximity (the same band-field structure can also be found in abstract expressionists like Barnett Newman). This produces a kind of temporal or successive perception of the field itself. Even in the other cases, where the proximity is assured by the line of a large, midsize, or small contour, this is a general rule: the smaller or more localized the contour is, the more aerial the triptych will be, as in the 1970 *Triptych* [60], where the blue circle and the ocher apparatuses seem to be suspended in a sky. But even here, the field becomes the object of a temporal perception that is raised to eternity as the form of time. Here then is the means by which the uniform field—that is, color—provides a structure or armature: it is made up intrinsically of one or more zones of proximity, which make up a kind of contour (the largest) or an aspect of the contour. The armature can then consist of the connection between the field and the horizontal plane as defined by a large contour, which implies an active presence of the shallow depth. But it can just as easily consist of a system of linear apparatuses that suspend the Figure in the field, denying all depth (the 1970 *Triptych* [60]). Or finally, it can consist in the action of a very particular section of the field that we have not yet considered: the field occasionally includes a black section, sometimes quite localized (*Pope No. II*, 1960 [27], *Three Studies for a Crucifixion*, 1962 [29], *Portrait of George Dyer Staring into a Mirror*, 1967 [45], *Triptych*, 1972 [70], *Portrait of a Man*

Walking Down Steps, 1972 [68]), sometimes even flowing (*Triptych,* 1973 [73]), and sometimes total or constituting the entire field (*Three Studies from the Human Body,* 1967 [44]). Now this black section does not produce the same effect as the other possible sections. It assumes the role that had been given to the curtain or blended colors in the *malerisch* period; it makes the field of color project itself forward, no longer either affirming or denying the shallow depth, but filling it completely. This is particularly evident in the portrait of George Dyer. In a single instance, the 1965 *Crucifixion* [35], the black section is, on the contrary, retreating from the field, which shows that Bacon did not reach this new formula for black all at once.

If we move on to the other term, the Figure, we now find ourselves before flows of color, in the form of broken tones. Or rather, the broken tones constitute the flesh of the Figures. As such, they are opposed to the monochrome shores in three ways: the broken tone is opposed to the tone that is perhaps the "same," but vivid, pure, or complete; thickened, it is opposed to the flatness of the field; finally, it is polychromatic (except in the remarkable case of a 1974 triptych [74], where the flesh is treated as a single broken green tone that resonates with the pure green of a ribbon). When the flow of colors is polychromatic, blues and reds often dominate, which are precisely the dominant tones of meat. Yet they not only appear in meat, but even more so in the bodies and heads of the portraits—for instance, in the large 1970 back of a man [63] or the 1959 portrait of Miss Muriel Belcher [26], with its reds and blues on a green field. And above all, it is in the portraits of heads [34, 48, 49, 54] that the flow loses the all-too-easily tragic and figurative aspect it still possessed in the meat of the Crucifixions, in order to assume a series of dynamic figural values. Many of the portraits of heads also combine the dominant blue-reds with other dominant colors, notably ochers. In each case, it is the affinity of the body or the flesh with meat that explains the treatment of the Figure through broken tones. In fact, the Figure's other elements, such as clothes and shadows, receive a different treatment: the crumpled clothes may conserve the values of bright and dark, of shadow and light; by contrast, the shadow itself, the Figure's shadow, will be treated with a pure, bright tone (hence the beautiful blue shadow in the 1970 *Triptych* [60]). Thus, just as the rich flow of broken tones gives shape to the Figure's body, we can see that color attains a completely different regime than it had previously. In the first place, the flow traces millimetrical variations in the body as the content of time, whereas the monochromatic shores or fields were raised to a kind of eternity as the form of time. In the second place, and more important, *color-structure* gives way to *color-force*. Each dominant color and each broken tone indicates the immediate exercise of a force on the corresponding zone of the body or head; it immediately renders a force visible. Finally, the internal variation of the field was defined in terms of a zone of proximity, which is obtained, as we have seen, in various ways (for example, the proximity of a ribbon). But it is with the diagram, as the point of application or agitated locus of all forces, that the flow of colors enters into relations of proximity. This proximity can certainly be spatial, as in the case where the diagram appears in the body or the head, but it can also be topological and act at a distance, as in cases in which the diagram is situated elsewhere or has spread elsewhere (for example, the 1967 *Portrait of Isabel Rawsthorne Standing in a Street in Soho* [47]).

Last, there remains the contour. We are familiar with its ability to multiply itself, since it can include a large contour (for example, a rug) surrounding a midsize contour (a chair), which itself surrounds a small contour (a round area). Or the three contours of the *Figure at a Washbasin* [80]. In all these cases, color seems to recover its old tactile-optical function and to be subordinated to the closed line. Most notably, the large contours have a curvilinear or angular line that indicates the manner in which a horizontal plane is freed from the vertical plane in the minimal depth. Yet color is subordinated to the line in appearance only. Precisely because this contour is not here the contour of the Figure but is executed as an autonomous element of the picture, this element is determined by color in such a way that the line is derived from it, and not the reverse. It is thus color that still creates the line and the contour. Many large contours, for example, are treated as rugs (*Man and Child*, 1963 [32], *Three Studies for a Portrait of Lucian Freud*, 1966 [38], *Portrait of George Dyer Staring into a Mirror*, 1968 [45]), and seem to constitute a decorative regime of color. This third regime can be seen even better in the existence of the small contour, within which the Figure is erected and which can deploy delightful colors—for example, the perfect lilac oval in the central panel of the 1972 *Triptych* [70], which gives way to an uncertain rose-colored pool in the left and right panels; or the golden-orange oval that radiates from the door in the 1978 *Painting* [81]. In these contours, we recover a function that is derived from the halos of premodern painting. Now placed at the foot of the Figure, in a profane use, the halo retains its function as a concentrated reflector of the Figure, a colored pressure that ensures the Figure's balance, and makes one regime of color pass into another.[3]

Colorism (modulation) consists not only of relations of warm and cool, of expansion and contraction, which vary in accordance with the colors considered. It also consists of regimes of colors, the relations between these regimes, and the harmonies between pure tones and broken tones. What is called haptic vision is precisely this sense of colors. This sense, or this vision, concerns all the more the totality insofar as the three elements of painting (armature, Figure, and contour) communicate and converge in color. One might ask whether this implies a kind of superior "good taste," as Michael Fried has done with regard to certain colorists: Can taste be a potentially creative force and not simply an arbiter of fashion?[4] Does Bacon owe this taste to his past as a decorator? Bacon's good taste would seem to have been exercised most intensely in the armature and the regime of the fields. But just as the Figures sometimes have forms and colors that make them look like monsters, so the contours themselves sometimes appear to be in "bad taste," as if Bacon's irony were exercised as a preference against decoration. Most notably, when the large contour is presented as a rug, it always seems to have a particularly ugly pattern. Commenting on *Man and Child* [32], Russell goes so far as to say that "the carpet itself is of a particularly hideous kind. Having once or twice espied Bacon walking by himself in just such a street as the Tottenham Court Road, I know with what a concentrated and baleful stare he examines shop-windows of this sort. (There are no carpets in his own apartment.)"[5] Nonetheless, the appearance itself only refers to figuration. The Figures seem to be monsters only from the viewpoint of a lingering figuration, but they cease to be so as soon as they are considered "figurally," because they then reveal the most natural of poses, in accordance with the everyday task that occupies them and the momentary forces that are confronting them. In the same way, the most hideous rug ceases to be hideous when one comprehends it "figurally," depending on the function that it exercises in relation to color. The rug in *Man and Child* [32], with its red veins and blue zones, decomposes the vertical field of violet horizontally, and makes us pass from the pure tone of the latter to the broken tones of the Figure. It is a color-contour, more like white water lilies than an ugly rug. There is indeed a creative taste in color, in the different regimes of color, which constitute a properly visual sense of touch, or a haptic sense of sight.

CHAPTER 17

The Eye and the Hand

*Digital, tactile, manual, and haptic — The practice of
the diagram — On "completely different" relations —
Michelangelo: the pictorial fact*

The two definitions of painting, by line and color, and by the trait
and the color-patch, do not overlap exactly, for the first is visual, but
the second is manual. To describe the relationship of the eye and the
hand, and the values through which this relation passes, it is obviously not enough to say that the eye judges and the hands execute.
The relationship between the hand and the eye is infinitely richer,
passing through dynamic tensions, logical reversals, and organic
exchanges and substitutions (Focillon's famous text, "In Praise of
Hands," does not seem to us to give an account of this).[1] The paintbrush and the easel can express a general subordination of the hand,
but no painter has ever been satisfied with the paintbrush. There are
several aspects in the values of the hand that must be distinguished
from each other: the digital, the tactile, the manual proper, and the
haptic. The *digital* seems to mark the maximum subordination of
the hand to the eye: vision is internalized, and the hand is reduced
to the finger; that is, it intervenes only in order to choose the units
that correspond to pure visual forms. The more the hand is subordinated in this way, the more sight develops an "ideal" optical space,
and tends to grasp its forms through an optical code. But this optical
space, at least in its early stages, still presents manual referents with
which it is connected: we will call these virtual referents (such as
depth, contour, relief, and so on) *tactile* referents. This relaxed
subordination of the hand to the eye, in turn, can give way to a ver-

itable insubordination of the hand: the painting remains a visual reality, but what is imposed on sight is a space without form and a movement without rest, which the eye can barely follow and which dismantles the optical. We will call this reversed relationship the *manual*. Finally, we will speak of the *haptic* whenever there is no longer a strict subordination in either direction, either a relaxed subordination or a virtual connection, but when sight discovers in itself a specific function of touch that is uniquely its own, distinct from its optical function.[2] One might say that painters paint with their eyes, but only insofar as they touch with their eyes. And no doubt this haptic function was able to reach its fullness, directly and immediately, in ancient forms whose secret we have lost (Egyptian art). But it can also be re-created in the "modern" eye, through violence and manual insubordination.

Let us begin with tactile-optical space, and with figuration. Not that these two characteristics are the same thing: figuration or the figurative appearance is rather like the consequence of this space. According to Bacon, this kind of space will inevitably be there, in one way or another: one has no choice in the matter (it will at least be there virtually, or in the head of the painter... and figuration will be there, preexistent or prefabricated).[3] Now what will disrupt this space and its consequences, in a catastrophe, is the manual "diagram," which is made up exclusively of insubordinate color-patches and traits. And something must *emerge* from this diagram and present itself to view. Roughly speaking, the law of the diagram, according to Bacon, is this: one starts with a figurative form, a diagram intervenes and scrambles it, and a form of a completely different nature emerges from the diagram, which is called the Figure.

Bacon first cites two examples.[4] In the 1946 *Painting* [3], he had wanted "to make a bird alighting on a field," but the lines he had drawn suddenly took on a kind of independence and suggested "something totally different," the man under the umbrella. And in the portraits of heads, the painter looks for organic resemblance, but sometimes "the paint moving from one contour into another" happens to liberate a more profound resemblance in which the organs (eyes, nose, mouth) can no longer be discerned. Precisely because the diagram is not a coded formula, these two extreme examples allow us to bring out the complementary dimensions of the operation.

We might assume that the diagram makes us pass *from one form to another*, for example, from a bird-form to an umbrella-form, and thus that it acts as an agent of transformation. But this is not the case in the portraits, where we only move across a single form. And with regard to *Painting* [3], Bacon even states explicitly that we do not pass from one form to another. In effect, the bird exists primarily in the intention of the painter, and it gives way to the *whole* of the really executed painting or, if one prefers, to the umbrella *series* — man below, meat above. Moreover, the diagram can be found, not at the level of the umbrella, but in the scrambled zone, below and to the left, and it communicates with the whole through the black shore. It is from the diagram—at the center of the painting, at the point of close viewing—that the entire series emerges as a series of accidents "mounting on top of another."[5] If we start with the bird as an intentional figurative form, we see that what corresponds to this form in the painting, what is truly analogous to it, is not the umbrella-form (which merely defines a figurative analogy or an analogy of resemblance), but the series or the figural whole, which constitutes the specifically aesthetic analogy: the arms of the meat that are raised as analogues to wings, the sections of the umbrella that are falling or closing, the mouth of the man as a jagged beak. What is substituted for the bird is not another form, but *completely different relations*, which create a complete Figure as the aesthetic analogue of the bird (relations between the arms of the meat, the sections of the umbrella, the mouth of the man). The diagram-accident has scrambled the intentional figurative form, the bird: it imposes nonformal color-patches and traits that function only as traits of birdness, of animality. It is from these nonfigurative traits that the final whole emerges, as if from a pool; and it is they that raise it to the power of the pure Figure, beyond the figuration contained in this whole. Thus the diagram acted by imposing a zone of objective indiscernibility or indeterminability between two forms, one of which was no longer, and the other, not yet: it destroys the figuration of the first and neutralizes that of the second. And between the two, it imposes the Figure, through its original relations. There is indeed a change of form, but the change of form is a deformation, that is, a creation of original relations that are substituted for the form: the meat that flows, the umbrella that seizes, the mouth that is made jagged. As the song says, *I'm changing my shape, I feel like an accident.*[6] The diagram has introduced or distributed formless forces throughout the painting, which have a necessary relation with the deformed parts, or which are made use of as, precisely, "places."

We thus see how everything can be done inside the same form (second case). Thus, for a head, one starts with the intentional or sketched-out figurative form. One scrambles it from one contour to the other, like a gray that spreads itself everywhere. But this gray is not the undifferentiated gray of white and black; it is the colored gray, or rather the coloring gray, out of which new relations will emerge (broken tones) that are completely different from relations of resemblance. And these new relations of broken tones produce a more profound resemblance, a nonfigurative resemblance for the same form, that is, a uniquely figural Image.[7] Hence Bacon's program: to produce resemblance with nonresembling means. And when Bacon tries to think of a very general formula capable of expressing the diagram and its action of scrambling and rubbing, he can propose a linear formula as much as a colorist one, a trait-formula as much as a patch-formula, a distance-formula as much as a color-formula. The figurative lines will be scrambled by extending them, by hatching them, that is, by introducing new distances and new relations between them, out of which the nonfigurative resemblance will emerge: "you suddenly see through the graph *[diagramme]* that the mouth could go right across the face." There is a diagrammatical line of desert-distance, just as there is a diagrammatical patch of gray-color, and the two come together in the same action of painting, painting the world in Sahara-gray ("you would love to be able in a portrait to make a Sahara of the appearance—to make it so like, yet seeming to have the distances of the Sahara").[8]

But Bacon's demand always remains valid: the diagram must remain localized in space and time, it must not cover the entire painting, which would be "sloppy" (we would once again fall into an undifferentiated gray, or a line of the "marshland" rather than the desert).[9] Being itself a catastrophe, the diagram must not create a catastrophe. Being itself a zone of scrambling, it must not scramble the painting. Being a mixture, it must not mix colors, but break tones. In short, being manual, it must be reinjected into the visual whole, in which it deploys consequences that go beyond it. The essential point about the diagram is that it is made in order for something to *emerge* from it, and if nothing emerges from it, it fails. And what emerges from the diagram, the Figure, emerges both gradually and all at once, as in *Painting* [3], where the whole is given all at once, while the series is at the same time constructed gradually. This is because, if we consider the painting in its reality, the heterogeneity of the manual diagram and the visual whole indeed indicates a difference in nature or a leap, as if we leapt a first time from the optical eye to the hand, and a second time from the hand to the eye. But if we consider the painting as a process, there is instead a continual injection of the manual diagram into the visual whole, a "slow leak," a "coagulation," an "evolution," as if one were moving gradually from the hand to the haptic eye, from the manual diagram to haptic vision.[10]

But this passage, whether abrupt or gradual, is the great moment in the act of painting. For it is here that painting discovers, deep in itself and in its own manner, the problem of a pure logic: how to pass from the possibility of fact to the fact itself?[11] For the diagram was only a possibility of fact, whereas the painting exists by making present a very particular fact, which we will call *the pictorial fact*. In the history of art, it was perhaps Michelangelo who made us grasp the existence of such a fact most forcefully. What we will call a "fact" is first of all the fact that several forms may actually be included in one and the same Figure, indissolubly, caught up in a kind of serpentine, like so many necessary accidents continually mounting on top of one another.[12] Hence *The Holy Family* [107]: the forms may be figurative, and there may still be narrative relations between the characters—but all these connections disappear in favor of a "matter of fact" or a properly pictorial (or sculptural) ligature, which no longer tells a story and no longer represents anything but its own movement, and which makes these apparently arbitrary elements coagulate in a single continuous flow.[13] Certainly there is still an organic representation, but even more profoundly, we witness the revelation of the body beneath the organism, which makes organisms and their elements crack or swell, imposes a spasm on them, and puts them into relation with forces—sometimes with an inner force that arouses them, sometimes with external forces that traverse them, sometimes with the eternal force of an unchanging time, sometimes with the variable forces of a flowing time. A piece of meat, a large back of a man: it is Michelangelo who inspires this in Bacon. And here again, the body seems to enter into particularly mannered postures, or is weighed down by stress, pain, or anguish. But this is true only if a story or a figuration is reintroduced: figurally speaking, these are actually the most natural of postures, as if we caught them "between" two stories, or when we were alone, listening to a force that had seized us. It was with Michelangelo, with *mannerism*, that the Figure or the pictorial fact was born in its pure state, and which would no longer need any other justification than "an acrid and strident polychromy, striated with flashes, like a metal plate." Everything is now brought into the clear, a clarity greater than that of the contour and even of light. The words Leiris uses to describe Bacon—hand, touch, seizure, capture—evoke this direct manual activity that traces the possibility of fact: we will capture the fact, just as we will "seize hold of life." But the fact itself, this pictorial fact that has come from the hand, is the formation of a third eye, a haptic eye, a haptic vision of the eye, this new clarity. It is as if the duality of the tactile and the optical were surpassed visually in this haptic function born of the diagram.

A Politics of Fact and Figure

Tom Conley

At the outset of *Cinema 1: The Movement-Image*, a book that can be pictured as the sinister panel of a textual diptych that includes *Cinema 2: The Time-Image*, Gilles Deleuze remarks that film generally draws its frame around either rarefied or saturated images. Sometimes a subject is isolated in space, as might be the lonely hero of a classical western shot on a mesa in New Mexico. At other times the subject is crowded into a compressed world of bodies and bric-a-brac, as would an unwitting protagonist in the dark interiors of a film noir. In both instances the frame teaches us that the image "is not merely given to be seen. It is as legible as it is visible."[1] As he puts it in his typically stenographic French, "elle est lisible autant que visible"; the same observation also applies to Deleuze's magnificent reading of the painterly oeuvre of Francis Bacon in a series aptly named La vue le texte (The Sight the Text). From a visual reading of the legible shapes of the paintings Deleuze builds the operative concept of a "logic of sensation." What exactly it is cannot be immediately discerned. The work refuses cursory reading.

The shape and aspect of the French edition of *The Logic of Sensation* are double. One volume contains textual reflections that are broken into seventeen chapters, designed, according to the preface, to take up separate aspects of the paintings in an order that moves toward greater complexity. But the progression is relative. It works "only from the point of view of a general logic of sensation." In other words, if the grounding tautology of the explanation of the title by the title is taken seriously, it means that what Deleuze is getting at is everywhere, throughout the book and beyond its borders. Each of the seventeen chapter-fragments can be taken as a sum and a mosaic fragment of a concept seen in a state of perpetual construction and revision. They have to be read in juxtaposition to the second volume, which includes reproductions of ninety-seven paintings by Francis Bacon that span the years 1944–1983. Sixty-six are reproduced in black and white, thirty-one in color. Twenty-one of the plates (thirteen in color) are triptychs that fold out from the spine of the volume, leaving an accordion-effect of a book of images whose sum is greater than its designated whole. At least forty-two plates— if two of each of the foldout triptychs is counted—supplement the ninety-seven entries, yielding a total of 139 illustrations.

Information concerning the titles, size and material, and location of each of the plates is found in an index at the end of the first volume. The list is organized not in a chronological sequence but according to a logic of citation and allusion found in the margins of the textual commentary. Each painting is queued by a number placed to the left of the text on both *recto* and *verso* sides of each page, somewhat like title-summaries in *manchettes* in early-modern printed books, in which the text itself can be seen at once as a "legend" underwriting the images or even as a component unit of a greater "fable" built from the composite character of words and pictures. Yet the order is deceptive. The index refers only to a first citation or allusion in the text to each painting, but not to its reiteration. Like others, *Painting* (1946) is first commented on in chapter 5 and thus indexed therein, but it then is taken up in subsequent discussion without further annotation in the index. It is up to the reader to figure out which paintings, if any, take command in the text. Admirers of Bacon will note that the catalogue, although copious, is not complete. The third edition of the book adds eleven paintings (figures 85–96) not cited in the body of the text or referred to by number along its margins, presumably because they were not yet available to be reproduced and examined. Some of the works figure in Bacon's own collection, and some others have private owners in Japan, Switzerland, London, San Francisco, New York, and Rome. Nine of the paintings are attributed to private collections without indication of place. *Two Figures in the Grass* [17] belongs to a private collection in Paris, while a *Triptych* [79] is owned privately "in France."

Would any of these eleven paintings be hanging on the walls of Deleuze's apartment? Would they be the furnishings of a baroque universe that would belong to the philosopher's fancy? Given the passion and detail of Deleuze's treatment it appears that the author had been living with a certain number of the paintings for a long time. A logic of sensation depends, it is implied, on an extended and extensive relation afforded by constant contact, first and foremost, with the paintings seen, touched, smelled, and felt over a long duration of time. Those that might not have been on the wall could, for the purpose of writing the text, be reproduced and taped to a panel or spread over a floor. The unlinked or paratactic quality of the observations suggests that the author is telling the reader to break frequently with the line of his reasoning by looking in detail at an ample quantity of pictures. We might say that what Deleuze calls the "systolic-diastolic" pulsations that emanate from the canvases owe to the leisure of sharing his life with Bacon's oeuvre.

And the text itself betrays well the rhythm of the relation. Certain chapters cite the paintings profusely (1, 3–6, 10, 16), some somewhat or slightly (7–9, 17), a few not at all (2, 11–15). The result is a dialogue in which Deleuze and Bacon intercede with each other. Following a trademark of the philosopher's writing, his words affirm over and over again that they cannot entirely account for Bacon's visual and chromatic effects. It is not because critical language would be at a loss to describe sensation; rather, it takes its task to be, like the paintings themselves, a *liberation of figures from figuration*. It entails, no less, loosening itself, insofar as it is a critical account, from a penchant to narrate, to relapse into a discourse that would tell a story based on "phases" of Bacon's career, its "turns" and "evolution" in the direction of holism, or a spurious sense of "reason" dictating the form and content of a *catalogue raisonné*. The art of commentary remains consonant with the painting where it also takes its own task to be one that must "break with representation, shatter narration, impede illustration," and thus "liberate" a "Figure" as does the artist himself.

Deleuze brings to Bacon a language that aims not to compete with the painting, as André Malraux might have wished, but to live and be liberated with it. He takes care not to incorporate the painting in a broader philosophy of aesthetics that would figure in the midst of what, when *The Logic of Sensation* was published in 1981, was a growing and increasingly self-contained and self-referential oeuvre. At that time, with Félix Guattari, he had just published *A Thousand Plateaus* (1980), the second volume of *Capitalism and Schizophrenia*, and was teaching and writing reflections on cinema soon to be published as *Cinema 1* (1983) and *Cinema 2* (1985). *The Logic of Sense* (1968), a work near in character to *The Logic of Sensation*, emphasizes the multilateral and infinitely bifurcating paths that reason finds in its creation of concepts. But here, thirteen years later, stress is placed on paintings that touch the "nervous system." Recall of the earlier work, especially *Proust and Signs*, informs the reader that sensation is discerned as movement that runs transversally, that "translates" affects, that is "what passes from one 'order' to another, from one 'level' to another, from one 'domain' to another. That's why sensation is the master cause of deformations, an agent that deforms the body." Translation or migration of affect was taken up in the study of passages and framings of signs in Proust. It is reiterated through the involuntary effects that move independently of figuration, illustration, or narrative. A sense of "Figure" would be captured in the site of "Combray," in a figural writing composed of images.[2] But in the world of painting, more than that of philosophy, sensation exceeds the intellectual and mimetic control, not only in the formal design of classical works, but even in the mental universe of abstract expressionism.

Given the proximity of Proust, the logic of "sense" in "sensation" can be taken as an implicit inflection of direction and seriality. Different "series" of forces are driven through the oeuvre. They are the celebrated images of crying Popes, contorted and coupled bodies on oval surfaces suspended in single fields of color, self-portraits in parallelepipeds, splayed carcasses—in dialogue with Rembrandt and Soutine—suspended in abstractly theatrical decors, seated figures witnessed by observers in the sides or background, or even nascent or unshaped allegories about painting itself. In all events sensation amounts to *Figure*, not to what is not figurative, not to what cannot be figured, but to what becomes a totalizing and also infinitizing *sense of figure*. Building on Bacon's own words, Deleuze remarks, "Toute sensation, et toute figure, est déjà de la sensation 'accumulée,' 'coagulée,' comme dans une figure de calcaire. D'où le caractère irréductiblement synthétique de la sensation" [Every sensation, and every Figure, is already an 'accumulated,' 'coagulated' sensation, as if in a limestone figure. Hence the irreducibly synthetic character of sensation]. Key, especially in the French, are not only the way Deleuze's remarks bleed into Bacon's words about the Figure ("a coagulation of nonrepresentative marks") but also a slippage of meaning that betrays well the logic of his own idiolect. Wherever Deleuze uses "Tout," as in "toute sensation," he emphasizes the presence of a totality that cannot be accorded a finite measure (hence the general cipher of "a thousand plateaus") but that nonetheless sums up a quantity and opens out onto new and other possibilities.

From the form and aspect of the dialogue the reader ascertains a new aesthetics that will prevail throughout the philosopher's writings after 1980. They loosen and soon lend a more reflective and even sensuous aspect to work in other areas. The complex and difficult "sensation" of Bacon's paintings infuses Deleuze so indelibly that many subsequent (but also anterior) concepts are virtually bathed in the artist's forms and colors. Among others, five interconnected terms are worth briefly pursuing. The "fact," the "diagram," the "cliché", the "event," and the "mold" gather force in the works published after *The Logic of Sensation*. In this work they have unique and strong inflection. How they shift and change in view of the paintings tells much about the character of the philosophy in a creative arena where picture and concept are confused.

The first sentences of the book set the stage: Deleuze begins with the oval base that could be a carpet on which two contorted human figures seem to embrace and wrestle with each other, the seat of a swing on which an athlete leans, or a suspended casserole on which a dressed figure sits while staring at the viewer (*Triptych* [61]); a round table or socle on which a muscular human form in an oval decor is posed but is bent and on the verge of melting [3, (*Study for a Portrait of Lucian Freud* [64]); a stool, also in front of an oval space, where a man whose head seems to be placed in an oblong frame under a hanging light (whose taut cord casts white and black shadows on either side), his arms and legs crossed, seemingly letting his calves dangle and drip into the shape of sheets of paper scattered on a floor whose rugged surface is suggested by thick parallel hatchings of pigment, though of a texture smoother than what is evoked through recall of Van Gogh's pigments that appeared to be applied to the canvas with a palette knife (*Portrait of George Dyer Talking* [37]); a field that could be another oval carpet, on which two rubbery peasants, arched over their hoes as might any of Millet's farmers, rake paint that would be a crust of soil (*Two Men Working in a Field* [66]); a corrida where a bull's head twists and draws a circular line extending the curve of its horns, almost concentric with the fuchsia border around the area in front of a mass of spectators, dots of pigment that somehow recall public space in the early Goya, seen through a bay window cutting into the color-field and standing at the edge of the circular arena (*Study for Bullfight No. 1* [56]). Deleuze notes that the paintings bear a "track, or a sort of circus ring as a place." The Figure immediately becomes a function of the ground from which an "operative field" emerges. The relation of the Figure to its isolating area, he notes, "defines a fact: the fact is . . . what takes place. . . . Thus isolated, the Figure becomes an Image, an Icon."

By dint of isolation the figurative dimension is lost, and so also is a narrative we would wish to invest in the image. The paintings do not allow the spectator to read into them allegories of couples sharing their sadomasochistic pleasures, nor do they invite us to elaborate on pyschoanalytical scenarios through the idea of the human figure (which is an avatar of Freud in some paintings, such as the portrait-blur in the left panel of *Triptych, Three Studies for a Crucifixion* [29], a work dated 1962, that distorts a photograph of the psychoanalyst often seen on book covers) meditating on the fantasies the painting is putting forward, or to speculate on thematics of source and variation through the presence of images derived from classical works and modified in the new decor. "Isolation is thus the simplest means, necessary though not sufficient, to break with representation, to disrupt narration, to escape illustration, to liberate the Figure: to stick to the fact" [s'en tenir au fait].

Here the "fact" becomes synonymous with what Deleuze elsewhere calls an "event," at once the experience of Bacon's paintings and the aim of philosophy. In the median chapter of *The Logic of Sensation* ("Couples and Triptychs"), he argues that sensation has the virtue not only of moving across different levels of space and affect but also of bringing together different zones of intensity. Such are those where bodies are entwined (*Two Figures in the Grass* [17]; the central panel of *Triptych, Studies from the Human Body* [61]; the blur of members and their viscous shadow in the center of *Triptych* [75]; and so on). They comprise a decisive coupling of sensation, what would be "the one and the same *matter of fact* for two Figures" (in English in the text). The word leads to broader speculation on the possibility of there existing among the figural elements certain relations—neither illustrative, narrative, nor logical—that, in order not to lapse into psychology or psychoanalysis, he would be impelled to call merely "matters of fact." The force of the Figure can be attributed to what has no cause. It is simply what it is, *here*, something complex, isolated, bearing all the traits of its quiddity and haecceity. Very few paintings are of such power. The event of Bacon's paintings can be defined as a sensation that in the same flash grasps and releases a governing perception of their composite elements.

Hence the attraction of the triptych: no causal or illustrative relation ties one panel to another. Resemblances between them are obvious, some kind of relation must be established, but progression or mimetic authentification in the passage from one point to the other cannot be determined. The various Figures incarnate a "common" trait or a "matter of fact" that would be at once human figures coupled and figures separated, as might also the composite pieces of a triptych. A new element is added in the figure of the "attendant," a human form that looks at what seems to be happening in the images (the dexter panel *Triptych* [74]; possibly the nude looking right in the sinister panel of *Triptych* [70]; *Triptych, Three Portraits* [71]; or surely the clothed figure in the curved window looking at the nude couple in the parallelepiped of the dexter panel of *Triptych Inspired by T. S. Eliot's Poem "Sweeney Agonistes"* [46]). Deleuze divests the figure of the witness of all residual voyeurism. The witness is neither the double of the spectator seen in the image nor a critical rendering of scopophilia. Rather, "the attendant only indicates a constant, a measure or cadence in relation to which we can appraise a variation," allowing the attendant-Figure to become a variation-Figure. Introduced thus is vibration that oscillates along the contours of the figures themselves in the panels and in the containing lines that define the spaces they inhabit. The "matter of fact," what the painting embodies and becomes, is made manifest in the greater rhythms of line, color, and form.

Deleuze's argument in these pages bears comparison with the definitions he put forward in *The Fold: Leibniz and the Baroque* (1988) concerning the event as a perception of point of view. Taking up John Russell's reading of Bacon's *Man and Child* [32], in which a seated male figure with a protracted and distorted face, set against the frame of a bright background, extends a pair of legs wearing enormous shoes—which seem to blend the forms of wingtips and peasants' clogs—onto a carpetlike floor with mottled outlines of tiles that vaguely resemble wafts of clouds. The child has oversized feet and calves that are attached backward to her thighs; she wears a short skirt and an ample sweater. Her face appears simultaneously canine and human. She looks at the scene of the portraiture to the right. Deleuze sums up Russell's perplexity about the painting: Is the girl in disgrace with a father who refuses to pardon her? Is she the man's guardian, a woman who looks sternly at him with her arms crossed as he contorts his body and looks in another direction? Is she some kind of mongoloid monster that returns from the "repressed" to haunt him? Or is he a character set on a pedestal, like a pope or a judge, who will pronounce judgment on the person with whom he refuses any visual contact? On each occasion Russell is obliged to respond in the negative. The narration that is disqualified by the response to one question requires each subsequent supposition to be rejected in turn. The spectator, concludes the art historian, will and ought never wish to know. Deleuze then adds decisively: the painting "is the possibility of all of these hypotheses or narrations at the same time" because in itself it is outside of any narration.

The painting can be seen orienting all of its potential narratives into the sensation of witnessing, what indeed in *The Fold* he will later define as a matter of "point of view." Point of view is generally assumed to be a key to the representation of subjectivity in the modern novel. It is what literary critics in the wake of Percy Lubbock's studies of Henry James's "reflectors" consign to relativity.[3] It would result from the staging of a statement uttered by figure x, consonant with his or her psychology and character that elicits a response, stated by y and in the tenor of his or her character, affecting the emotive condition both of x and of witness z; y emits a reaction that causes z to change the tenor of speech because of a frown seen on the forehead of x, and so on. Through his relation with Bacon's painting Deleuze takes the issue a step further. Point of view is a "point of view on variation"; that is, it is the condition in which an eventual subject grasps a variation. It is not a variation of truth according to the way a subject looks at something, "but the condition in which there appears to the subject the truth of a variation," what Deleuze calls "the very idea of Baroque perspective." Point of view is "enveloped in variation, just as variation is enveloped in point of view."[4] In Bacon the gazing figure bears witness or attends to the variation that it elicits. Thanks to a composition and treatment unique to Bacon's world, where it is impossible to reconstitute any plausible scenario, a sense of point of view is given.

A corollary point is that the sensation of point of view as variation qualifies as an *event*. Such would be the "Bacon-event" or the "painting-event" that Deleuze is getting at. The final pages of the section of *The Fold* devoted to inclusions take up the vagaries of perception. What is it that a subject decides to hold in the purview of his or her senses? To this question and the one that he poses in the title of the sixth chapter, "What Is an Event?," Deleuze responds that an event is something that happens, such as a man being crushed or the duration of a pyramid. It is the realization that hits Napoleon's soldiers, when they are marching across the Egyptian desert, that the pyramids are beholding them as much as they are beholding the pyramids. In Leibniz's world, perception of an event requires the placement of some kind of screen between the perceiver and the perceived. Without a screen, grid, or a filter, a surrounding chaos would be invisible.

Here Bacon implicitly intervenes in Deleuze's discussion of Leibniz's theory of the event. "Following a physical approximation, chaos would be depthless shadows, but the screen would extract its dark background, the 'fuscum subnigrum' that, for as little as it differs from black, contains all colors: the screen would be like the infinitely machinated machine that constitutes Nature."[5] By way of a complex reading (through Alfred North Whitehead's treatment of Leibniz), Deleuze concludes that the composite elements or conditions of an event include *extension*, where one figure becomes a sum of itself and everything that surrounds it. Figure and ground interpenetrate each other (across a limpid visual field soldiers become pyramids and pyramids soldiers). An extension (say, the distance between the marching troops and the great pyramids) dissolves where the mutual perception is perceived. Extension, however, depends on how passage to and from the figure and ground is effected. "Series," "waves," or "vibrations" are vital to the event. Hence a second attribute is the intrinsic quality of a given series—that might include tone, tint, chromatic value, or color saturation—that engages other series, such that *intensions or intensities* result from a concatenation of perceptions. The subject or object that perceives extension and intension must be an individual that is a "concrescence of elements," in other words, a site of *prehension* that becomes the matter prehended by another individual. What is prehended is in itself a preexisting or coextensive prehension, such that "all prehension is a prehension of prehension, and the event a 'nexus of prehensions,' in other words, at once the objectivation of one prehension and the subjectivation of another."[6]

However great its abstraction, it would not be wrong to see the subtlety and force of Deleuze's definition of the event in the "prehensive" qualities he discerns in Bacon's paintings. The coupled Figures create extension through their isolation. The intensities that result from their indeterminate state—they are amphibian, androgynous, polymorphous, simultaneously organic and inorganic—offer the viewer an intense experience of painterly variation that runs through the bodies, in and along the spinal columns and nervous systems, of both the Figures that are grasped and the viewer who grasps them. In the dexter panel of *Three Studies for a Crucifixion* [29], a splayed carcass reveals a dorsal column leading downward to a head with a gaping mouth whose teeth seem to be miniature vertebrae. The upper end of the body is a curved swath of lines of red and white pigment that surround an ellipse that might be a mouth above an eye. Its form resembles the incursion of what seems to be the black silhouette of a seal's or a dog's head, or even a cartoon character, that would be one of the "attendants" to the strange bodily event that is taking place above. Yet its resemblance to the contour of the upper part of the carcass makes the image waver between horror at the sight of vivisection and a reminders of "Loony Tunes," the comic creations of Tex Avery in which rubbery homunculi (Porky Pig, Bugs Bunny, Spike the dog, all cartoon clichés) are distended and bent in antic fashion. The viewer of this image prehends different forms in the painting that are in constant modulation, thanks in part to an extension that is created through the isolation of the object in an area of minimal depth of field. The intensity of the forms results from a transmutation taking place in the context of an anatomy lesson, and a sense of the fungibility of prehension is obtained from the point of view shared by the spectator with that of the uncanny witness to the carcass. As both fact and Figure (Deleuze takes care to capitalize the latter), in itself and in its relation to surrounding panels and to the oeuvre in general, the painting becomes an event.

Adepts of literature and philosophy who read *The Logic of Sensation* discover that Deleuze dismantles the myth of the blank page or white canvas that would be anterior to creation. "It is a mistake to think that the painter works on a white surface. The figurative belief follows from this mistake. If the painter were before a white surface, he could reproduce an external object functioning as a model, but such is not the case. The painter has many things in his head, around him, or in his studio." These things are *données*, givens, that can be qualified as a stockpile of images and clichés that are virtually on the canvas (or in the creator's brain) before the labor of painting ever begins. Here begins, by way of quotation of D. H. Lawrence's remarks on Cézanne's struggle to offer a new view of the applelike nature of apples, a reflection of greater scope on the artist's rapport with clichés. With wry humor and the slightest of irony Deleuze remarks, "The fight against clichés is a terrible thing." The artist does not merely mutilate, manhandle, or parody the cliché for comic or deformative ends. Creators of Bacon's order give themselves over to clichés. They invoke, accumulate, and multiply them in the name of "prepictorial givens," which they draw out of the canvas in the act of painting. They do not use them, as might a novelist or a poet, for underscoring stylistic deviation.[7] Rather, and here again Deleuze takes the theory and practice of the cliché a step further, the cliché figures in a "prepictorial idea" that disengages from the canvas as many ready-made forms as needed to discern "an entire order of *equal and unequal probabilities.*" By way of freely drawn markings within the painted image the painter might destroy nascent figuration and allow chance or accident—a vital element of an event in the broad and strong sense—to take place.

Bacon's painterly images are drawn and torn from clichés that subtend illustration and narration. Chance becomes a happening that is made to happen. It takes place by way of conceived or evident probabilities in the prepictorial arena. Chance becomes painterly when a Figure is extracted from a sum of figurative probabilities. In this way it shares much with the concept of point of view, and it thus bears a stronger and more active inflection than what is taken to be the art of chance in the work of Marcel Duchamp. Duchamp often lets things happen as they may; he gives the impression of passively using mixed media to record quasi-invisible occurrences. For Deleuze and Bacon an accident or an event is a result of a manipulation of things given, of affective investment made through a selection taken from thousands of clichés saturating a prepictorial field. Out of it emerges a painting, an image, that is both within and beyond the creator's control.

The visual formatting of *The Logic of Sensation* bears witness to the process. The back cover of the second volume displays four strips and one square of four and five photos that Bacon took of himself in a photo booth. In three sets he stands before a white backdrop, and in two others his face is seen against the folds of a curtain. The back cover of the volume might seem to be a sheet of photosensitive paper on which are placed the strips and a torn fragment of a black-and-white snapshot. Usually destined for identification cards, these miniature pictures of the artist display him now and again with a casual air, distracted, looking troubled, and posed theatrically. They would seem to have nothing to do with the paintings until their brute state as *clichés* is brought forward and grotesquely distorted within the paintings reproduced inside. Sometimes they are the basis for triptychs, taken as preparatory studies for portraits (*Three Studies for a Self-Portrait* [48]; *Three Studies of Isabel Rawsthorne* [54]) that turn the images into grotesquely attractive and perversely eroticized masses of flesh. At others, isolated, they resurface as pictures tacked to the wall of the arenas in which figures sit on stools or in chairs (the sinister and dexter panels of *Triptych, Three Portraits* [71]). A selection, transference, and distortion are aptly shown through the composition of the book and Deleuze's commentary.

Attesting to the fact that concepts move through and across his oeuvre analogously to the ways painterly forms migrate to and from many places in Bacon's paintings, the cliché acquires a different aspect in other studies. In *Cinema 1* the creative potential of the cliché begun with Bacon is amplified at a point where history determines some of the aesthetics of postwar cinema. At the end of *Cinema 1* Deleuze draws a line of demarcation between the first fifty years of cinema, in which movement is taken to be the essence of its images, and the work of the past sixty years, where attention to duration takes greater control. Five artistic and thematic elements, he argues, are symptomatic of the shift. Cineasts begin to portray events as they take place instead of recording them. Thus, an "open totality" is given in film, especially where cinema takes up "dispersive" situations where, second, lines that concatenated events become blurred, the ones becoming confused with the others. Suddenly, third, the camera begins to gain autonomy as the tracking shot and handheld camera liberate the image from a fixed position on a tripod. The camera begins to stroll on its own. In the thematic world, fourth, films treat of conspiracies and of strategies of control that they virulently denounce. Finally, viewers begin to wonder about what holds things together in a world lacking totality or linkage. "The answer is simple: what gives order to the sum are clichés and nothing more. Nothing but clichés, everywhere clichés."[8] Films are suddenly papered with clichés and readymade dialogues that turn the classical tensions of depth of field and the long take in classical film to a *shallow depth* in which the spectator is asked to see how clichés inform the image and how he or she must use them in creative and productive reading. A perception of a reign of clichés in the mental and visual world alike gives rise to a politics. The cineast who knows how to use them in a prefilmic way, as does Bacon in the preparation of his canvases, yokes aesthetics in the service of a politics.

In any respect the element of probability that Deleuze develops through his study of the paintings acquires prismatic inflection in the writing on Foucault and Leibniz. In *Foucault*, in a chapter in which he argues that the author of *Discipline and Punish* is a "new cartographer," Deleuze states that the modern age begins when institutions that have traditionally been archives turn into "diagrams."[9] Up until the French Revolution and its immediate aftermath institutions of knowledge had recorded and registered phenomena of the world pertaining to their disciplines. The historian wrote of the genealogy of the king and inhabited a library where knowledge was partitioned according to inherited visual and architectural schemes. With the advent of the modern prison there was implemented the need "to impose a given kind of behavior upon a given human multitude" (41). A new sense of things unformed and unorganized went hand in hand with that of functions not yet formalized or finalized. A mode that seeks to pattern these things would be a *diagram*. It is a new abstract dimension, in which present and future time are folded into the past of the archive. No longer the auditory or visual archive, "it is the map, it is cartography coextensive with the entire social field. It is an abstract machine" (42), a map "of relations of force, of density, intensity, that goes by way of primary linkages that cannot be localized, and that pass at every instant through all points, 'or rather in every relation from one point to another'" (44). Like Leibniz's subjects imbricated in their predicates,[10] or in events where predication is at once a cause and an effect of subjectivation, the diagram folds a cause into an effect: it seeks to produce the history of the future by using its archival knowledge (a cause) to map and to grid future behavior (an effect). The diagram is a model that will shape operations otherwise subject to chance. In our world, Deleuze notes in his reading, it would belong to logistics and the arts of strategy and control. Where the archive had been a "history of forms" the diagram is a "becoming of forces" (51). In these words are heard a history and a politics of what has shaped the contemporary world.

In *The Logic of Sensation* the diagram bears a different but comparable inflection. Relating it to Bacon's style of painting, it is the sum of creative actions that include marking and drawing lines by way of chance; then cleaning, sweeping, or wiping areas with spots or color; finally, applying paint from varied angles and at as many different speeds. Thus a mouth can be extended from one end of the head to another or a leg twisted into a distorted dorsal column. The diagram has an effect comparable to "inserting a Sahara, a zone of the Sahara," into our head, or of stretching the skin of a rhinoceros under a microscope or drawing and quartering two parts of a head with an ocean, units of measure moving indiscriminately to and from micrometric to cosmic proportion. In Bacon's paintings the diagram becomes the "operative set of asignifying and nonrepresentative lines and zones, line-strokes and color-patches," a *catastrophe* or chaos infused with a minimum of order or rhythm.

Like the political diagram in Foucault's world, in Bacon's studio the term designates a mapping of the elements of chance, a selection and distribution of clichés, and a condition that shapes creative accident. Through a comparison of Bacon and Action Painting, Deleuze deduces a "history" of the sweep and swath he draws in the works on cinema, Leibniz, and Foucault. Taken together, Jackson Pollock's early work (in which were mixed freely drawn lines, painted zones of color, and iconic and representative shapes) and later drip-canvases (said to be free of all illustration, the swirls of paint aspiring to pure rhythm and abstraction) betray a movement by which a "catastrophe-painting" becomes synonymous with a "diagram-painting." In his view, where painting executed on the floor is put on a wall, the spectator witnesses the "optical catastrophe and the manual rhythm" that extends "all over" the canvas and thus becomes, in view of the totality, an *event.* Yet the diagrammatic condition of the painting, Deleuze insists, is the possibility of its fact, but not quite its Fact. As might a Fact, a Figure emerges from the diagram when the latter extends—as it does in all of Bacon's canvases—across the whole picture, when it is conferred with a new radiance and power of vibration that cannot be limited to one zone or another.

Yet Bacon takes the spectator beyond abstract expressionism and Action Painting, we learn, when he offers new and other topographies of lines drawn by chance and zones of color washed and swept by means other than a freely active hand painting with a brush or wiping a surface with a cloth soaked in pigment. Deleuze brings to the operation of the diagram a notion of modulation and a sense of an "analogical" painting. It resembles that of a give-and-take between the canvas and the painter (as if each were the interlocutor of the other) that stands in contrast to a "digital" mode of communication (where discrete units of information or matter are displaced from one site to another).[11] Painting that builds its force through color would be analogical par excellence, in contrast to demarcations yielded by boldly drawn lines where the codes or signs of a digital art would be made manifest. By way of the diagram, a compositional strategy, there can be a breakage with representation or figurative resemblance. When forms and colors mix as they do in the areas of the human body and its ambient space in Bacon's work, distortions and modulations—especially across panels of given triptychs or the oeuvre in general—become painfully visible. Modulation is taken to be something of a "law of Analogy" that acts upon the painting as might "a variable and continuous mold."

But what, other than an obvious oxymoron, is a variable and continuous mold? Quite possibly, it is a flexible matrix in which expansions, contractions, shifts in mass, new shapes, and unforeseen torsions come forward. With it we pass from "the possibility of fact to the Fact, from the diagram to the painting," or from the figures to a Figure.[12] The diagram, which bears resemblance to a digital operation comprised of given codes, turns into a modulating agent, thanks to the work of the unconscious in creative speculation and action, that creates new and multiple forms and colors. Nothing attests to modulation better than the gamut of Bacon's human figures, especially those of the triptych, when they are splayed and displayed over different blocks and bands of color. The bodies are elastic, as if composed at times with silly putty that hardens into muscle and melts into puddles of flesh. Their extremities (knees, shoulder blades, heels) are sites of agglutinated swishes of white paint that give relief to the black areas of shadow, in the groins and armpits or even the neck and chest, where flesh melds into painterly contrast (the seated men in the sinister and dexter panels of *Triptych* [70]). Or else, appearing to follow a cruel law of geometry with which he composes his diagrammatic settings of framelike backgrounds set within the arc lines of abstract arenas or on rotund tables on which bodies are coupled, Bacon seems to make contours and curves grow into buttocks or muscular thighs from which also extend faces whose smiles resemble the curves of miniature dorsal columns (the central panel of *Triptych, Studies from the Human Body* [84]).[13] The bodies seem to be molded as much as they are drawn and painted. When seen together they are serialized and exist as variations or modulations.

Molding and modulation bear a different but comparable aspect in Deleuze's other writings on philosophy and aesthetics. The concepts cannot be detached from the images of these contorted bodies. *The Fold* inaugurates its grounding argument that the baroque style is the legacy of modern art and thinking and that Leibniz is its first and finest practitioner and theorist with a volley of *images*. The philosopher offered the fantasy of "a flexible or elastic body" with cohering parts that form a fold, such that "they are not separated in parts of parts, but rather are infinitely divided into smaller and smaller folds that always retain a certain cohesion," parts of matter being "masses or aggregates, as a correlation of compressive elastic force" (9). Folds become the matter and process of morphogenesis. In Leibniz Deleuze detects an affinity of matter and life. There prevails "a muscular conception of matter" that springs into everything. "Plastic forces" that "organize" (or give rise to bodily organs) extensive life are distinguished from "compressive or elastic forces" (11) that make organisms possible or cause them to be born from pre-existing organs.

It is impossible not to imagine these bodies without reference to the human shapes everywhere in Bacon's paintings. Where Deleuze writes of a "swarm" of folds of matter both organic and inorganic, and where he notes that in both Leibniz and the baroque world in general "the principles of reasons are veritable cries" (14), how can a reader not recall Bacon's treatment of flesh and color or the many paintings that portray figures that cry or shriek (*Head VI* [6]; *Fragment of a Crucifixion* [7]; *Three Studies of the Human Head* [13])? Bacon, admired because he creates "a painting of the cry," transforms the shriek into a material, visible, and plastic form. For Leibniz and the painter alike the Scream "captures or detects an invisible force."

Bacon's paintings seem to hang on the walls of the upper floors of the "baroque house" that Deleuze constructs as the edifice in which he gathers his reflections on the condition of modern life.

The paintings show how the philosopher can apply the concept of modulation and continually variable molding to social history. In *Foucault* we see that our era begins when diagrams take precedence over archives, or when licit illegalism, the regime of accepted practices of corruption replaces a fixed order where good and evil formerly had been built over other illegalisms. In *The Fold* the modern age begins when a "fluctuation of a norm replaces the permanence of a law." So also do industrially produced objects, no longer functions of standards, when they figure in a temporal modulation, a continuous development of form (26). Borrowing the words of the biologist Gilbert Simondon, Deleuze observes that molding amounts to modulating, but in a continuous and perpetually variable way.[14] Because they are always fluctuating and never in a state of inert permanence, objects, "manneristic" in quality, contrary to forces that would essentialize them—like what happens in Bacon's paintings when they are taken individually or in aggregate—"become an event."

Other lines of comparison could be drawn through *The Logic of Sensation* and Deleuze's philosophical, aesthetic, and political writings. The work on Bacon affirms not only an extraordinary savor and delight that might be less apparent in the earlier writings; it also makes clear what he means by "styles" of thinking, living, and doing. Some of the chapters—such as "Analogy," "Painters Recapitulate the History of Painting in Their Own Way," and "The Eye and the Hand"—are thumbnail summaries of a theory of aesthetics. Put into salient profile is Deleuze's taste for Aloïs Riegl's concept of the haptic way of reading and seeing; for Wilhelm Worringer's rhapsodic epiphanies to the endlessly creative and continuously bifurcating line of "Gothic" style, a line that conveys attraction and empathy, in opposition to the square and closed measure of its "classical" counterpart; for Cézanne and his readers, from D. H. Lawrence to Merleau-Ponty and Lyotard, who find in the paintings a vital and vibrant sense of things that cannot be essentialized or consigned to the language of the sublime; for the sculpted abstraction of Egyptian architecture and the way it makes visible energies of light.

The same taste can be found elsewhere in Deleuze's writings, but it suffices to observe that if there are hinges or turning points in the oeuvre the work on Bacon is a crucial one. Before *The Logic of Sensation* Deleuze philosophizes and conceptualizes; after the work on Bacon a greater and more supple sense of flow, flexion, transformation, and bodily force becomes evident. The style becomes the very image of what Deleuze draws from the life he lived with the paintings. As a result, the philosophy gains color, tone, and force that pull toward literature and art. If, as he had remarked of great writers and cinematic auteurs who left legacies of works whose whole is greater than the sum of their individual creations, Deleuze can be seen as a name referring to a considerable oeuvre made up of vastly different topics and inflections over the second half of the twentieth century. It follows that his study of Bacon remains a telling turning point. In the arena where he considered writing to be the drive to resist, to struggle, and to become,[15] and where *art* needs to be seen as a matter of fact for all politics, "the art of the possible," this book stands among one of Deleuze's greatest trophies.

Notes

Translator's Introduction

This translation might never have seen the light of day were it not for the tireless efforts of Tristan Palmer, to whom I owe a debt of gratitude.

1. Gilles Deleuze, *Francis Bacon: Logique de la sensation* (Paris: Éditions de la Différence, 1981), in the series La vue le texte, edited by Harry Jancovici, now out of print. A revised version appeared from Éditions de la Différence in 1983, incorporating fifteen new paintings by Bacon and one minor emendation to the text (on 25). The French book is currently available in a paperback edition published in 2002 by Éditions de Seuil in the series L'Ordre philosophique, edited by Alain Badiou and Barbara Cassin.

2. See, for instance, Patrick Vauday's early review in *Critique* 426 (1982), as well as Christine Buci-Glucksmann, "Le plissé baroque de la peinture," *Magazine littéraire* 257 (September 1988).

3. The two volumes of *Capitalism and Schizophrenia* include *Anti-Oedipus*, trans. Robert Hurley, Mark Seem, and Helen R. Lane (New York: Viking, 1977), and *A Thousand Plateaus*, trans. Brian Massumi (Minneapolis: University of Minnesota Press, 1987).

4. See Gilles Deleuze, *Cinema 1: The Movement-Image*, trans. Hugh Tomlinson and Barbara Habberjam (Minneapolis: University of Minnesota Press, 1986), and *Cinema 2: The Time-Image*, trans. Hugh Tomlinson and Robert Galeta (Minneapolis: University of Minnesota Press, 1989); *The Fold: Leibniz and the Baroque*, trans. Tom Conley (Minneapolis: University of Minnesota Press, 1993); and *Essays Critical and Clinical*, trans. Daniel W. Smith and Michael A. Greco (Minneapolis: University of Minnesota Press, 1997).

5. Ronald Bogue's magisterial three-volume work on Deleuze and the arts, which includes *Deleuze on Music, Painting, and the Arts, Deleuze on Cinema*, and *Deleuze on Literature* (New York: Routledge, 2003), is a definitive study of Deleuze's "philosophy of art." My comments here are deeply indebted to Bogue's pioneering work.

6. Gilles Deleuze, "8 ans après: Entretien 1980" (interview with Catherine Clément), *L'arc* 49 (rev. ed., 1980), special issue on Deleuze, 99.

7. Gilles Deleuze, *Negotiations 1972–1990*, trans. Martin Joughin (New York: Columbia University Press, 1995), 32, translation modified.

8. Deleuze, *The Movement-Image*, ix; *Negotiations*, 47.

9. Quoted in Milan Kundera, *The Art of the Novel*, trans. Linda Asher (New York: Grove Press, 1988), 5, 36.

10. Deleuze, *Negotiations*, 58.

11. John Russell, *Francis Bacon* (New York: Oxford University Press, 1971; rev. ed., 1979).

12. See Jean-François Lyotard, *Que peindre? Adami. Arakawa. Buren* (Paris: Éditions de la Différence, 1987), and Michel Butor, *Comment écrire pour Jasper Johns* (Paris: Editions de la Différence, 1992).

13. See Michel Leiris, *Francis Bacon: Full Face and in Profile*, trans. John Weightman (New York: Rizzoli, 1983), and *Francis Bacon*, trans. John Weightman (New York: Rizzoli, 1998).

14. See Michael Peppiatt, *Francis Bacon: Anatomy of an Enigma* (New York: Farrar, Straus and Giroux, 1996), 276.

15. See Gilles Deleuze, *Abécédaire*, "C as in 'Culture'" (overview by Charles J. Stivale available on-line at http://www.langlab.wayne.edu/Romance/FreDeleuze.html): Deleuze "doesn't believe in culture, rather he believes in encounters *(rencontres)*, but these encounters don't occur with people. People think that it's with other people that encounters take place, like among intellectuals at colloquia. Encounters occur, rather, with things, with a painting, a piece of music. With people, however, these meetings are not at all encounters; these kind of encounters are usually so disappointing, catastrophic."

16. Peppiatt, *Francis Bacon*, 305–6.

17. "La peinture enflamme l'écriture," interview with Gilles Deleuze by Hervé Guibert, *Le Monde*, 3 December 1981, 15.

18. David Sylvester, *The Brutality of Fact: Interviews with Francis Bacon 1962–1979*, 3d ed. (New York: Thames and Hudson, 1987).

19. From Bacon's introductory text to the "The Artist's Eye" exhibition at the National Gallery, London, as cited in Peppiatt, *Francis Bacon*, 310.

20. "La peinture enflamme l'écriture," interview with Deleuze by Guibert, 15, emphasis added.

21. Gilles Deleuze, "Preface to the English-Language Edition," in *Empiricism and Subjectivity: An Essay on Hume's Theory of Human Nature*, trans. Constantin V. Boundas (New York: Columbia University Press, 1991), ix.

22. Erwin Straus, *Vom Sinn der Sinne* (1935), translated as *The Primary World of the Senses: A Vindication of Sensory Experience*, trans. Jacob Needleman, 2d ed. (New York: Free Press, 1963).

23. Marius von Senden, *Space and Sight: The Perception of Space and Shape in the Congenitally Blind Before and After Operation*, trans. Peter Heath (London and Glencoe, Ill.: Free Press, 1960).

24. See Daniel N. Stern, *The Interpersonal World of the Infant: A View from Psychoanalysis and Developmental Psychology* (New York: Basic Books, 1985).

25. Straus, *The Primary World of the Senses*, 351.

26. Maurice Merleau-Ponty, *Phenomenology of Perception*, trans. Colin Smith (New York: Routledge, 1962), 102–6.

27. Deleuze, *Francis Bacon: The Logic of Sensation*, chapter 7.

28. This reading can be found in Deleuze's seminars of 28 March and 4 April 1978, which are available on-line at http://www.webdeleuze.com/sommaire.html under the title "Quatre Leçons sur Kant," translated into English by Melissa McMahon.

29. See Immanuel Kant, *Critique of Pure Reason*, trans. Norman Kemp Smith (London: Macmillan Press, 1929), A120, 144: "There must exist in us an active faculty for the synthesis of the manifold. To this faculty I give the title, imagination."

30. Gilles Deleuze, *Kant's Critical Philosophy: The Doctrine of the Faculties*, trans. Hugh Tomlinson and Barbara Habberjam (Minneapolis: University of Minnesota Press, 1984), 15–16.

31. Kant, *Critique of Pure Reason*, A68/B93, 105: "The only use which the understanding can make of these concepts is to judge by means of them."

32. Immanuel Kant, *Critique of Judgment*, trans. J. C. Meredith (Oxford: Oxford University Press, 1978), §26, 105.

33. Jacques Derrida, *The Truth in Painting*, trans. Geoff Bennington and Ian McLeod (Chicago: University of Chicago Press, 1987), 140.

34. See Maurice Merleau-Ponty, *The Primacy of Perception*, ed. James M. Edie (Evanston: Northwestern University Press, 1964), 5. See also Eva Schaper, "Kant's Schematism Revisited," *Review of Metaphysics* 18 (1964), 267–92.

35. Kant, *Critique of Judgment*, §26, 98.

36. See Henri Maldiney, "L'Esthetique des rhythmes," in *Regard Parole Espace* (Lausanne: Éditions l'Age d'Homme, 1973), 147–72: 149–51.

37. Seminars of 28 March and 4 April 1978.

38. "La peinture enflamme l'écriture," interview with Deleuze by Guibert, 15.

39. Deleuze, *Francis Bacon*, chapter 6.

40. Joachim Gasquet, *Cézanne: A Memoir with Conversations*, trans. Christopher Pemberton (London: Thames and Hudson: 1991), 160.

41. Seminar of 28 March 1978. Deleuze is referring to a passage in Paul Klee, *On Modern Art*, trans. Paul Findlay (London: Faber and Faber, 1966), 43, as cited in *A Thousand Plateaus*, 312.

42. In Kant, sensibility is a mere *receptive* faculty: it simply presents a diversity of a manifold in space and time. The task of the imagination (through synthesis), the understanding (through concepts), and reason (through Ideas) is to *unify* this diversity (the form of recognition and common sense).

43. Deleuze, *The Movement-Image*, 50–51.

44. Deleuze, *The Movement-Image*, 208–9, translation modified.

45. Gary Genosko, *Félix Guattari: An Aberrant Introduction* (London and New York: Continuum, 2002), 180. Genosko presents an excellent analysis of Guattari's "diagrammaticism" on 178–85.

46. Charles Sanders Peirce, *The Collected Papers*, ed. Charles Hartshorne and Paul Weiss (Cambridge, Mass.: Harvard University Press, 1935–1966), vol. 4, 531 (as cited in Genosko, *Félix Guattari*, 179). For a useful discussion of Peirce's theory of the diagram, see James Feibleman, *An Introduction to Peirce's Philosophy Interpreted as a System* (New York and London: Harper and Brothers, 1946), 137–40.

47. See Deleuze and Guattari, *A Thousand Plateaus*, 531, note 41: Deleuze and Guattari note that they "borrow his [Peirce's] terms, even while changing their connotations," such that they are able to assign to the diagram "a distinct role, irreducible to either the icon or the symbol." For their use of the term *diagram*, see 141–44.

48. Deleuze and Guattari, *A Thousand Plateaus*, 142.

49. Deleuze, *Francis Bacon*, chapter 12.

50. Deleuze and Guattari, *A Thousand Plateaus*, "1837: Of the Refrain," 310–50.

51. Deleuze and Guattari, *What Is Philosophy?*, 203: "The struggle with chaos that Cézanne and Klee have shown in action in painting, at the heart of painting, is found in another way in science and in philosophy."

52. Deleuze nonetheless occasionally makes use of this term; see, for instance, *A Thousand Plateaus*, 497: "The figurative as such is not inherent to any 'will to art.'"

53. Maldiney, *Regard Parole Espace*, 195.

1. The Round Area, the Ring

1. Jean-François Lyotard uses the word *figural* as a substantive in order to oppose it to the "figurative." See *Discours, Figure* (Paris: Klincksieck, 1972).

2. See David Sylvester, *The Brutality of Fact: Interviews with Francis Bacon, 1962–1979*, 3d ed. (New York: Thames and Hudson, 1987). The critique of the "figurative" (both "illustrative" and "narrative") is a constant theme of the book, which we will cite hereafter as *Interviews*.

3. *Interviews*, 23.

4. [In English in the original, and thus throughout this book.—*Trans.*]

5. *Interviews*, 12–13.

6. [*Traits asignifiants*. The French word *trait*, like its English equivalent, is derived from the Latin *tractus*, the past participle of *trahere*, to draw. The term has two primary senses: etymologically, it refers to a graphic line, or more specifically, to the action of drawing a line or set of lines (a stroke, a draft, a "touch" in a picture); by extension, it is also used to designate a distinguishing quality or characteristic mark, a feature that allows one to identify or recognize a thing. Deleuze often refers to both meanings: it is the marks or strokes on the canvas that introduce traits of animality into the human figure, thereby constituting a "zone of indiscernibility" between the human and the animal. Since the English term is most commonly used in the latter sense, however, we have occasionally translated *trait* as "stroke" in those contexts where the literal meaning is predominant, that is, when Deleuze is referring to the activity of the artist's hand on the painting (as when one speaks of "a stroke of the pencil" or "brush stroke").—*Trans.*]

7. [Deleuze is here following the terminology of Aloïs Riegl, who distinguished between the tactile *(taktisch)* perception of the work of art, for which the viewer has to be close to the object *(Nahsicht)*; and an optical *(optisch)* perception, for which a view from a distance *(Fernsicht)* is best suited. We have generally translated *vue proche* as "close viewing," and *vision éloignée* as "distant viewing." Erwin Panofsky, in *Meaning in the Visual Arts* (Garden City, N.Y.: Doubleday Anchor Books, 1955), notes that the German word *taktisch*, "normally denoting 'tactical' as opposed to 'strategic,' is used in art-historical German as an equivalent of 'tactile' or even 'textural' as well as 'tangible' or 'palpable'" (330). For the term *haptic*, see note 2 to chapter 14.—*Trans.*]

8. We cite here the complete text: Francis Bacon: "In thinking about them as sculptures it suddenly came to me how I could make them in paint, and do them much better in paint. It would be a kind of structured painting in which images, as it were, would arise from a river of flesh. It sounds a terribly romantic idea, but I see it very formally." David Sylvester: "And what would the form be?" Bacon: "They would certainly be raised on structures." Sylvester: "Several figures?" Bacon: "Yes, and there would probably be a pavement raised high out of its naturalistic setting, out of which they could move as though out of pools of flesh rose the images, if possible, of specific people walking on their daily round. I hope to be able to do figures arising out of their own flesh with their bowler hats and their umbrellas and make them figures as poignant as a Crucifixion" (*Interviews*, 83). And on 108, Bacon adds: "I've thought about sculptures on a kind of armature, a very large armature made so that the sculpture could slide along it and people could even alter the positions of the sculpture as they wanted."

9. Writing of Jacques Tati, who is also a great artist of fields, André Bazin says: "Indistinct sound elements are rare.... On the contrary, Tati's shrewdness consists of destroying clarity with clarity. The dialogues are not incomprehensible but insignificant, and their insignificance is revealed by their very precision. Tati succeeds in this by deforming the relations of intensity between planes." André Bazin, *Qu'est-ce que le cinema?* (Paris: Éditions du Cerf, 1958), vol. 1, *Ontologie et langage*, 114. [The abridged English translation of Bazin's work, *What Is Cinema?*, 2 vols., trans. and ed. Hugh Gray (Berkeley: University of California Press, 1971), does not include this text.—*Trans.*]

10. Michel Leiris, *Au verso des images* (Montpellier: Fata Morgana, 1975), 26. [For Leiris's writings on Bacon in English, see Michel Leiris, *Francis Bacon: Full Face and in Profile*, trans. John Weightman (New York: Rizzoli, 1983), and Michel Leiris, *Francis Bacon*, trans. John Weightman (New York: Rizzoli, 1998).—*Trans.*]

2. Note on Figuration in Past Painting

1. See *Interviews*, 28–29. (Bacon is asking himself how Velázquez could stick so close to "figuration." And he answers, on the one hand, that photography did not yet exist; and on the other hand, that painting was still connected to a religious sentiment, even if it was a vague one.)

2. *Interviews*, 30. We will have to return to this point, which explains Bacon's attitude toward photography, which is one of both fascination and mistrust. In any case, Bacon criticizes the photograph for something completely different than being figurative.

3. Athleticism

1. Samuel Beckett, *The Lost Ones*, in *Samuel Beckett: The Complete Short Prose, 1929–1989*, ed. S. E. Gontarski (New York: Grove Press, 1995), 202.

2. Joseph Conrad, *The Nigger of the "Narcissus,"* in *The Portable Conrad*, ed. Morton Dauwen Zabel (New York: Viking Press, 1947), 355.

3. William S. Burroughs, *Naked Lunch* (New York: Grove Press, 1959), 91.

4. [See *Interviews*, 78.—*Trans.*]

4. Body, Meat, and Spirit

1. Félix Guattari has analyzed these phenomena of the disorganization of the face: "faciality traits" are liberated, which also become the animal traits of the head. See *L'inconscient machinique: Éléments de schizo-analyse* (Paris: Recherches, 1979), 75 ff.

2. *Interviews*, 46–47.

3. Franz Kafka, "The Sword," in *Diaries, 1914–1923*, ed. Max Brod, trans. Martin Greenberg with Hannah Arendt (New York: Schocken Books, 1949), 109–10.

4. *Interviews*, 23, 46.

5. Jean-Christophe Bailly has included extracts of this very beautiful text by Karl Philipp Moritz (1756–1793), titled *Anton Reiser*, in his *La légende dispersée: Anthologie du romantisme allemand* (Paris: Union Generale d'Editions, 1976), 35–43.

6. *Interviews*, 58: "Well, if you think of the great Rembrandt self-portrait in Aix-en-Provence, for instance, and if you analyze it, you will see that there are hardly any sockets to the eyes, that it is almost completely anti-illustrational."

5. Recapitulative Note

1. *Interviews*, 56: "You would love to be able in a portrait to make a Sahara of the appearance—to make it so like, yet seeming to have the distances of the Sahara."

2. *Interviews*, 58: "I've always wanted and never succeeded in painting the smile."

3. Lewis Carroll, *Alice in Wonderland*, chapter 6: "It vanished quite slowly...ending with the grin, which remained some time after the rest of it had gone." *The Complete Works of Lewis Carroll* (New York: Modern Library, n.d.), 74.

4. *Interviews*, 48.

5. We cannot here follow John Russell, who confuses the order of the triptych with the succession of panels from left to right: he sees on the left a sign of "sociability," and in the center, a public discourse. Even if the model were a prime minister, it is not clear how the disquieting smile could pass for a sociable one, or the scream in the center, for a discourse. See John Russell, *Francis Bacon*, rev. ed. (New York: Oxford University Press, 1979), 94.

6. *Mal* derives from "macula," the color-patch *[tache]* (hence *malen*, "to paint," *Maler*, "painter"). Wölfflin uses the word *malerisch* to designate the pictorial in opposition to the linear, or more precisely, the mass in opposition to the contour. See Heinrich Wölfflin, *Principles of Art History: The Problem of the Development of Style in Later Art*, trans. M. D. Hottinger (New York: Dover, 1950), 3. [Following Deleuze, we have left the term *malerisch* untranslated in the text. In justifying this practice, Herbert Read, in his introduction to Wölfflin's *Classic Art*, trans. Peter and Linda Murray (London: Phaidon Press, 1952), writes that the term *malerisch* "is a word absolutely essential to the discussion of stylistic problems in art, and purists must admit it into our language, for no other word is exact enough. It stands for that depreciation and gradual obliteration of line (outline and tangible surface) and for the merging of these in a 'shifting semblance' of things—it is an attempt to represent the vague and impalpable essence of things. English readers who are familiar with the distinction Blake made between 'the hard and wiry line of rectitude' and the 'broken lines, broken masses, and broken colours,' which he denounced as 'bungling,' will have already seized the full meaning of the word" (vi). On possible English equivalents, Panofsky notes that "the ubiquitous adjective *malerisch* must be rendered, according to context, in seven or eight different ways: 'picturesque' as in 'picturesque disorder'; 'pictorial' (or, rather horribly, 'painterly') as opposed to 'plastic'; 'dizzolved', 'sfumato,' or 'non-linear' as opposed to 'linear' or 'clearly defined'; 'loose' as opposed to 'tight'; 'impasto' as opposed to 'smooth'" (Panofsky, *Meaning in the Visual Arts*, 330).—*Trans.*]

7. On the three periods distinguished by Sylvester, see *Interviews*, 118–20.

8. We are currently familiar with six paintings of this new abstraction—other than the four previously cited, a *Landscape* of 1978, and the 1982 *Water Flowing from a Faucet*.

6. Painting and Sensation

1. Henri Maldiney, *Regard Parole Espace* (Lausanne: Éditions l'Age d'Homme, 1973), 136. Phenomenologists like Maldiney or Merleau-Ponty see Cézanne as the painter par excellence. They analyze sensation, or rather, "sense experience" *[le sentir]*, not only insofar as it relates sensible qualities to an identifiable object (the figurative moment), but insofar as each quality constitutes a field that stands on its own without ceasing to interfere with the others (the "pathic" moment). Hegel's phenomenology short-circuits this aspect of sensation, which nonetheless forms the basis for every possible aesthetic. See Maurice Merleau-Ponty, *Phenomenology of Perception*, trans. Colin Smith (London: Routledge and Kegan Paul, 1967), 207–42, and Maldiney, 124–208.

2. D. H. Lawrence, "Introduction to These Paintings," in *Phoenix: The Posthumous Papers of D. H. Lawrence* (1936: New York: Viking Press, 1972), 578–79.

3. TN. *Interviews*, 58 (and also 53, 66).

4. *Interviews*, 18.

5. *Interviews*, 63.

6. *Interviews*, 65.

7. These are all constant themes in the interviews.

8. [See *Interviews*, 21, 28, 43, 44, 46, 56, 58–59, 66.—*Trans.*]

9. *Interviews*, 28.

10. *Interviews*, 84–86.

11. *Interviews*, 58 ("coagulation of non-representational marks").

12. [*Interviews*, 48.—*Trans.*]

13. *Interviews*, 76–81 (and 47: "I have never tried to be horrific").

14. *Interviews*, 43. Bacon seems to rebel against psychoanalytic suggestions, and when Sylvester, on another occasion, says to him that "the Pope is the Father," Bacon politely responds, "I'm not quite sure I understand what you're saying" (*Interviews*, 71). For a more developed psychoanalytic interpretation of Bacon's paintings, see Didier Anzieu, *Le corps de l'oeuvre* (Paris: Gallimard, 1981), 333–40.

15. *Interviews*, 83, 108–12.

16. [See Bailly, ed., *La légende dispersée*, 35–43.—*Trans.*]

17. See Maldiney, *Regard Parole Espace*, 147–72, on sensation and rhythm, systole and diastole (and the pages on Cézanne in this regard).

18. *Interviews*, 78–80.

7. Hysteria

1. Antonin Artaud, "The Body Is the Body," trans. Roger McKeon, *Semiotext(e)* 2, no. 3 (1977), 38–39.

2. Wilhelm Worringer, *Form in Gothic* (New York: G. P. Putnam, 1927), 32–151.

3. William S. Burroughs, *Naked Lunch* (New York: Grove Press, 1959), 9.

4. Burroughs, *Naked Lunch*, 131.

5. One might consult any nineteenth-century manual on hysteria, but see especially the study by Paul Sollier, *Les phénomènes d'autoscopie* (Paris: Alcan, 1903), who created the term *Vigilambulator*.

6. Antonin Artaud, "The Nerve Meter," in *Antonin Artaud: Selected Writings*, ed. Susan Sontag, trans. Helen Weaver (New York: Farrar, Straus and Giroux, 1976), 86.

7. Ludovic Janvier, in his *Beckett par lui-meme* (Paris: Seuil, 1979), had the idea of making a lexicon of Beckett's principal notions. These are operative concepts. The articles on "Corps," "Espace-temps," "Immobilité," "Témoin," "Tête," and "Voix" ["Body," "Space-Time," "Immobility," "Witness," "Head," and "Voice"] should be noted in particular. Each of these articles has parallels with Bacon. And it is true that Bacon and Beckett are too close to know this themselves. But one should refer to Beckett's text on the painter Bram van Velde, "La peinture des van Valde, ou le monde et le pantalon" (1948), in *Disjecta: Miscellaneous Writings and a Dramatic Fragment*, ed. Ruby Cohn (New York: Grove Press, 1984), 118–32. Many things in it could apply to Bacon—notably the absence of figurative and narrative relations as a limit of painting.

8. Michel Leiris has devoted a superb text to this action of "presence" in Bacon. See *Ce que m'ont dit les peintures de Francis Bacon* (Paris: Maeght, 1966).

9. *Interviews*, 48.

10. Sartrean themes such as excessive distance (the root of the tree in *Nausea*) or of the flight of the body or the world (as if down the toilet drain in *Being and Nothingness*) have their place in a hysterical painting.

11. *Interviews*, 28–29.

12. *Interviews*, 37.

13. Marcel Proust, *In Search of Lost Time*, vol. 3, *The Guermantes Way*, trans. C. K. Scott Moncrieff and Terence Kilmartin; rev. D. J. Enright (New York: Modern Library, 1993), 55; Marcel Proust, *A la Recherche du temps perdu*, *Le côté de Guermantes*, part 1 (Paris: Pléiade, 1954), vol. 2, 48.

14. Marcel Moré, *Le dieu Mozart et le monde des oiseaux* (Paris: Gallimard, 1971), 47.

8. Painting Forces

1. See Russell, *Francis Bacon*, 123: Duchamp "was interested in process as a subject for painting, and in the way in which a human body makes a coherent structure when it walks downstairs, even if that structure is never revealed completely at any one moment in time. Bacon's object is not to show successive appearance, but to superimpose appearances, one on top of the other, in ways different from those vouchsafed to us in life. Henrietta Moraes in the *Three Studies* of 1963 is not moving from left to right or from right to left." [All references are to the 1979 edition.— *Trans.*]

2. Lawrence, "Introduction to These Paintings," in *Phoenix: The Posthumous Papers of D. H. Lawrence*, 580.

3. [*Interviews*, 48.—*Trans.*]

4. See Bacon's statements on the scream in *Interviews*, 34–37 and 48–50 (it is true that, in the latter text, Bacon regrets that his screams still remain "too abstract," because he thinks he has missed "what causes someone to scream." But it is a question of forces, not of the spectacle).

5. Franz Kafka, letter to Brod, as cited in Klaus Wagenbach, *Franz Kafka: Années de jeunesse, 1883–1912* (Paris: Mercure, 1967), 156: "Diabolical powers, whatever their message might be, are knocking at the door and already rejoicing in the fact that they will arrive soon."

6. *Interviews*, 78–80: "If life excites you, its opposite, like a shadow, death, must excite you. Perhaps not excite you, but you are aware of it in the same way that you are aware of life.... One's basic nature is totally without hope, and yet one's nervous system is made out of optimistic stuff." (And on what Bacon calls his "greed for life," his refusal to make the game a deadly wager, see 122–25.)

9. Couples and Triptychs

1. *Interviews*, 104: "I wanted to make an image which coagulated this sensation of two people in some form of sexual act on the bed ... and if you look at the forms, they're extremely, in a sense, unrepresentational."

2. Russell, *Francis Bacon*, 30–31.

3. Marcel Proust, *In Search of Lost Time*, vol. 6, *Time Regained*, trans. C. K. Scott Moncrieff and Terence Kilmartin; rev. D. J. Enright (New York: Modern Library, 1993), 274 (translation modified); Marcel Proust, *A la Recherche du temps perdu*, *Le temps retrouvé* (Paris: Pléiade, 1954), vol. 3, 879.

4. Marcel Proust, *In Search of Lost Time*, vol. 1, *Swann's Way*, trans. C. K. Scott Moncrieff and Terence Kilmartin; rev. D. J. Enright (New York: Modern Library, 1993), 500, translation modified; Marcel Proust, *A la Recherche du temps perdu*, *Du côté chez Swann*, part 2 (Paris: Pléiade, 1954), vol. 1, 352.

5. Marcel Proust, *In Search of Lost Time*, vol. 5, *The Captive*, trans. C. K. Scott Moncrieff and Terence Kilmartin; rev. D. J. Enright (New York: Modern Library, 1993), 346–47; Marcel Proust, *A la Recherche du temps perdu*, *La prisonnière*, part 2 (Paris: Pléiade, 1954), vol. 3, 260.

6. *Interviews*, 39–43.

7. *Interviews*, 63–64.

8. Russell, *Francis Bacon*, 121.

9. On the essential notion of the "rhythmic character," see Messiaen's analysis in Claude Samuel, *Conversations with Olivier Messiaen*, trans. Felix Aprahamian (London: Stainer and Bell, 1976), 36–38; and Antoine Goléa, *Rencontres avec Olivier Messiaen* (Paris: Julliard, 1961).

10. Paul Claudel, *The Eye Listens*, trans. Elsie Pell (Port Washington, N.Y.: Kennikat Press, 1969), 40–48.

10. Note: What Is a Triptych?

1. On this notion of retrogradable rhythm and, later, of added or subtracted value, see Messiaen's comments in Samuel, *Conversations with Olivier Messiaen*, 43 ff. It is not surprising that the same problems are posed in painting, notably from the point of view of colors: Paul Klee has shown this in his practice of painting as much as in his theoretical texts.

2. Witold Gombrowicz, *Pornographia*, trans. Alastair Hamilton (London: Calder and Boyars, 1966), 131.

3. Immanuel Kant, *Critique of Pure Reason*, trans. Norman Kemp Smith (London: St. Martin's Press, 1929), "Anticipations of Perception," 201–8, A166/B207–A176/B218.

4. Sartre, in his analysis of Flaubert, showed the importance of the episode of the fall, from the point of view of a "hysterical engagement," but he gives it far too negative a meaning, even though he recognizes that the fall fits into a long-term, active, and positive project. Jean-Paul Sartre, *The Family Idiot: Gustave Flaubert, 1821–1857*, trans. Carol Cosman (Chicago: University of Chicago Press, 1981).

5. Writing of Rembrandt's *Nightwatch*, Claudel spoke of the "disintegration brought to a group by light." Paul Claudel, *Oeuvres en prose* (Paris: Pléiade, 1965), 1429.

11. The Painting before Painting

1. Lawrence, "Introduction to These Paintings," in *Phoenix: The Posthumous Papers of D. H. Lawrence*, 569, 576, 577, 579–80.

2. D. H. Lawrence, *Lady Chatterley's Lover* (New York: Grove Press, 1959), 346.

3. *Interviews*, 37. (And Bacon's condemnation of all his paintings that still contain a figurative violence.)

4. *Interviews*, 30 ff.

5. *Interviews*, 56–57. In his *Francis Bacon*, John Russell has analyzed Bacon's attitude toward the photograph in his chapter titled "The Prehensile Image," 54–71.

6. Foucault, writing on Gérard Fromanger, has analyzed several types of relation between photography and painting; see Michel Foucault, "Photogenic Painting," in Sarah Wilson, ed., *Photogenic Painting: Gilles Deleuze, Michel Foucault, Gerard Fromanger* (London: Black Dog, 1999), 81–104. The most interesting cases, like Fromanger, are those where the painter integrates the photograph, or the photograph's action, apart from any aesthetic value.

7. *Interviews*, 13.

8. The theme of marks by chance, or by accident, appears constantly in the interviews, especially on 50–67.

9. See Puis Servien, notably *Hasard et probabilité* (Paris: Presses Universitaires de France, 1949). In the framework of his distinction between a "language of the sciences" and a "lyrical language," the author opposed probability as the object of science, and chance as the mode of a choice that was neither scientific nor aesthetic (to choose a flower by chance, that is, a flower that is neither "specified" nor "the most beautiful").

10. *Interviews*, 50–53. (Clearly Bacon does not make roulette a type of action: see his considerations of Nicolas de Staël and Russian roulette, *Interviews*, 122–24.)

11. *Interviews*, 92.

12. Bacon notes that his best friends contest what he calls "chance" or "accident": see *Interviews*, 95–99.

13. *Interviews*, 100: "I know what I want to do, but I don't know how to do it" (and 12: "I don't know how the form can be made").

14. *Interviews*, 126: "When we've talked about the possibility of making appearance out of something which was not illustration, I've over-talked about it. Because, in spite of theoretically longing for the image to be made up of irrational marks, inevitably illustration has to come into it to make certain parts of the head and face which, if one left them out, one would then only be making an abstract design."

15. *Interviews*, 105–7.

12. The Diagram

1. [*"Traits et taches."* The *Robert* dictionary defines *tache* most generally as "a small space of different color in a field of uniform color," and the English language presents a rich variety of possible equivalents, such as spot, blot, stain, patch, mark, blotch, splotch, smudge, dab, or daub. The term *tachisme* was coined to refer to "pointillists" such as Seurat, who used juxtaposed dabs or touches of uniform color to produce their figurative works, and later, to the nonfigurative works of abstract expressionism or *art informel*. Deleuze introduces the term here in order to distinguish between two different conceptions of painting: the *optical* (the visual perception of line and color by the eye) and the *manual* (the application of traits and patches of color by the hand). We have rendered the term as "patch" or "color patch." For the translation of the term *trait*, see chapter 1, note 6.—*Trans.*]

2. [See *Interviews*, 20–21.—*Trans.*]

3. Here is the very important text from the interviews: Bacon: "Very often the involuntary marks are much more deeply suggestive than others, and those are the moments when you feel that anything can happen." Sylvester: "You feel it while you're making those marks?" Bacon: "No, the marks are made, and you survey the thing like you would a sort of graph *[diagramme]*. And you see within this graph the possibilities of all types of fact being planted. This is a difficult thing; I'm expressing it badly. But you see, if you think of a portrait, you maybe have to put the mouth somewhere, but you suddenly see through this graph that the mouth could go right across the face. And in a way you would love to be able in a portrait to make a Sahara of the appearance—to make it so like, yet seeming to have the distances of the Sahara" (*Interviews*, 56). In another passage, Bacon explains that when he does a portrait, he often looks at photographs that have nothing to do with the model—for example, a photograph of a rhinoceros for the texture of the skin (*Interviews*, 32).

4. *Interviews*, 90–92.

5. *Interviews*, 89–90, on the possibility that involuntary marks contribute nothing and botch the painting, leading to a "kind of marshland."

6. *Interviews*, 56: "You see within this graph *[diagramme]* the possibilities of all types of fact being planted." Wittgenstein invoked a diagrammatic form in order to express "possibilities of fact" in logic.

7. *Interviews*, 56.

8. Henri Maldiney has compared Cézanne and Klee on this point in *Regard Parole Espace*, 149–51.

9. [See Auguste Herbin, *Herbin: The Plastic Alphabet* [exhibition catalogue] (New York: Galerie Denise Renée, 1973).—*Trans.*]

10. This tendency to eliminate the manual has always been present in painting, as when one says of a work, "I no longer feel the hand in it." Henri Focillon analyzes this tendency, "ascetic frugality," which culminates in abstract painting, in "In Praise of Hands," in *The Life of Forms in Art*, trans. Charles B. Hogan and George Kubler (New York: Zone Books, 1989), 173–74. But, as Focillon says, the hand is felt all the same. In order to distinguish a true Mondrian from a false one, Georg Schmidt refers to the intersection of the two black sides of a square, or the disposition of the layers of color along right angles. See his *Mondrian* (Paris: Réunion des musées nationaux, n.d.), 148.

11. See Elie Faure's famous text on Velázquez, in *History of Art*, vol. 4, *Modern Art*, trans. Walter Pach (New York: Harper and Brothers, 1924), 124–36.

12. [In English in the original, referring to Pollock's "all-over" drip paintings of 1947–1950.— *Trans.*]

13. On these new blind spaces, see Christian Bonnefoi's analysis of Robert Ryman, "A propos de la destruction de l'entité de surface," *Macula* 3–4 (1978), 163–66; and Yves-Alain Bois's analysis of Bonnefoi, "Le futur antérieur," *Macula* 5–6 (1979), 229–33.

14. Clement Greenberg (*Art and Culture* [Boston: Beacon Press, 1961]) and Michael Fried ("Three American Painters: Kenneth Noland, Jules Olitski, Frank Stella" [1965], in *Art and Objecthood: Essays and Reviews* [Chicago: University of Chicago Press, 1998]) were the first to analyze the spaces of Jackson Pollock, Morris Louis, Barnett Newman, Kenneth Noland, etc., and to define them by a "strict opticality." The aim of these critics was doubtless to break with the extra-aesthetic criteria invoked by Harold Rosenberg when he coined the term "Action Painting." They reminded us that Pollock's works, no matter how "modern" they might be, were paintings first and foremost, and therefore subject to formal criteria. But the question is whether or not opticality is the best criterion for these works. It seems that Fried had some doubts that he passed over far too rapidly (see 227–28, 232), and that the term "Action Painting" might turn out to be aesthetically justified.

15. Greenberg strongly emphasized the importance of this abandonment of the easel, especially in Pollock. He raises the theme of the "Gothic" in this context, but without seeming to give this term the full meaning it assumes in Worringer's analyses (one of Pollock's paintings is called, precisely, *Gothic*). Greenberg seems not to see any alternative other than "easel painting" or "mural painting" (which seems to us instead to correspond to Mondrian's case). See "Dossier Jackson Pollock," *Macula* 2 (1977), 41–62.

16. Bacon often criticizes abstraction for remaining "on one level," and for botching the "tension" (*Interviews*, 59–60). And Bacon will say, when speaking of Duchamp, that he admires him more for his attitude than for his painting; to Bacon, Duchamp's painting seems to be a symbolism or a "shorthand of figuration" (*Interviews*, 105).

17. *Interviews*, 94: "I hate that kind of sloppy sort of Central European painting. It's one of the reasons I really don't like abstract expressionism." And 61: "Michaux is a very, very intelligent and conscious man . . . and I think that he has made the best *tachiste* or free marks that have been made. I think he is much better in that way, in making free marks, than Jackson Pollock."

18. See Gregory Bateson, "Why Do Things Have Outlines?" in *Steps to an Ecology of Mind* (New York: Ballantine Books, 1972), 27–32. What drove Blake mad, mad with rage and wrath, were people who took him for a madman, but it was also "some artists who painted pictures as though things didn't have outlines. He called them the 'slobbering school'" (28).

19. *Interviews*, 94: Sylvester: "You would never end a painting by suddenly throwing something at it. Or would you?" Bacon: "Oh yes. In that recent triptych, on the shoulder of the figure being sick into the basin, there's like a whip of white paint that goes like that. Well, I did that at the very last moment, and I just left it."

13. Analogy

1. See Joachim Gasquet's famous text in *Conversations with Cézanne*, ed. Michel Doran, trans. Julie Lawrence Cochran (Berkeley: University of California Press, 2001), 114–15. The editor's reservations about the value of Gasquet's texts appear to us to be unfounded; Maldiney seems to be justified in using this text as the center of his commentary on Cézanne.

2. The two criticisms leveled against the impressionists by Cézanne are, in general, to have remained at a confused state of sensation through their treatment of color, and, for the best of them, like Monet, to have remained in an ephemeral state: "I wanted to make impressionism something solid and enduring like the art of museums ... In these paintings of Monet, a solidity, a framework in the present, has to be put in the flight of the whole." The solidity or endurance that Cézanne calls for must at the same time agree with the pictorial material, the structure of the painting, the treatment of colors, and the state of clarity to which the sensation is led. For example, a viewpoint does not create a motif because it lacks the necessary solidity and duration ("I have here beautiful viewpoints, but that does not at all make a motif"; Paul Cézanne, *Correspondence*, ed. John Rewald [Paris: Grasset, 1978], 211). One finds in Bacon the same demand for clarity and endurance, which he himself opposes not to impressionism but to abstract expressionism. And he attaches this "possibility of enduring" first of all to the material: "think of the Sphinx made of bubble gum" (*Interviews*, 58). Significantly, Bacon thinks that oil painting is a medium of both long duration and a high clarity. But the possibility of enduring also depends on the framework or armature, and on the particular treatment of colors.

3. See Doran, *Conversations with Cézanne*, 178, which is the text in which Maurice Denis cites Sérusier, but precisely in order to oppose him to Cézanne.

4. [*Interviews*, 105.—*Trans.*]

5. In his theory of the sign, Peirce attaches great importance to the analogical function and to the notion of the diagram. Nonetheless, he reduces the diagram to a similitude of relations. See Charles S. Peirce, *Ecrits sur le signe*, ed. Gérard Deledalle (Paris: Seuil, 1978); *Peirce on Signs: Writings on Semiotic by Charles Sanders Peirce*, ed. James Hoopes (Chapel Hill and London: University of North Carolina Press, 1991).

6. We borrow the preceding analysis from Richard Pinhas, *Synthèse analogique, Synthèse digitale* (unpublished). [A revised portion of this text has since appeared in Richard Pinhas, *Les Larmes de Nietzsche* (Paris: Flammarion, 2001).—*Trans.*]

7. Gregory Bateson has a very interesting hypothesis on the language of dolphins in *Steps to an Ecology of Mind*, 372–74. After having distinguished analogical language, founded on relations, and digital or vocal language, founded on conventional signs, Bateson comes up against the problem of dolphins. Because of their adaptation to the sea, they have renounced the kinesic and facial signs that characterize the analogical language of mammals; they nonetheless remained condemned to the analogical functions of this language, but found themselves in the situation of having to "vocalize" them, to codify them as such. This is something like the situation of the abstract painter.

8. On all these points, see Doran, *Conversations with Cézanne* (and for color, see especially the text by R. P. Rivière and J. F. Schnerb, "Cézanne's Studio," 84–90). In a fine article, "Cézanne: The Logic of Organized Sensations" (in *Conversations with Cézanne*, 180–212), Lawrence Gowing has analyzed the modulation of color that Cézanne himself presented as a law of Harmony. This modulation can coexist with other uses of color, but in Cézanne it takes on a particular importance around 1900. Although Gowing reduces it to a "conventional" code (191) or a "metaphoric system" (192), it is much more like a law of analogy. Chevreul used the term "harmonies of analogues."

9. Clement Greenberg's French translator, Marc Chenetier, suggests that "shallow depth" be translated as *profondeur maigre*, an oceanographic expression that describes shallows or shoals *[hauts-fonds]* ("Dossier Jackson Pollock," *Macula* 2, 50).

10. This would be a second point common to both Bacon and abstract expressionism. But Gowing notes that, already in Cézanne, colored patches "imply not only volumes but axes, armatures at right angles to the chromatic progressions," an entire "upright scaffolding" that, it is true, remains virtual. See Gowing, "Cézanne: The Logic of Organized Sensations," 204.

14. Painters Recapitulate the History of Painting in Their Own Way

1. Cited in Russell, *Francis Bacon*, 99.

2. See Aloïs Riegl, *Late Roman Art Industry*, trans. Rolf Winkes, 2d ed. (Rome: Giorgio Bretschneider Editore, 1985). *Haptic*, from the Greek verb *aptō* (to touch), does not designate an extrinsic relation of the eye to the sense of touch, but a "possibility of seeing *[regard]*," a type of vision distinct from the optical: Egyptian art has not yet made up its mind with regard to the gaze, which it thinks must see things from close-up. As Maldiney says, "in the spatial zone of closeness, the sense of sight behaves just like the sense of touch, experiencing the presence of the form and the ground *at the same place*" (*Regard Parole Espace*, 195).

3. *Interviews*, 83, 114.

4. Paul Claudel, *The Eye Listens*, 47; and 42: "Before a picture of Rembrandt's one never has the sensation of permanence and definiteness; it is a precarious realization, a phenomenon, a miraculous beginning again of what has already expired: the curtain, raised for an instant, is ready to fall again." Russell, in *Francis Bacon*, cites a text by Leiris that struck Bacon very much: "For Baudelaire, beauty cannot come into being without the intervention of something accidental. . . . We can call 'beautiful' only that which suggests the existence of an ideal order—supraterrestrial, harmonious, and logical—and yet bears within itself, like the brand of an original sin, the drop of poison, the rogue element of incoherence, the grain of sand that will foul up the entire system" (88).

5. On organic representation, see Worringer, *Form in Gothic*, chapter 5, "Classical Man." In *Abstraction and Empathy: A Contribution to the Psychology of Style*, trans. Michael Bullock (London: Routledge and Kegan Paul, 1963), 28, Worringer writes: "This will did not consist in the wish to copy the things of the outer world or to render their appearance. Its aim was to project the lines and forms of the organically vital, the euphony of its rhythm and its whole inward being, outward in ideal independence and perfection."

6. Maldiney, *Regard Parole Espace*, 197–98 (and further on Maldiney analyzes Byzantine art in detail as inventing a purely optical space, thereby breaking with Greek space).

7. It is Wölfflin, in particular, who has analyzed this aspect of tactile-optical space, or of the "Classic" world of the sixteenth century: light and shadows, and colors, can have a very complex play, but they nonetheless remain subordinate to the plastic form that maintains its integrity. We must wait for the seventeenth century to witness the liberation of shadow and light in a purely optical space. See Wölfflin, *Principles of Art History*, especially chapters 1 and 5. A particularly striking example is given in the comparison of the two church interiors of Neefs the Elder and E. de Witte (213).

8. Wölfflin, *Principles of Art History*, 21, translation modified.

9. Worringer, *Abstraction and Empathy*, 112–15 (it is Worringer who invented the word *expressionism*, as Dora Vallier shows in her preface to the French translation of this work). And in *Form in Gothic*, Worringer insists on the two movements that are opposed to classical organic symmetry: the infinite movement of the inorganic line, and the peripheral and violent movement of the wheel or turbine (55–57).

10. Claudel, *The Eye Listens*, 36.

11. See Giorgio Vasari, "Life of Michelangelo Buonarroti," in *Lives of the Artists*, trans. George Bull (London: Penguin Books, 1965), vol. 1, 325–442.

12. Defining the pure optical space of Rembrandt, Wölfflin shows the importance of the straight stroke and the broken line that replace the curve; and with the portraitists, the expression no longer comes from the contour, but from strokes dispersed inside the form (23, 32–34). But all this leads Wölfflin to state that optical space does not break with the tactile connections of form and contour without liberating new tactile values, notably weight ("the more the attention is withdrawn from the plastic form as such, the more active is the interest in the surface of things, in how objects feel. Flesh in Rembrandt is clearly rendered as a soft material, yielding to pressure …" [33–34]).

13. [Wölfflin, *Principles of Art History*, 19, translation modified.—*Trans.*]

14. The warm or cool tonality of a color is essentially relative (which does not mean subjective). It depends on its surroundings, and a color can always be "heated" or "cooled." And green and red are in themselves neither warm nor cool: green is the ideal point of the mixture of warm yellow and cool blue, and red, on the contrary, is that which is neither blue nor yellow, so that warm and cool tones can be represented as separating from each other starting from green, and then tending to be gathered together in red through an "ascending intensification." See Johann Wolfgang von Goethe, *Goethe's Color Theory*, ed. Rupprecht Matthaei, trans. Herb Aach (New York: Von Nostrand Reinhold, 1970), 168, §§764–802.

15. On the relations of tonality in Byzantine art, see André Grabar, *Byzantine Painting: A Historical and Critical Study*, trans. Stuart Gilbert (Geneva: Skira, 1953), and Maldiney, *Parole Regard Espace*, 241–46.

16. Gowing, in "Cézanne: The Logic of Organized Sensations" (in Doran, *Conversations with Cézanne*, 180–212), analyzes numerous examples of these colored sequences (191–201). But he also shows how this system of modulation could coexist with other systems in relation to a single motif: for example, in *Seated Peasant*, the watercolor version works through sequence and gradation (blue-yellow-rose), whereas the oil version works through light and local tone; or the two portraits of a woman wearing a jacket, one of which "is massively modeled in light and dark" (201), while the other, though it still maintains chiaroscuros, renders the volumes through the sequence rose-yellow-emerald-cobalt blue. See 191 and 200–1, with reproductions.

17. Rivière and Schnerb, "Cezanne's Studio," in Doran, *Conversations with Cézanne*, 87 (and 88: "a succession of colors progressing from warm to cool," "a scale of very high tones"). If we return to Byzantine art, the fact that it combines a modulation of colors with a rhythm of values implies that its space is not uniquely optical; despite Riegl, "colorism" seems to us to be irreducibly haptic.

18. Black and white, light and dark, present a movement of contraction or expansion analogous to the warm and the cool. But even Kandinsky, in the passages where he oscillates between a primacy of tones or values, recognizes in the light-dark values only a static and "stationary" movement. See Wassily Kandinsky, *Concerning the Spiritual in Art*, trans. M. T. H. Sadler (New York: Dover Publications, 1977), 36–39.

19. [*Interviews*, 120.—*Trans.*]

20. It was Buffon who, in relation to problems concerning the reproduction of living beings, proposed the notion of the internal mold, while emphasizing the paradoxical character of this notion, because the mold is here supposed to "penetrate the mass." See Comte de Georges-Louis Leclerc Buffon, *Histoire naturelle des animaux* in *Oeuvres complètes* (Paris, 1885), vol. 3, 450. And in Buffon himself, this internal mold is related to the Newtonian conception of light. On the technical difference between molding and modulation, we can refer to the recent analyses of

Simondon: in modulation "there is never time to turn something out, to remove it from the mold *[demoulage]*, because the circulation of the support of energy is equivalent to a permanent turning out; a modulator is a continuous, temporal mold.... To mold is to modulate in a definitive manner, to modulate is to mold in a continuous and perpetually variable manner." Gilbert Simondon, *L'individu et sa genèse physico-biologique* (Paris: Presses Universitaire de France, 1964), 41–42.

15. Bacon's Trajectory

1. *Interviews*, 120.

2. "Suffice it to say that black and white are also colors, for in many cases they can be looked upon as colors." Vincent Van Gogh, letter B6, to Émile Bernard (second half of June 1888), in *The Complete Letters of Vincent Van Gogh*, 3 vols., trans. C. de Dood (London: Thames and Hudson, 1958), vol. 3, 490.

3. "When the complementary colors are produced in equal strength, that is to say in the same degree of vividness and brightness, their juxtaposition will intensify them each to such a violent intensity that the human eye can hardly bear the sight of it." Van Gogh, letter 401, to Theo, in *Complete Letters*, vol. 2, 365. One of the principal interests of Van Gogh's correspondence is that he turned color into a kind of initiatory experience, after a long trek through chiaroscuro, and black and white.

4. See Rivière and Schnerb, "Cézanne's Studio," in Doran, *Conversations with Cézanne*, 88: "Cézanne's entire working method is determined by this chromatic concept of modeling.... If he avoided blending two tones by a simple turn of the brush, it was because he saw modeling as a succession of colors progressing from warm to cool. His great interest lay in determining each of the colors exactly. He believed that to replace one of them with the mixture of two neighboring ones would not be art.... Modeling by color, which was his language, requires the use of a sophisticated array of colors that allows him to observe oppositions down to half-tones and to avoid white lights and black shadows." In the preceding letter to Theo (letter 401), Van Gogh introduces the principles of colorism, which he derives from Delacroix rather than the impressionists (he sees the opposite in Delacroix, but also the analogous in Rembrandt: what Rembrandt is to light, Delacroix is to color). And next to pure tones, which are defined by primary and complementary colors, Van Gogh introduces *broken tones:* "If one mixes two complementary colors in unequal proportions, they only partially destroy each other, and one gets a *broken tone*, which will be a variety of gray. This being so, new contrasts may be born of the juxtaposition of two complementary colors, one of which is pure and the other, broken.... Finally, if two similar colors are placed next to each other, the one in the pure state, the other broken, for instance pure blue and gray-blue, another kind of contrast will result, which will be toned down by the analogy.... In order to intensify and to harmonize the effect of his colors he [Delacroix] used the contrast of the complementary and the concord of analogous colors at the same time; or in other terms, *the repetition of a vivid tint by the same broken tone*." Van Gogh, *Complete Letters*, vol. 2, 365–66.

5. See Gowing's analysis in "Cézanne: The Logic of Organized Sensations," in Doran, *Conversations with Cézanne*, 190–92.

6. Georges Duthuit, *Le feu du signes* (Geneva: Skira, 1962), 189: "In effect, painting tends to disengage itself from impressionism by putting the dispersion of the tints—which are supposed to be reconstituted in our vision—back into the large colored planes, which allow them to circulate more freely. Rather than being recomposed in our vision, the image, always new, creates itself: the form will be all the better by assuring its unforeseen vigor, and the line, its essential cleanness."

7. Cézanne reproached Gauguin for having stolen from him his "small sensation," while misunderstanding the problem of the "passage of tones." In the same way, Van Gogh has often been reproached for the inertia of the background in certain of his canvases; see the very interesting text by Jean Paris, *Miroirs de Rembrandt. Le Sommeil de Vermeer. Le Soleil de Van Gogh. Espaces de Cézanne* (Paris: Éditions Galilée, 1973), 135–36.

8. Van Gogh, letter 520, to Theo (in *Complete Letters*, vol. 3, 6): "to finish [the painting], I am now going to become an arbitrary colorist."

9. Van Gogh, letter to Bernard, early August 1888, in *Complete Letters*, vol. 3, 510 (and 6: "instead of painting the ordinary wall of the mean room, I paint the infinite, a plain background of the richest, intensest blue"). And Gauguin, letter to Shuffenecker, 8 October 1888: "I have done a self-portrait for Vincent.... The color is a color remote from nature; imagine a confused collection of pottery all twisted by the furnace! All the reds and violets streaked by flames, like a furnace burning fiercely, the seat of the painter's mental struggles. The whole on a chrome background sprinkled with childish nosegays. The room of a pure young girl..." Paul Gauguin, *Letters to His Wife and Friends*, ed. Maurice Malingue, trans. Henry J. Stenning (Cleveland: World Publishing, 1949). Gaugin's *La Belle Angèle* (1889) presents a formula that Bacon will also follow: the field, the head-Figure surrounded by a circle, and even attendant-object...

10. Van Gogh, letter to his sister, 1890 (in *Complete Letters*, vol. 3, 470): "What impassions me most—much, much more than all the rest of my *métier*—is the portrait, the modern portrait. I seek it in color."

11. *Interviews*, 112.

12. According to Huysmans's critique, there are "scabby and dull colors" in Gauguin, especially at the beginning, that he did not know how to avoid. Bacon is thrown into the same problem in the *malerisch* period. As for the other danger, the inert ground, Bacon also confronts it; it is even the reason why he most often criticizes acrylics. Oil has its own life, whereas one knows in advance how acrylic paint is likely to behave. See *Interviews*, 93.

16. Note on Color

1. Marc Le Bot, "Espaces," *L'Arc* 73 (special issue on Francis Bacon).

2. [Title of a work by Olivier Messiaen incorporating eighteen birdsongs.—*Trans.*]

3. In *L'Espace et le regard* (Paris: Editions du Seuil, 1965), Jean Paris makes an interesting analysis of the halo from the viewpoints of space, light, and color. He also studies arrows as spatial vectors, in the cases of St. Sebastian, St. Ursula, and so on. In Bacon, the purely indicative arrows seem to be the last residues of these saintly arrows, just as the gyratory circles for the coupled Figures are residues of halos.

4. Fried, "Three American Painters: Kenneth Noland, Jules Olitski, Frank Stella" (1965), in *Art and Objecthood: Essays and Reviews*, 245.

5. Russell, *Francis Bacon*, 121.

17. The Eye and the Hand

1. [Focillon, "In Praise of Hands," in *The Life of Forms in Art*, 157–84.—*Trans.*]

2. The word *haptisch* was coined by Riegl in response to certain criticisms. It did not appear in the first edition of *Spätrömische Kunstindustrie* (1901), which was content with the word *taktische*.

3. [See *Interviews*, 126.—*Trans.*]

4. *Interviews*, 11–13.

5. *Interviews*, 11. Bacon adds: "And then I made these things, I gradually made them. So that I don't think the bird suggested the umbrella; it suddenly suggested this whole image" (11). This text seems obscure, since Bacon invokes two contradictory ideas at the same time: a gradual series and a sudden whole. But both are true. In any case, he means that there is not a relationship between one form and another (bird-umbrella), but a relationship between an intention at the beginning, and an entire series *or* ensemble at the end.

6. [In English in the original. The reference is to the song "Crosseyed and Painless," by David Byrne, Chris Frantz, Jerry Harrison, Tina Weymouth, and Brian Eno, from the Talking Heads album *Remain in Light*, produced by Brian Eno, Sire Records, 1980. I thank Timothy Murphy for this reference.—*Trans.*]

7. The mixture of complementary colors produces gray; but the "broken" tone, the unequal mixture, conserves the sensible heterogeneity or the tension of colors. The painting of the face will be *both* red and green, etc. Gray as a power *[puissance]* of broken color is very different from gray as the product of black and white. It is a haptic, and not optical, gray. Of course, the color could be broken with the optical gray, but much less so, even with a complementary: in effect, we are already given what is in question, and we lose the heterogeneity of the tension, or the millimetric precision of the mixture.

8. *Interviews*, 56.

9. *Interviews*, 12: "The next day I tried to take it further and tried to make it more poignant, more near, and I lost the image completely." See also 90, 94.

10. *Interviews*, 56, 58, 100 ("these marks that have happened on the canvas evolved into these particular forms").

11. See *Interviews*, 56: the diagram is only a "possibility of fact." A logic of painting here meets up with notions analogous to those of Wittgenstein.

12. This was Bacon's formula; see *Interviews*, 12.

13. In a short text on Michelangelo, Luciano Bellosi has shown how Michelangelo destroyed the narrative religious fact in favor of a properly pictorial or sculptural fact. See *Michelangelo: The Painter*, trans. Pearl Sanders (New York: Grosset and Dunlap, 1971).

Afterword

1. *Cinéma 1: L'Image-mouvement* (Paris: Minuit, 1983), 24. Here and elsewhere all translations from the French are mine.

2. Gilles Deleuze, *Proust et les signes* (Paris: Presses Universitaire de France, 1964), especially "Niveaux de la Recherche," 158–73. The "capture" of Combray and of Albertine is mentioned in *The Logic of Sensation*.

3. Percy Lubbock, *The Craft of Fiction* (New York: Viking Reprint, 1966). The first edition appeared in 1921, on the heels of the career of Henry James and as the later volumes of Proust began to reach French readers. French enthusiasts of point of view, including Deleuze, no doubt began with Sartre's studies of the American novel (Dos Passos and Faulkner), which mostly appeared in *Situations, 1* (Paris: Gallimard, 1947).

4. *Le Pli: Leibniz et le Baroque* (Paris: Minuit, 1988), 27 and 29.

5. *Le Pli*, 104.

6. *Le Pli*, 105–6.

7. Such is the hypothesis of Michael Riffaterre in his *Essais de stylistique structurale* (Paris: Flammarion, 1971), in an elegant and terse reading of Victor Hugo and the Romantic tradition.

8. *Cinéma 1*, 280.

9. *Foucault* (Paris: Minuit, 1985), 31–51.

10. *Le Pli*, 55–56.

11. The vocabulary, familiar to every user of the computer, finds an early and effective demonstration in Anthony Wilden, *System and Structure* (London: Tavistock, 1972). He applies it to the *Essais* of Montaigne, in which the reader's reactions are anticipated and accounted for in the writing itself. The author is used to develop a theory of feedback and communicational "loops" based on the work of Gregory Bateson, a key figure in Deleuze's canon.

12. A strange play of the signifier is seen in the French of Deleuze's text. The *diagramme*, as he demonstrates, gives rise to the painting, but the painting is seen culminating in an uncanny play of color that he describes as "une intense clarté diffuse sur les gammes" (78) [an intense diffuse clarity on the color fields]. The spectrum of color, the *gamme*, emerges from its containment in *diagramme*.

13. Bacon's bodies would be an ideal extension of Erwin Panofsky's treatment of the relation of geometry and perspective to the body in *Meaning in the Visual Arts* (New York: Doubleday, 1955) or *Perspective as Symbolic Form*, trans. Christopher S. Wood (New York: Zone Books, 1991).

14. Simondon's same words are cited in *The Logic of Sensation*, in respect to the "analogical" language of color, but they are inflected by the eighteenth-century natural historian Buffon, in whose *Histoire naturelle des animaux* a notion of an "inner mold" is seen bearing resemblance to Newtonian concepts of light. Deleuze thus synthesizes Buffon and Simondon: "if there remains a molding by color, it is no longer even an inner mold, but a temporal, variable and continuous mold that can only, strictly speaking, bear the name of *modulation*." Note 18 (in chapter 14) anticipates the work in *Le Pli* where Bacon and Leibniz are blended.

15. "Whence the triple definition of writing: to write is to struggle, to resist; to write is to become" (*Foucault*, 51).

Paintings

Paintings by Francis Bacon

[1] *Triptych, Three Studies for Figures at the Base of a Crucifixion*, 1944. Oil and pastel on hardboard, each panel 94 x 74 cm. The Tate Gallery, London.

[2] *Figure in a Landscape*, 1945. Oil and pastel on canvas, 145 x 128 cm. The Tate Gallery, London.

[3] *Painting*, 1946. Oil and tempera on canvas, each panel 198 x 132 cm. Museum of Modern Art, New York.

[4] *Figure Study I*, 1945–46. Oil on canvas, 123 x 105.5 cm. Private collection, Great Britain.

[5] *Head II*, 1949. Oil on canvas, 80.5 x 65 cm. Ulster Museum, Belfast.

[6] *Head VI*, 1949. Oil on canvas, 93 x 77 cm. The Arts Council of Great Britain, London.

[7] *Fragment of a Crucifixion*, 1950. Oil and cotton wool on canvas, 140 x 108.5 cm. Stedelijk Van Abbemuseum, Eindhoven.

[8] *Landscape*, 1952. Oil on canvas, 139.5 x 198.5 cm. Brera Museum, Milan.

[9] *Study for a Figure in Landscape*, 1952. Oil on canvas, 198 x 137 cm. The Phillips Collection, Washington, D.C.

[10] *Study for a Crouching Nude*, 1952. Oil on canvas, 198 x 137 cm. Detroit Institute of Arts.

[11] *Study for a Portrait*, 1953. Oil on canvas, 152.5 x 118 cm. Kunsthalle, Hamburg.

[12] *Two Figures*, 1953. Oil on canvas, 152 x 116.5 cm. Private collection, Great Britain.

[13] *Triptych, Three Studies of the Human Head*, 1953. Oil on canvas, each panel 61 x 51 cm. Private collection, Switzerland.

[14] *Study of a Baboon*, 1953. Oil on canvas, 198 x 137 cm. Museum of Modern Art, New York.

[15] *Man with Dog*, 1953. Oil on canvas, 152 x 117 cm. Albright Knox Art Gallery, Buffalo, New York (gift of Seymour H. Knox).

[16] *Study after Velázquez's Portrait of Pope Innocent X*, 1953. Oil on canvas, 153 x 118 cm. Des Moines Art Center, Iowa.

[17] *Two Figures in the Grass*, 1954. Oil on canvas, 152 x 117 cm. Private collection, Paris.

[18] *Sphinx*, 1954. Oil on canvas, 198 x 147.5 cm. Brera Museum, Milan.

[19] *Pope*, 1955. Oil on canvas, 152.5 x 116.5 cm. Private collection, Switzerland.

[20] *Study for Portrait II, after the Life Mask of William Blake*, 1955. Oil on canvas, 61 x 51 cm. The Tate Gallery, London.

[21] *Study for Portrait III, after the Life Mask of William Blake*, 1955. Oil on canvas, 61 x 51 cm. Private collection.

[22] *Man Carrying a Child*, 1956. Oil on canvas, 198 x 142 cm. Private collection.

169

[23] *Study for a Portrait of Van Gogh II*, 1957. Oil on canvas, 198 x 147.5 cm. Edwin Janss Thousand Oaks Collection, California.

[24] *Study for the Nurse in the Film "Battleship Potemkin,"* 1957. Oil on canvas, 198 x 142 cm. Städelsches Kunstinstitut und Städtische Galerie, Frankfurt.

[25] *Lying Figure*, 1959. Oil on canvas, 198 x 142 cm. Kunstsammlung Nordrhein-Westfalen, Düsseldorf.

[26] *Miss Muriel Belcher*, 1959. Oil on canvas, 74 x 67.5 cm. Gilbert Halbers Collection, Paris.

[27] *Pope No. II*, 1960. Oil on canvas, 152.5 x 119.5 cm. Private collection, Switzerland.

[28] *Reclining Woman*, 1961. Oil on canvas, 198.5 x 141.5 cm. The Tate Gallery, London.

[29] *Triptych, Three Studies for a Crucifixion*, 1962. Oil on canvas, each panel 198 x 145 cm. The Solomon R. Guggenheim Museum, New York.

[30] *Figure Turning*, 1962. Oil on canvas, 198 x 147.5 cm. Private collection, New York.

[31] *Lying Figure with Hypodermic Syringe*, 1963. Oil on canvas, 198 x 147.5 cm. Private collection, Switzerland.

[32] *Man and Child*, 1963. Oil on canvas, 198 x 147.5 cm. McCrory Corporation Collection, New York.

[33] *Triptych, Three Figures in a Room*, 1964. Oil on canvas, each panel 198 x 147.5 cm. Musée national d'Art moderne, Centre Georges-Pompidou, Paris.

[34] *Triptych, Three Studies for a Portrait of George Dyer (on Light Ground)*, 1964. Oil on canvas, each panel 198 x 147.5 cm. Private collection.

[35] *Triptych, Crucifixion*, 1965. Oil on canvas, each panel 198 x 147.5 cm. Staatsgalerie Moderner Kunst, Munich.

[36] *After Muybridge—Woman Emptying a Bowl of Water and Paralytic Child on All Fours*, 1965. Oil on canvas, 198 x 147.5 cm. Stedelijk Museum, Amsterdam.

[37] *Portrait of George Dyer Talking*, 1966. Oil on canvas, 198 x 147.5 cm. Private collection, New York.

[38] *Triptych, Three Studies for a Portrait of Lucian Freud*, 1966. Oil on canvas, each panel 198 x 147.5 cm. Marlborough International Fine Art.

[39] *Portrait of George Dyer Staring at Blind Cord*, 1966. Oil on canvas, 198 x 147.5 cm. Maestri Collection, Parma.

[40] *Portrait of George Dyer Riding a Bicycle*, 1966. Oil on canvas, 198 x 147.5 cm. Jerome L. Stern Collection, New York.

[41] *Study of Isabel Rawsthorne*, 1966. Oil on canvas, 35.5 x 30.5 cm. Michel Leiris Collection, Paris.

[42] *Portrait of George Dyer and Lucian Freud*, 1967. Oil on canvas, 198 x 147.5 cm. (Destroyed in a fire.)

[43] *Three Studies of Isabel Rawsthorne*, 1967. Oil on canvas, 119.5 x 152.5 cm. Nationalgalerie, Berlin.

[44] *Three Studies from the Human Body*, 1967. Oil on canvas, 198 x 147.5 cm. Private collection.

[45] *Portrait of George Dyer Staring into a Mirror*, 1967. Oil on canvas, 198 x 147.5 cm. Private collection, Caracas.

[46] *Triptych Inspired by T. S. Eliot's Poem "Sweeney Agonistes,"* 1967. Oil on canvas, each panel 198 x 147.5 cm. The Hirshhorn Museum and Sculpture Garden, Washington, D.C.

[47] *Portrait of Isabel Rawsthorne Standing in a Street in Soho*, 1967. Oil on canvas, 198 x 147.5 cm. Nationalgalerie, Berlin.

[48] *Triptych, Three Studies for a Self-Portrait*, 1967. Oil on canvas, each panel 198 x 147.5 cm. Private collection.

[49] *Four Studies for a Self-Portrait*, 1967. Oil on canvas, 91.5 x 33 cm. Brera Museum, Milan.

[50] *Two Studies for a Portrait of George Dyer*, 1968. Oil on canvas, 198 x 147.5 cm. Sara Hildén Tampere Collection, Finland.

[51] *Portrait of George Dyer in a Mirror*, 1968. Oil on canvas, 198 x 147.5 cm. Thyssen-Bornemisza, Lugano.

[52] *Two Studies of George Dyer with a Dog*, 1968. Oil and pastel on canvas, 198 x 147.5 cm. Gilbert de Botton Collection.

[53] *Triptych, Two Figures Lying on a Bed with Attendants*, 1968. Oil on canvas, each panel 198 x 147.5 cm. Private collection, New York.

[54] *Triptych, Three Studies of Isabel Rawsthorne*, 1968. Oil on canvas, each panel 198 x 147.5 cm. Mrs. Susan Lloyd Collection, Nassau.

[55] *Triptych, Three Studies of Lucian Freud*, 1969. Oil on canvas, each panel 198 x 147.5 cm. Private collection, Rome.

[56] *Study for Bullfight No. 1*, 1969. Oil on canvas, 198 x 147.5 cm. Private collection.

[57] *Second Version of "Study for Bullfight No. 1,"* 1969. Oil on canvas, each panel 198 x 147.5 cm. Jerome L. Stern Collection, New York.

[58] *Lying Figure*, 1969. Oil and pastel on canvas, 198 x 147.5 cm. Private collection, Montreal.

[59] *Study of Nude with Figure in a Mirror*, 1969. Oil on canvas, 198 x 147.5 cm. Private collection.

[60] *Triptych*, 1970. Oil on canvas, each panel 198 x 147.5 cm. National Gallery of Australia, Canberra.

[61] *Triptych, Studies from the Human Body*, 1970. Oil on canvas, each panel 198 x 147.5 cm. Jacques Hachuel Collection, New York.

[62] *Triptych, Studies of the Human Body*, 1970. Oil on canvas, each panel 198 x 147.5 cm. Marlborough International Fine Art.

[63] *Triptych, Three Studies of the Male Back*, 1970. Oil on canvas, each panel 198 x 147.5 cm. Kunsthaus, Zurich.

[64] *Study for a Portrait of Lucian Freud (Sideways)*, 1971. Oil on canvas, 198 x 147.5 cm. Private collection, Brussels.

[65] *Second Version of "Painting, 1946,"* 1971. Oil on canvas, 198 x 147.5 cm. Wallraf-Richartz Museum, Ludwig Collection, Cologne.

[66] *Two Men Working in a Field*, 1971. Oil on canvas, 198 x 147.5 cm. Private collection, Japan.

[67] *Lying Figure in a Mirror*, 1971. Oil on canvas, 198 x 147.5 cm. Museo de Bellas Artes, Bilbao.

[68] *Portrait of a Man Walking Down Steps*, 1972. Oil on canvas, 198 x 147.5 cm. Private collection, London.

[69] *Triptych, Three Studies of Figures on Beds*, 1972. Oil on canvas, each panel 198 x 147.5 cm. Private collection, San Francisco.

[70] *Triptych*, August 1972. Oil on canvas, each panel 198 x 147.5 cm. The Tate Gallery, London.

[71] *Triptych, Three Portraits*, 1973. Oil on canvas, each panel 198 x 147.5 cm. Private collection, San Francisco.

[72] *Self-Portrait*, 1973. Oil on canvas, 198 x 147.5 cm. Private collection, New York.

[73] *Triptych*, May–June 1973. Oil on canvas, each panel 198 x 147.5 cm. Saul Sternberg Collection, New York.

[74] *Triptych*, March 1974. Oil and pastel on canvas, each panel 198 x 147.5 cm. Private collection, Madrid.

[75] *Triptych, May–June 1974* (later retitled *Triptych 1974–77*). Oil on canvas, each panel 198 x 147.5 cm. Property of the artist.

[76] *Sleeping Figure*, 1974. Oil on canvas, 198 x 147.5 cm. A. Carter Pottash Collection.

[77] *Seated Figure*, 1974. Oil and pastel on canvas, 198 x 147.5 cm. Gilbert de Botton Collection.

[78] *Three Figures and a Portrait*, 1975. Oil and pastel on canvas, 198 x 147.5 cm. The Tate Gallery, London.

[79] *Triptych*, 1976. Oil and pastel on canvas, each panel 198 x 147.5 cm. Private collection, France.

[80] *Figure at a Washbasin*, 1976. Oil on canvas, 198 x 147.5 cm. Museo de Arte Contemporáneo de Caracas.

[81] *Painting*, 1978. Oil on canvas, 198 x 147.5 cm. Private collection, Monte Carlo.

[82] *Jet of Water*, 1979. Oil on canvas, 198 x 147.5 cm. Private collection.

[83] *Sphinx — Portrait of Muriel Belcher*, 1979. Oil on canvas, 198 x 147.5 cm. National Museum of Modern Art, Tokyo.

[84] *Triptych, Studies from the Human Body*, 1979. Oil on canvas, each panel 198 x 147.5 cm. Private collection.

[85] *Carcass of Meat and Bird of Prey*, 1980. Oil on canvas, 198 x 147.5 cm. Private collection.

[86] *Sand Dune*, 1981. Oil and pastel on canvas, 198 x 147.5 cm. Private collection, New York.

[87] *Study of Man Talking*, 1981. Oil on canvas, 198 x 147.5 cm. Private collection, Switzerland.

[88] *A Piece of Waste Land*, 1982. Oil on canvas, 198 x 147.5 cm. Property of the artist.

[89] *Study from the Human Body, Figure in Movement*, 1982. Oil on canvas, 198 x 147.5 cm. Marlborough International Fine Art.

[90] *Study of the Human Body from a Drawing by Ingres*, 1982. Oil and pastel on canvas, 198 x 147.5 cm. Property of the artist.

[91] *Study of the Human Body*, 1982. Oil on canvas, 198 x 147.5 cm. Musée national d'Art moderne, Centre Georges-Pompidou, Paris.

[92] *Study for a Self-Portrait*, 1982. Oil on canvas, 198 x 147.5 cm. Private collection, New York.

[93] *Statue and Figures in a Street*, 1983. Oil and pastel on canvas, 198 x 147.5 cm. Property of the artist.

[94] *Oedipus and the Sphinx after Ingres*, 1983. Oil on canvas, 198 x 147.5 cm. Private collection, California.

[95] *Study from the Human Body*, 1983. Oil and pastel on canvas, 198 x 147.5 cm. Menil's Foundation Collection, Houston.

[96] *Triptych*, 1983. Oil and pastel on canvas, each panel 198 x 147.5 cm. Marlborough International Fine Art.

[97] *Sand Dune*, 1983. Oil and pastel on canvas, 198 x 147.5 cm. Ernst Beyeler Collection, Basel.

Paintings by Other Artists

[98] Paul Cézanne, *The Bathers*, 1900–1906. Oil on canvas, 130 x 195 cm. National Gallery, London.

[99] Paul Cézanne, *A Modern Olympia (The Pasha)*, c. 1873–1874. Oil on canvas, 46 x 55.5 cm. Musée d'Orsay, Paris.

[100] Paul Cézanne, *Woman in a Green Hat (Madame Cézanne)*, 1894–1895. Oil on canvas, 100.2 x 81.2 cm. The Barnes Foundation, Merion, Pennsylvania.

[101] Edgar Degas, *After the Bath: Woman Drying Herself,* c. 1888–1892. Pastel on tracing paper, 104 x 98 cm. National Gallery, London.

[102] Marcel Duchamp, *Nude Descending a Staircase (No. 2)*, 1912. Oil on canvas, 146 x 89 cm. The Louise and Walter Arensberg Collection, Philadelphia Museum of Art.

[103] Marcel Duchamp, *Three Standard Stoppages*, 1913–1914. Three threads glued on three glass panels, each 125.4 x 18.4 cm. Museum of Modern Art, New York.

[104] Paul Gauguin, *La Belle Angèle*, 1889. Oil on canvas, 92 x 73 cm. Musée d'Orsay, Paris.

[105] Ambrogio Bondone Giotto, *Legend of St. Francis:* panel 19, *Stigmatization of St. Francis*, 1297–1300. Fresco, 270 x 230 cm. Upper Church, San Francesco, Assisi, Italy.

[106] El Greco (Doménikos Theotokópoulos), *The Burial of the Count of Orgaz*, 1586–1588. Oil on canvas, 480 x 360 cm. Iglesia de Santo Tomé, Toledo, Spain.

[107] Michelangelo Buonarotti, *The Holy Family with the Infant St. John the Baptist (Tondo Doni)*, 1504–1506. Oil on canvas, 71.1 x 71.1 cm. Galleria degli Uffizi, Florence.

[108] Rembrandt van Rijn, *Nightwatch (The Company of Frans Banning Cock Preparing to March Out)*, 1642. Oil on canvas, 363 x 437 cm. Rijksmuseum, Amsterdam, The Netherlands.

[109] Jacopo Tintoretto, *Creation of the Animals*, c. 1550. Oil on canvas, 151 x 258 cm. Gallerie dell'Accademia, Venice.

[110] J. M. W. Turner, *Snowstorm—Steam Boat off a Harbour's Mouth Making Signals in Shallow Water, and Going by the Lead*, 1842. Oil on canvas, 91.5 x 122 cm. The Tate Gallery, London.

[111] Vincent Van Gogh, *Portrait of the Postman Joseph Roulin*, Arles, early August 1888. Oil on canvas, 81.2 x 65.3 cm. Museum of Fine Arts, Boston.

[112] Diego Velázquez, *Pope Innocent X*, 1650. Oil on canvas, 152.5 x 116.5 cm. Galleria Doria-Pamphili, Rome.

Index

175

Kafka, Franz, 21, 36, 51; Bacon's
resemblance to, 14
Kandinsky, Wassily, xiii, 84–85, 86, 88,
164n.16, 164n.18
Kant, Immanuel, 67; theory of perception,
xv–xxii
Klee, Paul, xxi, xxiii, 48, 83, 159n.1

Landscape, 8
landscapes: distinction between geography
and, xiv–xv; involuntary, 7–8
Lawrence, D. H., 32, 72–73, 79, 141, 148
Le Bot, Marc, ix, 116
Leibniz, Gottfried Wilhelm von, 147; theory
of event, 139
Leiris, Michel, ix, x, 9, 129, 163n.4
levels of sensation: hypothesis of, 33–38:
motor hypothesis of, 35–37; phenomenological hypothesis of, 37–38, 39;
psychoanalytic hypothesis of ambivalence,
35; represented object, 33–35
line: derived from color, 121; Gothic, 40–41,
85, 88, 104–5, 148
local scrubbing, 8, 19–20
Logic of Sense, The (Deleuze), 133
Louis, Morris, 85, 161n.14
Lubbock, Percy, 138
luminism, 106, 108
Lying Figure, 21
Lying Figure in a Mirror, 17, 56
Lying Figure with Hypodermic Syringe, 17, 21
Lyotard, Jean-François, x, xiii, 148

Maldiney, Henri, xv, xviii, 156n.1
malerisch period/treatment, 27, 89, 97, 110,
115, 156n.6, 166n.12; diagram in, 111
Malraux, André, 10, 133
Man and Child, 59, 122, 123, 137–38
Man Carrying a Child, 36
manipulated chance, 77, 78
mannerism, 129
manual, tendency to eliminate the, 85,
161n.10
manual conception of painting, 160n.1
manual eye-hand relationship, 125
manual power: diagram as, 110–11
manual space, xxv, 105; evolution toward
imposition of violent, 103
manual traits, 82
Man with Dog, 8, 27
materials and forces: relationship of, xxix
material structure. *See* field of color (material
structure)

material synthetic unity of sensation: makeup
of, 33–38
mathematical sublime, xxi
mathematics: role of diagrams in, xxiii–xxiv
matter(s) of fact, 6–7, 58, 129, 136, 137;
coupled Figures as, 55, 70; triptych as
union that separates, 70; types of, in
triptych, 58
measure, units of: aesthetic comprehension
of, as grasping of rhythm, xviii–xix; human
body as, xvii–xviii
meat: affinity of mouth with, 23–24; body as,
20–24; head and, relationship between,
22–24; as object of Bacon's pity, 21–22, 24
memory, involuntary, 56–57
Merleau-Ponty, Maurice, xv, xviii, 148,
156n.1
Messiaen, Olivier, xxxii, xxxiii, 60, 61
Michaux, André, 89
Michelangelo, 105, 167n.13
Millet, Jean François, 49
mirrors: cube or parallelepiped replicated
in, 17
misérabiliste painter, 40, 53
Miss Muriel Belcher, 23, 120
modeling: chromatic concept of, 165n.4
modern painting: man's experience of self as
accident and, 101
modulation of color, xxvi, 96–97, 98, 106–7,
108, 113–14, 115, 116, 118, 146, 147–48,
162n.8, 164n.16, 164n.17, 164n.20,
168n.14
modulator: diagram as analogical, xxiv, 98,
112
molding: by color, 108, 164n.20; variable and
continuous, 146–48, 168n.14
Mondrian, Pieter Cornelis, xiii, xxv, 84, 86,
88, 161n.10
Monet, Claude, 107, 162n.2
Moritz, K. P., 22
mosaic, Byzantine, 106
motif as diagram, 91–92
motor hypothesis of levels of sensation, 35–37
mouth: affinity with meat, 23–24; escape of
body through screaming, 16, 25
movement: between elements of painting,
28–30; motor hypothesis of levels of
sensation, 35–37
Multiplicity: Bacon's work as components of,
xii–xiv
music, 60; comparing painting to, 47; task of,
defined, 48
Muybridge, Eadweard, 35, 58, 74

Gilles Deleuze (1925–1995) was professor of philosophy at the University of Paris, Vincennes–St. Denis. With Félix Guattari, he coauthored *Anti-Oedipus*, *A Thousand Plateaus*, and *Kafka: Toward a Minor Literature*. He was also the author of *The Fold*, *Cinema 1: The Movement-Image*, *Cinema 2: The Time-Image*, *Foucault*, *Kant's Critical Philosophy*, and *Essays Critical and Clinical*. All of these books are published in English by the University of Minnesota Press.

Daniel W. Smith teaches philosophy at Purdue University. He has translated Gilles Deleuze's *Essays Critical and Clinical* and Pierre Klossowski's *Nietzsche and the Vicious Circle*.

Tom Conley is professor of Romance languages at Harvard University. He is the author of *Film Hieroglyphs* and *The Self-Made Map*. His translations include Gilles Deleuze's *The Fold: Leibniz and the Baroque*; Michel de Certeau's *The Capture of Speech and Other Political Writings* and *Culture in the Plural*; and Marc Augé's *In the Metro*, all published by the University of Minnesota Press.